# IMAGINE
# MEANDER

Journeys of Reflection,
Serendipity, and Delight

By Josephine Carubia
Illustrations by Teah Glorie

**Imagine Meander: Journeys of Reflection, Serendipity, and Delight**
Copyright © 2023 Josephine Carubia

Produced and printed by Stillwater River Publications.
All rights reserved. Written and produced in the
United States of America. This book may not be reproduced
or sold in any form without the expressed, written
permission of the author and publisher.

Visit our website at
**www.StillwaterPress.com**
for more information.

First Stillwater River Publications Edition

ISBN: 978-1-958217-88-7

1 2 3 4 5 6 7 8 9 10
Written by Josephine Carubia.
Cover and interior design by Elisha Gillette.
Illustrations by Teah Glorie.

Published by Stillwater River Publications,
Pawtucket, RI, USA.

# Table of Contents

# One Foot on the Ground

*A good traveler has no fixed plans and is not intent upon arriving.*
—Lao Tzu

*There is wisdom in turning as often as possible from the familiar to the unfamiliar: it keeps the mind nimble, it kills prejudice, and it fosters humility.* —George Santayana

When I hear the phrase, one foot on the ground, I think, Where is the other foot? In a literal sense, the other foot might be poised in the air, in liminal space, neither here nor there but utterly capable of landing fore or aft, higher or lower. The literal quickly gives way to the metaphorical, however, and I begin to imagine that other foot in seven-league boots at the end of a telescoping leg worthy of Dr. Seuss and extending across several pages to land quite anywhere in this galaxy or another.

Well, that isn't exactly my story!

I have strong roots in several specific places and I love my home and family, but there have been times when I've been beguiled by the notion of reincarnation. At those times, I have felt strongly that my spirit once sailed with explorers on uncharted seas. Seated at the very tip of the bow of a sailboat on a 360-degree plate of Atlantic Ocean in this very life, I tingled with the excitement of recognition. Maybe today we would make safe landfall, but if not, if never, this extraordinary elation might be enough. Sleeping out alone under the stars, albeit on my own farm, I felt the earth at my back and the deeply bright universe meeting me as surely as the familiar local views approaching through the windshield of my Prius. I would have lifted **both** feet willingly if my call to be taken by extraterrestrials had been answered in those nights.

I DO have one foot on the ground, a solid foundation for building a nest, loving children, and serving a community, but the other foot is a rambling rover. It has walked in heavy boots in the fresh furrow and in red high heels up and down the avenues. It has been tickled with my fancy for crossing bridges literally on foot, and humored my delight in walking down the middle of the street (not to be confused with the middle of the road) at any opportunity. My itinerant foot has helped me cross many a line in the sand when that foot wasn't stuck in the mud or in my mouth.

It was on both my feet that I walked into the woods near Walden Pond where Henry David Thoreau created a small base for his peripatetic musings. With one foot on the ground, I appreciate his encouragement to keep the other firmly in the air along with scores of castles thriving in the celestial atmosphere. "If you have built castles in the air, your work need not be lost; that is where they should be. Now put the foundations under them."

My nomadic foot has had a more profound influence on my career than its steadier mate. I embarked on an adult career path as a school teacher, one of the steadiest jobs in town. I heard my peers declare in our mid-twenties, "I have secured tenure and my own classroom, and I never need to do anything new for the rest of my life!" I nearly tripped over my foot bent on skipping off that path where a dim horizon spooled off slowly like a narrow rope waiting to hang me.

Taking risk after risk walking in different shoes has rubbed my skin raw in some spots and built up calluses in others. There were some years when I willingly soaked *both* feet in lukewarm water and rested for the next incitement. Fortunately, we now have a term for the zig-zag career path I've had a hard time defending as an early adopter. This generation of workers who build skill sets that can be transported across professions and platforms is called "Generation Flux." All in all, I've felt extremely fortunate to work and walk in locations as diverse as farm fields, hospital corridors, classrooms, and Rockefeller Center with people ranging in age from pre-school to the 95-year-old senior partners in a NYC law firm.

These essays are witness to life when my rambling foot has been ascendant, taking me around the block, over the mountain, or to another continent. It is written in a state of mind produced when that foot has been given free rein to meander down a grassy lane, subway steps, jetway, or simply along a train of thought. Both my feet adopted a motto from Thoreau and infused my life with it: "I wanted to live deep and suck out all the marrow of life ... and not, when I came to die, discover that I had not lived."

I've been on a journey—not entirely footloose, but not tethered or blindfolded either—and these stories are the souvenirs that I've collected along the way. Some are as ephemeral as the rainbow I embraced with my naked body in an outdoor shower, and some are the same souvenirs that **you** carry because every time I put one foot forward, my human experience is both similar to and different than yours. This is not a chronological narrative of one or even of several travel adventures, but you will find many stories and anecdotes where vivid characters will do a holographic dance in front of your eyes. Most of all, I hope you will experience the wonder of imagining where your feet will take you next, and that you will enjoy meandering along the pathways of your own marvelous adventures!

CHAPTER ONE

# Preparations

*Chance favors the prepared mind.* —Louis Pasteur

All travel begins, long before the first step away from home, with the open mind that imagines a deep breath of sea air, the surround-sound of a city street, or the panoramic view from a precarious-yet-secure height. Once the imagination creates the scene, that first step may be inevitable, but there are many stages and many hours between image, intention, and fulfillment. Preparations for a journey may seem onerous to some, while to others, the imagined itinerary with its glossy, photo-quality scenes, is quite the best aspect of an experience that inevitably will include non-photo-worthy situations and the bite of pesky inconveniences, both miniscule and massive.

# The Valise and the Tortoise

My father always called our family suitcase, "the valise." Much later, when I learned a few words in Italian, it became clear that this was a cognate for the Italian word "valigia," but still it is, for me, a foreign word that allows me to focus on an experience that otherwise would be quite ordinary.

When traveling for a week or more, the valise becomes the tortoise shell, your home on wheels that follows you around. It is a microcosm of all our habits and household customs, a snapshot of illusions and fantasies, and a ball and chain fettering dreams of mobility and freedom.

I have managed over the years to reduce my baggage—with the strong encouragement of my husband—to one suitcase that can fit into the overhead compartment of most large aircraft (if I can manage to lift it over my head). In addition, I carry a piece of hand luggage, often a medium-sized backpack. Years ago, my husband and I went to Paris for a week with an army's worth of luggage. We could have fit into those bags! I packed three changes of clothes per day. What were we carrying around with us? Was it all the accumulated guilt of two divorces, children's struggles, and career vicissitudes from our two adult lives? Probably. We are carrying less luggage now.

But think of what you put into your valise: the practical articles for comfort and the fanciful items for imagined ways you'll be different while traveling. For example, silk long johns are almost weightless in the bag and almost priceless on an unexpectedly chill day in Rejkyavik. What about the bathing suit? Will you spend time at the pool or beach when you could be viewing magnificent art in temples and museums? A bathing suit takes up little room, and when absent is missed far more than the extra pair of socks.

## Ready

We've been getting ready for this trip for months, so when the day arrives, today, we are <u>ready</u>. Whatever it means to be ready—itinerary

99% scheduled and distributed to family and friends, new sandals for me and shoes for V (both of us in "Clarks" known to be comfortable right out of the box), emails answered, books carefully selected, conference papers written or at least planned. One thing feels different this year for me—the balance of excitement and anxiety feels slightly shifted toward the anxious. Or maybe that's not the right word. I seem to miss the kids more and more every year when we travel, especially when going overseas. Is that natural with age? Are my father's genes becoming more active in me?

## Succession Planning for Parents

This is more than just making a will before you travel. Even when your children are grown, they need to have surrogates. Who will they call when they think of calling you? Who will call them on birthdays and holidays? Who will continue to integrate them into the extended family? Last year before we left for Brazil, I made my daughter promise to call my only sister if she felt like talking to me and I wasn't around. On the surface, I meant while I was traveling in Brazil, but it's always good to give hints for longer, more permanent kinds of absences as well. I think my sister and I are potential surrogates for each other's children.

## Last Kiss

Last Kiss at the curb is never enough. The shuttle driver and the hotel bellman holding the door are both waiting for me to step away from you. The first step is the hardest, the only. Shock of departure, sudden on my face; this time you are watching me go. Which is harder, watching or going? For hours all I want is another long hug and full-body-kiss goodbye. No, not goodbye...hello.

# Travel Anxiety: Zip it Up (airport anywhere)

I have a new four-wheeler suitcase. My older, bright red two-wheeler has been roughed around for six or seven years; for the last two of these I've snapped a rainbow strap around it, especially when I check it in for an independent adventure in baggage handling. I've been envying the four-wheelers for some time. These pieces of luggage seem to float along beside the travelers presenting a side approach for narrow passages (into bathroom stalls, for example) and easily gliding to a front-on stance facing the counter of the newsstand when purchasing Reese's Pieces or *The Atlantic Monthly* before a flight. An ache in my shoulder and back from pulling my two-wheeler with an accessory backpack through airports hastened this upgrade.

My new suitcase has three shallow zippered compartments on its topside, a large (it's a carry-on, so how large is that?) zippered main compartment, and one of those confusing expansion zippers that increase the depth of the bag by another two inches. My back pack has three zippered compartments and a small front mesh pouch, also with a zipper. I'm not even counting the zippers on the insides of both bags, or the zippers in my wallet and cosmetics case, or the quart-size ziplock bag with my travel liquids. Let's say, I have about a dozen zipped areas readily available for expressing travel anxiety.

Travel anxiety?

When asked, I will deny it.

When observed, I will fake it. I love to travel, so why am I creating so much activity around the contents of all the little segmented compartments of my baggage?

My checking and rechecking of the stuff in all of these sections and partitions approaches an OCD symphony. Dollar bills for the water machine inside the security lounge? Band-Aids and tea bags? Slippers, pajamas, pens, pencils, paper? Phone charger, camera charger, extra batteries? Even at the airport, finally relaxing with a cup of hot tea, I'm un-zipping and checking little side pockets and pouches to find my travel notebook, Dramamine just in case, and the tiny card that has the codes for remote accessing my home phone voice mail. Picture a man wearing a suit and an overcoat trying to find the parking ticket stub he put in a pocket early this morning. He will be patting himself and reaching in and out of perhaps ten potential locations in his pockets. Women have fewer pockets in their clothing, so we compensate by accessorizing with bags, packs, and suitcases that do have a multitude of places to hide our small, infinite, and indispensable accessories.

## Departure Panic

I am useless for the twenty-four hours before my departure for any trip! It doesn't really matter where I'm going or whether it is a car trip, bus or train trip, or air travel. The anxieties, feelings, and preparations are the same.

I actually begin a week before travel by doing all the laundry of possible clothing for the trip. It's good to have several days to get all socks, underwear, blouses, slacks, sweaters that might go along clean and hanging in the closet or neatly folded in drawers.

At some point, about three days before the trip, I ask myself, "Why am I going on this trip?" I regret offering to go, or even planning the trip myself! Even so, I am keeping my eye on magazines arriving in the mail to put aside as reading material for the trip. I avoid starting a new book so that I will have this to look forward to while traveling.

The day before travel is my packing day because I am not good with last minute decisions and time constraints. As part of my packing ritual, I check the small hiding places where I have stashed some cash so that if one bag is stolen, I might still have enough resources for my own rescue.

CHAPTER TWO

# Transportation

*It matters not where or how far you travel--the further commonly the worse --but how much alive you are.*

—H.D. Thoreau

Even at home, we limit or expand our experience by our transportation choices. In our individual private cars we are isolated from most casual encounters with other travelers, aside from the moments stretching legs at rest stops along the highway. Public transportation is a richly overflowing cornucopia of experience! It may be pungent and a bit grimy along the edges, but colors and stories flow and overflow in the arena right before your eyes. In my view, everyone in America should be required to make at least one journey of four hours or more by bus each year. Learn what is available to those for whom this is the only option. In other countries, the byways of ordinary folks surround touristic features and conveniences. On a tour bus, riverboat, or airplane, encounters with ordinary life are limited to the guide and perhaps the workers who service the tour. Instead, maneuver as a pedestrian to feel the texture of life in this place with only a padding of leather between you and the pebbled way.

# Bicycle-Friendly City

Ferrara defines itself as a city friendly to bicycles. We read the welcome signs as we follow instructions towards *Centro* on our first day in Italy. At first the streams of bicycles are just one more category of vehicle, one more vector of motion, on the crowded streets. We concentrate all of our effort on avoiding collision, adjusting our courtesy and consciousness as they glide into spaces we routinely assume are vacant, between the car and the curb to the right or to the left ... . it wouldn't surprise us to realize that a bicycle was suddenly inside the tiny Fiat with us!

The bicycle experience in Ferrara is nothing like what we would assume to be a parallel experience in the U.S. if, for example, a city like Philadelphia transformed itself into a bicycle friendly city. It appears that bicycle transportation agrees with all ages of riders, not just athletic youth showing plumage. In fact, we have seen very few adolescent males on bikes. The riders we see are women and men going about their daily occupations with a briefcase, loaf of bread, and other assorted hand baggage of the moment. The elderly women, some even in the stereotypical black garb, seem to ride with more alacrity than they walk. It seems more remarkable to see an elderly woman pedaling than any other demographic group, and I think about all the ways we limit expectations for women as they age.

The bicycles themselves are remarkable, that is, remarkable in their ordinariness. These are unadorned, simple bicycles of functional form. Even in my childhood, I prized a new fluorescent turquoise machine. No, these are mostly of spare frame and muted colors, many with a basket on front or back for carrying groceries. Almost entirely without "bells and whistles." We did hear some of the old-style bicycle bells that ring out a mechanical b-r-r-r-i-n-g to alert pedestrians. These bicycles are transportation, not toys, not status symbols, not accessories. The riders of these bicycles are purposeful; they are not wearing clothes for cycling, but for the many occupations of their lives.

## Grey Day by Car

Grey day, rain and wind. It's hard to keep a lot of energy going. A good day to sleep and read.

After V lectures we immediately get into the car with K and begin the journey in the rain to downtown Sofia (Bulgaria) to meet K and P for dinner and jazz. An hour and a half of traffic and pouring rain! The benefit of this time with K is the story he tells us about his father being one of the first disc jockeys in Bulgaria. The tourists asked for entertainment at their hotels in the evening, so the Communist Party decided to authorize a few DJ's to entertain the tourists. K's father was trained as an engineer so he was able to manage the equipment, and eventually he became the chief DJ and managed the music as well. He even trained the subsequent DJ's to serve tourists at other hotels. This was in the 70's. Of course, the youth also got wind of this and began to flock to the tourist hotels to hear western music. K was very young but remembers how great it was to have this amazing music in their home. His father traveled a lot acquiring music and equipment and training DJ's, and the marriage between his parents eventually broke up. His Dad is now on pension and loves to go trout fishing in the mountains.

We meet K and P on a rainy corner of Eagle's Bridge and get immediately into another cab for another half hour to a small restaurant. It was two hours from New Bulgarian University to that restaurant !! K drove us home at 1:38 a.m after dinner and music and we arrived back at our hotel at 1:53 a.m., only 15 minutes! No traffic and no rain!

# Travel Night

Travel days are always a bit difficult. Today is hot, hot, hot, and I can feel myself alternate from cranky to happy depending on my body temperature.

We are on the overnight train from Budapest to Krakow. It pulled out of Budapest on the dot of 6:30 pm (18:30). We have a sleeper compartment, bunks #42 and 46, and I love it ! It's my first sleeper. Everything is built in for efficiency: hooks, lights, ladder, hangers, sink under a lift-up countertop and a small cabinet with two bottles of water, two croissants, and 2 wrapped towels with small bars of soap. Our bunks are dark wine red velvet with very white sheets and pillows. When we are moving the breeze flows across us and I love it !!

"All I want is a room somewhere, far away from the cold night air, and one enormous chair, and wouldn't it be loverly?"

There is an "ugly American" just down the narrow passageway. He has been complaining to the conductor that he wants his beer. He spent lots of money coming to Europe to drink beer and he needs his beer. American beer is shit (Budweiser) and he is in Europe and he needs his beer. He is commiserating with the Irish couple down the hall. When we discovered that the conductor keeps our tickets until we get off the train, the young Irishman threatened to knock him down if we don't get the tickets in the morning. So much aggression so close to the surface and immediately activated! I think the two of them are plotting how to get beer at the next stop.

The fields outside the window are sliding by in broad strokes of greens and yellows (sunflowers) and a light tan (?) Is it cut wheat? I don't know. There are villages in the near view and mountains in the distance.

# Travel Day

We had a wake-up call at 7 am so we could pack and be ready to leave the Hilton Helsinki Kalastajatorrpa for the "Congress Train" to

Imatra. I hated to leave this comfortable (and expensive, 121 Euro/ night) hotel by the sea. I loved the seamless bathroomand shower on dark grey stone tiles. The shower door has a rubber bottom edge along its curved shape, but this doesn't entirely keep the water within its curve. This seems acceptable in this place because the floor is heated from below and dries quickly. Stones wet under my feet feel natural here. At home I hate a wet floor and wet feet! I loved our tram #4 just one block down the hill reliably coming for us on a six minute schedule all day long. This is the last/first stop on the red line, # 4 or 4T. The tram is also expensive at 2 Euro each way, but very civilized!

So, we pack again after these six days of spreading out; then we checked out and boarded our tram for the last time to travel to the train station. Others were going to work or school. Women—young women—with patient, calm babies go on and off the tram with strollers with the aid of ready hands of anyone near by.

At the train station we changed US $ for Euro—another experience of deflation as our $300 brought only 214 Euro. We sat in a restaurant for breakfast. V had a banana, juice, and coffee and I had tea and half of a ham, lettuce, and tomoato sandwich. We bought a bottle of water; I used the toilet for 1 Euro; and then we met our friends who were also waiting for the train, our own "Congress train." We were warned not to mistake the 10 am train for Imatra for our train, but one friend we met later had done just that, paying another fare and riding the scheduled train. After hoisting our heavy suitcases, two couples ( J and V, N and A) sat in facing seats to enjoy the ride! We laughed and talked and the time went quickly. Scenery was not spectacular, fields and light forest—cultivated forest, not natural. Logging and paper production seem to be important industries here.

Upon descending from the train, we were "herded" to buses to transport us to hotels. For the size of this village, we are a herd or horde of strange creatures! Just this morning I was lamenting a large group of Asian businessmen who might impede our individual efforts to check out of the hotel. Now, I am part of the horde as we disembark from buses to line up outside the entrance to the lovely hotel castle with its intimate lobby that can allow only four or five persons at a time.

The hotel desk is prepared for us, just taking the time to verify each name and hand us keys. We are lucky to be in the castle and not the adjacent newer annex, called Congress Hotel. Very lucky as everything is very graceful here—wide stairways with low-rise steps (reminds me of a castle somewhere where we were told these shallow steps allowed the soldiers to ride their horses right up the stairs! Here they are carpeted and soft with large landings, each one comfortably furnished with a seating arrangement, floor to ceiling mirror, and flowers. We refresh briefly and are thrilled to find a wireless internet connection functioning at the small desk in our room. We walk downstairs to join the others for lunch, a buffet of whitefish with tiny shrimp, chicken in brown sauce, vegetables, rice, potatoes.

## Following

We are about twenty people playing follow-the-leader. After the tour bus drops us off at the Suzhou(China) train station, we will take the bullet train from Suzhou back to Nanjing and then then take the subway back to our hotel on Zhongshan Road. Follow the leader: Step One: We each hand over 100 RMB and our passport to E and G. There is a feeling of vulnerability in letting that passport out of our hands, but this is at least the third time we've had to do so on this trip and it is just for brief periods. That feeling isn't as unpleasant as the thought of approaching the ticket counter one by one to purchase tickets with E or G having to translate for each of us. We stack ourselves like large pieces of luggage against a wall, just slightly out of the path of other travelers rushing down the stairs and towards their destinations.

E and G return with a fistful of tickets and our passports. We follow them as if on individual leashes. Really we are following the cluster of passports in their hands. Back up the stairs to the departure hall where we can see the big board with train numbers and track assignments.

Our leaders have already divided the tickets into two groups, one for Car #6 and one for car #8. We each receive a passport and a ticket with seat assignment and then move to the gate for our train. Everything is marked in both Chinese and English. We use eye contact to reorganize ourselves into Car #6 and Car #8 groups as we move forward through the gate and down the stairs to the track. I think about how nice it would be if this station were organized to the point of having signs to tell us where each car stops so we can wait exactly at the correct car. At first I see only the orderly lines of people who seem to have ESP. Then I see the tiles on the floor with the car numbers indicating where to stand.

How quickly we reshape our allegiances and friendships for this minor instance of travel survival! I am now best friends and seatmate with B for the next ninety minutes as we bullet through the city, suburbs, and countryside between Suzhou and Nanjing.

Reserved seats is such a civilized way to travel! We disperse into our seats, secure in knowing that our leaders cannot escape from us until we stop in Nanjing. Following is suspended for this period.

Our journey from Nanjing to Suzhou took nearly five hours by bus yesterday, but traveling at up to 297 km/hour, we make the return in about ninety minutes. This includes several station stops in between.

I've been in Penn Station in NYC enough to know that it is likely that the metro is located somewhere within the maze of the station. This is a small bit of comfort for me; others are anxious about how far it will be between train and subway stations. We were advised to bring just an overnight bag and many of us are just carrying our hand luggage.

The distance we must follow-the-leader doesn't have to be far for it to be treacherous in the unexpected crowds of mid-day Saturday. Our leaders are stepping lively out in front. The obstacle course thickens behind them as rolling suitcases take up rushing space and necessitate glances downward as well as onward to avoid a stumble, trip, or fall. The imaginary ribbon or thread connecting us stretches to a few dashes and we begin to lose visual contact when the person we are trying to follow turns a corner. I am somewhere in the middle of the pack this time, trying to keep connected both before and behind, eyeing a tall comrade far in advance over the sea of heads and turning back to encourage the one following behind me.

At a certain point I realize that I must let go of the one behind. I must step up my own pace regardless of whether he or she can keep up with me. Suddenly, the game has changed for me; it is now "every man/woman for herself!" I find this extremely disturbing and experience the cut thread fluttering behind me as a breach beyond bearing. I feel I've broken a bond with my follower in order not to lose track of the person I am following. It was a decision to be made because of the rigorous circumstances of followership survival. My only alternative seemed to be to let go of the one ahead and then I and those behind me would have been lost together.

Ultimately, no one is lost on this journey, but it seemed a bit of a broken compact that the ones in front of me never did turn around to see if anyone was still attached to the thread holding us all together in a line stretching thinner and thinner. Or were the leaders simply trusting us, knowing that if one adult was detached from the umbilical cord, he or she would revert to the competent and intelligent person they were before being turned into a follower by the unfamiliar circumstances of being in China with such competent and willing leaders. Ultimately, we were all capable of both keeping up with them in the maze of the station AND of finding our own way to the metro ticket area to buy a token and find our way home to the New Era Hotel by subway or by taxi.

## Airport Vignette

There are young men and a few young women in army fatigues carrying duffel bags everywhere in this airport (BWI)! These are the dusty tan color fatigues for dessert warfare, not the deep greens of jungles. They are leaving for Iraq. Their families bring them to the airport, some are alone, some with sweethearts, some bonding into new friendships as they form lines to begin the process of "shipping out." It isn't often that we are in a place filled with the immediacy of war. There is no laughing; no antics; all of these people are serious-faced with unfathomable thoughts, possibly of what they are leaving, and probably of what is ahead of them, or maybe of absolute terror of the unknown. It is sobering to stand on our line for Icelandair, knowing that we are off on a holiday, while these somber youth are leaving for months of constant fear of immanent death, either their own deaths or the deaths of those around them, friend or foe.

Icelandair was the airline of young travelers in the sixties and seventies, with cheap flights to Europe via a brief layover in Reykjavik. That elusive destination, intriguing for me as a former "wanna-be" 1970's traveler (when I was a very young wife and mother) and because of Jules Verne and a colorful article on its nightlife and music scene in a popular magazine. Snaefells volcano near Reykjavik was the starting point for "The Journey to the Center of the Earth." My imagination—along with countless others—was deeply impressed by Jules Verne's stories in my early teens. Like post traumatic stress syndrome, I possibly have permanent notches on my psyche from these early imaginary expeditions. Come to think of it, much of my adolescent reading informs my desires and dreams. I owned a complete set of Nancy Drew mysteries although they were like small sweet cookies compared to the meat of heavier books I was reading from my father's small shelf of classics and from our local library.

CHAPTER THREE

# Wandering, Lingering, Losing

*There is a saying among mountain climbers that you can learn more from climbing one mountain one hundred times than one hundred mountains one time.* —Alice Steinbach

*May your trails be crooked, winding, lonesome, dangerous, leading to the most amazing view.* —Edward Abbey

## Fluid Dynamics

I love the walk from the Port Authority Bus Terminal to Penn Station along Eighth Avenue. Was I fearful that this morning at 9:30 a.m. New York City would be too quiet to excite me? No worries! Pushing open a door to exit the Port Authority Terminal, I entered a full torrent of activity on the street. My diagonal aim to the corner was diverted slightly to avoid the opposite diagonal aim of a mail cart pushed by a determined young man. I read somewhere that the flow of pedestrians in a busy city is an example of fluid dynamics (or was it chaos theory?). As we eastbound-avenue-crossers meshed perfectly with the westbound pedestrians, I felt that there was some principle of dynamics at work. I scarcely had to adjust my stride or trajectory to avoid anyone and yet we were a multitude, each one of whom had a dotted line stretching out in front toward a goal. A woman pulling a bright blue suitcase caught my eye. Was she walking in parallel with me from station to station? I noticed a man approaching and waving to a young girl handing out flyers in front of a store. So, even here, a person could encounter someone they know! I drink deep sustenance from the massed bolts of colors inside the fabric stores. Are there any buttons in there? If I had more time I would seek out the button specialists within this garment district. Is garment industry in my blood through my mother, aunts, and uncle? Does that inheritance of cloth-matters flow down through nature or nurture? I feel at home here. I feel alive in a more visceral way. I think it is something to do with molecules rushing at the same frequency as these people, so we are microcosm and macrocosm; the city is I and I am the city. Just for these few minutes and then I cut to the left and enter under Madison Square Garden into Pennsylvania Station, labyrinth of longitude.

## Following vs. Wayfinding

On the first day in this city, our host K met us all in the lobby of Hotel Mercure at 8:45 am and led us in a group to Villa Academica. I was walking beside L who was wearing high heeled shoes on the cobblestone streets. We were both following the people directly in front of us with our eyes on the uneven pavement. I saw only her small feet selecting the flat spots among curved and uneven stones. It seemed like a long winding walk that morning although I had identified this destination on our maps and it looked like a relatively straight shot from the hotel. That morning we followed blindly, it felt as though we turned corners several times and I was very confused at the turns which were not in my mental map. After one session of the meetings, I left and K pointed out the route back to the hotel. It was, indeed, just one street directly across from our hotel—a straight shot! This morning, four days later, I walked to Villa Academica with V who seemed to follow that original route. Because of sidewalk width, we crossed the street from right to left side and then walked across a bridge to where the street split off to the right. We continued straight, but crossed the street again back to the right side after the split. Following on that first day, these two crossings felt like corner turns to me. With my head up and eyes open, it was an easy straight path out the front door of the hotel!

As a driver, I've noticed the same phenomenon. When I am in the back seat or even in the passenger seat observing or just talking, my focus is on persons within the vehicle, not on the route. When I am driving the car, I pay attention to distances, landmarks, route names, and directions. When I am passively following or riding along, I do not. In Sao Paulo we were picked up for the ride from hotel to university and it took us several years to figure out the bus route and even how to walk. Without traffic, it takes about 10 minutes to drive what takes almost an hour in traffic.

How much we miss as passengers or spectators that we would observe and learn during our own wayfinding process!! Even by getting lost we are finding more than when we are carried like packages from one destination to another. My first visit to Florence was a blur because tour buses picked us up and dropped us off for each destination, leaving little room for wayfinding on our own.

## Hotel Europa

The Hotel Europa is old and of gracious proportions. I want to linger here. In the lobby sipping my Campari and soda, I learn that

Benito Mussolini, Giuseppe Verdi, and the Prince Von Bulow have lingered here as well. Our room, # 30, has a fresco on the ceiling! This could be a first for us! It is quite delicious to lie down and view a fresco on the ceiling; a ceiling at least double in height than any I have ever seen. As a child I would imagine rooms turned upside down with the ceiling serving as the floor. This room could accommodate another story between floor and ceiling, either upside down or right-side up. I could have a full loft with a spiral staircase right inside this room. High ceilings are probably created by economic wealth, having enough means to afford the building materials. Is that what I feel in this air that invites me to linger? We visit "foreign" experiences not only in the churches and galleries, but also in the private spaces, like Room #30 at the Hotel Europa in Ferrara, Italy. Breathing the air under this high and decorated ceiling, I am slightly transported, slightly ecstatic from the novelty, just the right mood to enhance the rest of the city when I am rested and refreshed from travel.

## Lingering Over Maps

I love maps. Maps are affordable gateways to movement and transformation; the intrinsic pleasure of stretching out an arm and reaching deep into the universe to grasp a star or a starfish. They are finite in shape, size, and data, but infinite as sinkholes into a jungle, desert, city, pyramid, marketplace, river, cave, museum, tundra, or fireside. Love of maps is similar to love of travel, and Pico Iyer describes that joy as "the luxury of leaving all my beliefs and certainties at home, and seeing everything I thought I knew in a different light, and from a crooked angle." (www.salon.com, March 18, 2000).

I love maps. When I taught seventh grade in my twenties, I petitioned AAA to donate a classroom set of USA road maps. I created individual student assignments to write directions from, say, Ypsilanti, Michigan to Portola, California. Each student would slowly read his or her directions while everyone else traced the route at their own desks. The goal was to skillfully guide everyone in the class from the starting point to the destination. It was a lot of fun, everyone participated, and I hope they learned something about giving (and following) directions! When my own two children were about middle school age, we bought a white van, customized it with a plywood seat/convertible bed, and set out across the country. Each day, one of the kids would be in charge of maps and directions, letting us know where we were, how far to the next destination, what crossroads or major intersections we should encounter, etc. That was a long car trip for young adolescents and I devised quite a few activities in addition to maps to occupy them through long stretches between territorial targets. There were no seatbelts in the van, the air conditioning stopped functioning before we hit Texas, and we had more than a few battles over who sleeps in the tent vs. the van!

I love maps. Several years after being lost on a highway near the wrong Las Vegas, I was clutching a subway map and learning the byways of Manhattan. One of my first assignments upon joining a small publishing house at the very bottom of the pecking order was to go to the map room of the New York Public Library and identify maps for a book called *Christianity Comes to the Americas.* It was a plum of a mission; I was the proverbial "kid in a candy store." With the authority of being on assignment, I looked at many more maps than necessary, completely fascinated by early perspectives of territory and experience. I recently came across this quote attributed to Christopher Columbus, "For the execution of the voyage to the Indies, I did not make use of intelligence, mathematics or maps." (www.brainyquote.com) Columbus does not, however, disavow using stories which long-preceded maps as inspiration for exploration.

Philosopher Michel de Certeau comments on the evolution of present day maps from narratives. "Maps of medieval times, which were really illustrated stories telling of journeys made and of memorable encounters along the way, were gradually supplanted during the early history of modernity by spatial representations of the earth's surface."[*]

I love maps. While I am out in the world spinning my own narrative thread, I often integrate a variety of maps. I superimpose maps one on another: for example, a simple grid marked only with numbers keyed to an index of site names is superimposed in my mind with a full color map that has little pictures of churches, monuments, tramcars, fountains, ships, etc. On a trip to Helsinki, Finland, I collected and carried around four maps: a guidebook map cut with a razor out of the big fat travel book, a color grid of streets, a tram map superimposed over light grey streets, and a sketch of the city with destinations of interest highlighted. I studied my maps frequently, seeking the layered knowledge of the city they offered. I was a visitor to Helsinki, but when a city dweller knows her or his own city, it becomes a series of layered internalized maps, many more than my four maps of Helsinki. For example, one layer would be a map of daily routines; another might be a map of significant sites in this person's life as lived in this city.

I love maps! My most recent map purchase is a world map called, "What's Up? South!" by ODT, Inc. It is based on the simple premise that our typical representation of north at the top of a map is somewhat arbitrary. How strange and unfamiliar the continents look when the whole scheme is reversed! I should have learned this lesson years ago from my favorite Sesame Street animation and jingle, "That's about the size of it....The big becomes the little when you see it back a bit....The huge becomes the dinky which is just the opposite." It's a lesson about relative sizes to be sure, but the refrain of "where you put your eyes" is significant when considering the perspective of a snail versus the whole universe, and those of us wandering in between, both near and far.

---

[*] According to Tim Ingold ("Up, Across, and Along" p. 48, accessed online at http://www.spacesyntax.tudelft.nl//media/Long%20papers%20I/tim%20 ingold.pdf) who reports on de Certeau The Practice of Everyday Life. 1984: 120-1)

### *Extra*

Getting to know a new city means inscribing a mental image, first by studying a grid of streets and neighborhoods and then strolling and exploring on the ground, beginning at the center or a particular neighborhood. For example, I need a bird's eye view of the magnitude of Central Park and its setting in Manhattan before walking through it from the Museum of Natural History on the west side to the Metropolitan Museum of Art on the east. That picture is also an aid in understanding a stroll down 5th Avenue from the Met to the New York Public Library's twin lions, and then all the way to Washington Square Park.

### *Extra*

Occasionally when I am working with maps of various perspectives, I am catapulted back to a nightmare I had as a child. I believe the images of the nightmare were acquired from a puzzle with figures of Disney characters playing ice hockey. The dominant color was an olive green, like a dark, underwater scene. Characters in the lower half of the puzzle—the foreground—were large, and characters in the top half—the background—were small. Goofy was swatting at a puck in the central foreground. Being small and inexperienced, I didn't know how or why these figures got so small or big and in my dream, I couldn't control their size, or, more frightening still, my own size. My thumb, it seemed, would balloon in size to match Goofy in that grey/green murky light and I couldn't stop it. Size was out of control; things grew and shrank with no rationale that I could grasp. I wonder if this was my first experience with perspective in a flat image? I wonder if the image itself was distorted and thus didn't match the world I saw? Anyway, sometimes a similar color will bring back the feeling of swelling out of all proportion to my ability to manage.

Josephine Carubia

# Searching for Lou Lou:
## Seeking, Not-finding, Finding

After long hot walking, a cool afternoon shower and three-hour nap, we were refreshed and ready to go out for dinner and music in Budapest, Hungary. We were both wearing socks and sneakers because of the blisters on our feet. We set out in a new direction from our hotel. After locating our final destination for the evening, a jazz club called "Jazz Garden" but which was underground, we continued our searching for a bistro called "Lou Lou" that our guide book lauded with words like "glowing ... intimate charm ... succulent . .. . mouth-watering." We tried several strategies, searching in what we thought was the right neighborhood, asking other tourists for directions, and feeling frustrated with one another for not being able to make this elusive destination appear around any of the corners we turned.

Finally, we settled for a nice sidewalk restaurant along the main walking street and enjoyed the fresh salads tremendously. They sated our appetites but not our longing for Lou Lou. At 9:30 we moved over to the Jazz Garden, that was not in a walled garden as we suspected and hoped, but was underground. After one set, we returned to Hotel Anna for another cool shower and a deep, heat-induced slumber.

After breakfast, I suggested we continue our search for Lou Lou. We were departing later that day, so we packed and checked out of the hotel, did some window shopping and then began to search in earnest for Lou Lou. We continued farther in the indicated direction than last night and gave ourselves a gift of coffee, water, and ice cream at Café Romantico for encouragement of our persistence. The café name also reminded us to enjoy our quest, rather than having it tamper with our moods. Our waitress at Café Romantico took our map into her own hands and scanned it until she found the street we sought. It was not too much further. V scouted while I stayed in the cool, shady breeze of the café whose tables were in a small park across the street from the building. The spirit of adventure (and romance) had been revived! My scout returned with a reservation for lunch in about 20 minutes, so I gathered up my notebook, magazine, and camera and we strolled to the anticipated pleasure of Lou Lou.

Lou Lou was an excellent special environment and culinary treat. We ordered a bottle of sauvignon blanco, a 3 course lunch for me and a mahi mahi for V. You know it's a fine restaurant when they bring you a porcelain spoon with tiny vegetables bits topped with smoked swordfish as a special appetizer from the chef. My salad with sautéed mushrooms and goose liver was great. There is a lot of goose on menus in Hungary! My main course was sea bass with manioc (like stiff mashed potatos) and violet potato with some lovely sauce. The dessert was fruit with zabaglione, a sweet cream. It was a very special meal—excellent food and wine, loving company, a beautiful day, more strolling ahead of us, and all this in an oasis of cool air! Were we lost in space or time the night before? We were trying to force circumstances that wouldn't yield. We couldn't find Lou Lou the previous evening because we were not in the right neighborhood, and possibly because we were not in the right frame of mind. I like to think of the perfect Lou Lou lunch waiting for us like an orb dangling in a fold between train whistles and jazz.

## Mostly Wandering and Eating

Wednesday: Walking day; change $, phone card, national museum Dieter Rot ; coffee at museum; up church tower; lunch at Lackjarbrekka salad and fish soup. Salon for beer and tea and books; Nap; FLIS jazz group at "Idno." Dinner, tortellini in our little studio apt. at Luna Hotel Apts. on Spitalastigur # 1, Reykjavik, Iceland.

Thursday: Walk to geothermal pool, closed. Jazz at Pravda ...what time? Plan for Friday tour, Call P. Buy tickets for Bach at church, art museum Dieter Rot. "Quantity not quality." Outdoor café with snacks and pils. Fish soup (not stew). Paris café: quiche and Chivas Regal and Pils.

Friday: Bus Excursion to "Golden Circle": volcanic crater, greenhouses with bananas growing indoors. Waterfall, geyser, tectonic plates separating ; Parliament. Nap. Dinner at Enrico's lamb, chicken diavolo. In the Pingvellir National Park, Icelanders revere a heritage of assembling every year from all parts of the island to affirm their laws and to deliberate on matters of communal import. The park is also a site of volcanic activity where the American and Eurasian tectonic plates seem to be pulling apart very, very slowly (3mm annually).

Saturday: Cultur Festival. Paris Café for French press coffee and cappuccino. Marathon: Oobla di, oobla da warming up with Puffin! Photography exhibit in park: Iceland, Greenland, Faroe Islands. Roast bull and grilled fish in center. Classical Music by Icelandic composers. Jazz trio at information center. Opera singers outside at Solon. Dinner at Solon chicken salad, shrimp and noodles. African drumming at Library, photo exhibit. Fireworks over harbor.

Sunday: Sleep late. Paris café for French press coffee, quick brunch with café Americano reading New Yorker and James Salter. Flea market for mittens for A and T. Art museum for more Dieter Rot (Roth) and Rube Goldberg video of flames, balloons, candles, dry ice, tires, boards, etc. Art makes meaning .. .. Radhus café on Tjorn for scotch, beer and reading and postcards. Anniversary dinner at Seafood Cellar "sjávarkjallarinn": mojito and white wine. Bread with olive oil and crushed nuts with anise. Plaice marinated in mandarin (appetizer taste from kitchen), wild asia soup and salmon bento box; salad and monkfish with Jerusalem artichoke and spinach. Vermouth sweet wine (complimentary) Wow!

Monday: Buy tickets for Blue Lagoon. Paris café. Radhus for topographical map. National museum of Iceland for history and culture. Shopping for kids souvenirs and J (artist's design pin, silver with moss agate) Bus to Blue Lagoon—fantastic! Solon Bistro for nightcap of Chivas and carrot cake, Viking beer.

Tuesday: Alarm clock 7 am; 9 am bring luggage to Hotel Odensve for bus to airport at 1:30 pm. Paris Café by way of window shopping.

Coffee, tea. Library for wireless internet and browsing. Bar Thorvaldsen lunch: Viking pils, soup Tamzum, chicken and fries with arugula. Gifts for children: woolen mittens, angora socks; puffin hand puppet; Icelandic charm for "strength in battle."

# Helsinki Wanderday

I woke up still tipsy from the champagne, red and white wine, and cordial liquor served at the conference Gala Banquet last night. I suppose the two Campari and sodas before the banquet didn't help much! After some time on email, I went back to bed for two hours from 8:45 to 10:45 am. I took the tram downtown to the University and the conference sites. I wanted to use my lunch ticket at the university, but neglected to notice I was in the wrong building! Oh, well, it was good soup and salad for 5.70 Euro! I couldn't make up my mind among options for the afternoon—an art museum that S recommended, a couple of conference sessions by friends, a session on Chinese medicine, or wandering. When the sky cleared and the sun came out, my mind was easily made up! I wandered to a market noted in guidebooks for both outdoor and indoor goods. I love markets! Why do we love outdoor or indoor markets? Is it the prospect of making a discovery among the many small stalls? Is it nostalgia for a shopping experience of yesteryear, when the purchaser engaged directly with the producer or proprietor? Is it the small size of establishments? For tourists it is probably all of the above plus the chance to get a good deal—shop where the locals shop. Thinking back to Salvador da Bahia, Brazil and the indoor market there, I had a sense that all the little stalls were part of one large business showing the same products for nearly the same prices. If I were cynical, I would conjecture that all of the small stalls at all of the tourist markets in most of the world are part of a network of outlets for a single gigantic factory in China somewhere producing "hand-made" lace table cloths and pashmina scarves.

After my lunch mistake that cost me an unnecessary 5.70 Euro, about $8., I have decided the rest of the afternoon is a no-spending zone, and opportunity to have fun without spending! The walk to find the market was part I, and touring the market itself was part II. I wandered a bit of the nearby shore where a floating café and benches were a possible stop. There is always a finger of water nearby in Helsinki. I aimed myself back towards the university, but I wasn't ready to end my adventure time and re-enter familiar territory.

My map showed that just across the street is the Botanical Garden. Not much is visible from the street, and I always hesitate to enter a wooded area in a city, being a New Yorker of the era of several horrific attacks on women jogging in Central Park. Yet, I decided to make a sudden detour here. My fear of wandering into a secluded and dangerous park was soon allayed as I followed signs to "Glass Houses," ornate botanical greenhouse buildings set in a large open area with sample plantings arranged geometrically around a circular fountain and a small, rectangular lily pond. I considered entering the huge glass buildings, but the fee of 4.20 Euro would destroy my happy commitment to enjoying the sunshine for its typical fee of zero. So, I'm sitting on a bench beside the lily pond with my sandals unbuckled and no sunscreen, soaking up vitamin D in advance of the rain predicted for tomorrow. A pair of mated ducks were enjoying the pond also, snacking on something I wouldn't recognize as food. The male more colorful, the female soft brown and purposeful. They waddled slowly away as two toddlers in pink hats approached. There are small groups of people sitting on benches and grass or strolling casually—a very relaxing garden oasis, though as soon as I begin to focus on sounds, I hear the trams and traffic through the trees.

Toddlers love water as much as ducks. And these two tiny girls alternate between the fountain and the lily pond where I predict one of them will topple by out-running her adult keepers. They can lean over the side of the fountain and dabble in the water so the fountain is more popular.

Here she comes eluding capture! Of course, she falls, but on the gravel path two feet from the edge of the lily pond. If not for the premature fall, Mama in pursuit would not have caught her until she was in the water. They'll have a wonderful day, though not perhaps as good a story to tell through the years. Like the time D tumbled into the stream behind our house on South Street. I saw him go head first and upside down into the water from the kitchen window and I ran to pull him out and carry him right to the shower to wash the mud off. He was probably about his daughter Anna's age, 4 years old. Here they come again with Mama and grandmother much closer in pursuit this time.

Difficult travel seems to make better stories in retrospect. SP recalled the time years ago before cell phones when V never showed up in Rome and I had to make the decision to get on the plane to Bari without him. I had no idea where he was though I had waited in the Rome airport for him all day. I was weeping quietly in my seat as that plane took off. Of course he was safe and fine, in a travel vortex of one delay causing an entire new itinerary routing him through another city.

Today's serendipitous gifts include a mermaid singing in the prow of an ancient boat parked on a trailer just outside the entrance of the main building of Helsinki University where I was sitting for a few last minutes of sunshine before going indoors for the plenary lecture. She (the mermaid) had long curly blond mermaid hair and she was sitting so as to comfortably rest her tail on the bench seat of the boat while she gracefully waved her arms and sang a few notes of the plaintive mermaid's song. At first I thought it was opera, but once I identified the source, all the mermaid memories of my life rushed back to fill these sounds with mermaid significance: luring sailors to the rocks, enchanting all who hear her.

My Helsinki Wanderday reminds me of the main character and narrator of Mark Helperin's novel, *Memoir from Ant Proof Case*, who worked for a huge investment bank where his job was to explore a country at the miniscule level, talking to small shop owners, fisherman on their boats, women selling their own vegetables, workers leaving a factory, etc. to determine the grassroots truth about the economy and whether it was wise to invest or not. I'm feeling ready to invest in Helsinki!

## Losing Farther

Elizabeth Bishop says "Lose something every day, embrace the fluster...Then practice losing farther, losing faster..."

By taking her advice just one or two steps further, you may experience the adventure of losing yourself.

I set out for a walk this morning and came back with a story of small adventure. Around the block in the right mood can usually yield a small adventure of some sort. Rather than venture out with no goal at all—mostly my preference—I set out with two small goals: sparkling water and black coffee.

Crossing two busy streets of cars, buses, motor scooters, and bicycles was easy; just wait for the light and the other pedestrians. They know the unmarked conventions of safe crossing. I took tiny steps, almost marching in place, rather than get out in front of the crowd crossing two wide thoroughfares to the diagonal corner away from New Era hotel in Nanjing, China. As I walked away from the hotel in the direction I vaguely recall from one year ago as leading to a grocery supermarket, I reminded myself to keep my eyes on the pavement. Setting aside ferocious lions, pools of water, twisted glass edifices, marble from unknown quarries, signs readable and unreadable, and all the perambulating bipedal stories, I must not be diverted from the transformations of flat surface into gradual steps, fragments of broken concrete, loose blocks of pavement, and shifts in texture.

I thought I was on the right track because I noticed a few adults carrying tote bags with what might have been groceries in them. After just one long and one short block, I recognized the signs of the business I recalled. An easy aid was the long line of familiar shopping carts being corralled through the open door by a young male employee.

Shopping carts are the same the world over? But where had these carts been dispersed? There didn't seem to be a parking lot.

Inside the door, I remembered the ground floor line-up of small shops—jewelry, tea, snacks—and followed other entering shoppers to the mechanical ramp leading up. I knew we had gone upward last year, but I didn't know how far. This morning I followed up and up, entering the merchandise area with everyone else. This was not what I remembered. I had been to a grocery store with fresh fruits and vegetables, meats, beverages, dry goods, and a bakery all in separate departments. This store had sections devoted to books, shoes, household items, electronics, clothing, bedding, and cosmetics. Might as well browse.

I picked up a bright blue basket and placed a few items inside: "Angry Birds" notepads, mini Chinese checkers, and a few small toys. After reading symbols on every different brand of bottled water, I placed two labeled "soda" water into my basket hoping this meant carbonated or sparkling water. I tried to identify the pattern of shoppers with full baskets to discern how they were paying and exiting. No pattern; they seemed to be circulating but not leaving. My next strategy was to ask an alert young clerk in the electronics department if he spoke English. He knew just enough to shake his head "No."

In the next aisle, I tried a taller young man with longish spiked hair who seemed very modern and worldly. "No." This time, I pointed to an item in my basket meaning that I wanted to pay for this item. He motioned me towards a section of the store. I realized that he was sending me toward the toy department, which made sense since I had pointed to a toy in my basket.

I took a 10 Yuan note from my wallet and approached several young women in uniform to ask them, first if they spoke English, and then to indicate the cash and my basket. They all turned me down. I noticed the first young clerk I had approached coming toward me and indicating that I should follow him. It was a crowded aisle, but I hoisted my blue basket high and followed. He took me to a desk in the cosmetics department. We smiled at one another and I said thank you with a big smile, hoping this would convey international appreciation. The two women at this desk began to shake their heads "No" as soon as I turned towards them with my questions and cash. They pointed downwards. It appeared that I was not only linguistically and horizontally misplaced, but vertically as well. They gave me a little hint as to how I could adjust my vertical attitude and, of course, that's when I saw the signs in several languages pointing to "Exit" and "Cashier."

I descended one level and found myself in the grocery store I remembered from a year before. By spying down all the aisles, I could finally see the goal, and I approached the long row of cashiers.

Every culture has a different etiquette of lines. In some, it is acceptable to crowd forward until one unit at a time is squeezed ahead of all the others toward the goal. In others, the correct moves require more patience and structure. This was a quiet and orderly maneuver across the many cashier desks and through the narrow aisles between. I had brought my own sack and this matched the expectations of the process. Soon I was on my way to discovering the street exit along both the vertical and horizontal coordinates. I stopped at Kentucky Fried Chicken to purchase the cup of black coffee and complete my morning's mission.

Elizabeth Bishop ends her poem, "The Art of Losing," with the struggle to accept "disaster." Fortunately, my adventure was almost entirely successful: my only minor "disaster" was that the "soda" water I imagined to be lively and sparkling was as flat and mild as newborn rain.

## Chaos and Complexity

The day in Istanbul began as we made the decision to skip breakfast and enjoy a more leisurely morning in our room. I had granola bars and pecans left from my travel cache of food and that made a simple breakfast. V doesn't eat breakfast anyway.

K knocked on our door when we were both naked, but we managed to communicate through the door that we would leave in about

30 minutes (around 11 am). My understanding was that we would skip out on the conference meetings to spend the day with the cultural attractions of Istanbul, the city.

When I emerged from our room to meet the three men in the lobby, they were waiting for me in the car. K wanted to return to the conference, to meet an Italian scholar who is scheduled to participate in the Early Fall Semiotic Seminar on the Black Sea (we hope to be invited). I resolved to be a Zen team member and go with the flow of the collective day.

Yes, the drive was taking minutes (because we were not lost this time), even though complicated by the "all entry-all exit" ramps we had to traverse to get from one side of an 8-lane highway to the other. Oh! At the last minute, a missed ramp! After an endless wait in the car, imagining reams of paperwork, hard benches in the police station, traffic prison for foreigners, and a beautiful sunny day wasted, K tells us he has persuaded the police officer to forgive us for an illegal U-turn.

The breeze picks up, refreshing us with morning energy again as we quickly arrive at the university, park the car, and enter the conference lobby. It is very nice to greet people we met the day and evening before, to eat delicious Turkish cookies and nuts, to sip tea, and to use the free computers.

K connects with M and we meet his lovely wife, S. We make decisions and let conference people know we will NOT attend the Gala dinner that evening. Hmmm, it seems they are setting up the conference lunch banquet. Shall we just stay and have a marvelous free lunch before setting out? "Yes!" is our collective decision, but waiting almost an hour for the lunch to begin is frustrating. We use the time to make connections with people and use the restrooms. We are positioned to be first on line for the buffet and we secure a table near the door to eat quickly and depart. I make the mistake of inviting a young Turkish instructor of English literature to join us for lunch as we are entering the room. She joins us as we are nearly finished with our quick lunch. It would be extremely rude to abandon her at the table. Finally, I excuse myself and all of us by saying we have made an appointment to meet someone and must leave. K backs us up by taking out his cell phone to let them know we are late. What I don't realize is that we are truly going to meet someone, and we are truly late for our appointment.

We walk out of the building and as we reach the street, IV decides he wants his backpack out of the car. We wait for him to go and return. We walk to the Metro station and then by metro and tram travel to the "center." K guides us to the "galleria" and we enter a labyrinth tunnel lined with small but extravagant shops with all kinds of carpets, clothing, glassware, gold and silver, etc. It is known for gold and silver and leather goods. Oh, the beautiful bags! It is like Arabian nights, glittering and inviting one to turn down each small way, through low arches to hidden, secret, exquisite, unique treasures waiting for your magic key to be found. We actually move quickly through on our way to rendezvous with three friends from Sofia. I'm wondering why we are rushing through this marvel to connect with people we will see for the next week. We do find them sitting at an outdoor café enjoying their lunch. We've already had lunch of course. I am cordial, but confused. Will this negotiation result in our sitting down to keep them company while they eat? V and I are eager to see something of the city! It is now about 4 pm and we are leaving in the morning. I'm trying to persuade myself that interpersonal connections are the most important experience of travel, not the historic sites and atmosphere of ancient ruins. The negotiations eventually result in a round of partings, and we head off to follow signs for the Sultanamet, finally.

V and I take off our shoes—and I accept a bright turquoise blue scarf to cover head and shoulders—and we enter the sacred space. The multi-domed space soars exultantly above an entirely carpeted floor. We later hear that this is the largest carpet in the world. I had thought it was simply pieced together of many small carpets. We don't linger because our friends are waiting, but we quietly absorb the massive pillars steadily supporting the uprush of spirit. We exit and head to the benches to meet our friends as arranged in advance. Without cell phones we are helpless to discover where they might be other than the benches, where they are not. Eventually, they realize that there is more than one exit to the building and we reunite.

After exploring a possible entrance to the Hagia Sophia, we examine the Egyptian obelisks and then seek a café for an afternoon beer. Of three along the street, we select the center one, the most modest, and rest our feet with our eyes on the dome and minarets of Sultanamet. K and IV leave us to retrieve the car from the university, drive back to our hotel, change clothes, and then meet us in about 3 hours at "the end of the bridge" that has a long arcade of restaurants—Galata Koprusu (two dots over all vowels).

As they walked away, we were overjoyed to be free of car, train, tram, taxi travel and group decisions for the next three hours! We strolled and sat, strolled and sat, enjoying the sights, sun, breeze, atmosphere of the city itself. After meandering to the body of water called "Halic" (dot under c) or "Golden Horn" we surveyed the busy waterway and shoreline. So many ferries carrying workers home for the evening! Far off in the distance we could see the outline of the bridge linking the European and Asian parts of the city (and continents). We crossed the bridge, previewing restaurants, and debated what K meant by the "end of the bridge" where we were to meet. Is it the definite line where water meets land? Or is it the place where the surface of the bridge extends in a gentle slope to meet the street? Should we wait on the left side or right, upper deck or lower? Appointing a meeting place is quite difficult, especially in unfamiliar places. For the second time today we were alone waiting at our appointed place and time. After several delays, a friend with cellphone found us and we reconnected with our group.

We were six for dinner, M and S having joined us. Making a decision based on six sets of expectations and appetites is not for the faint of heart ! Unfortunately, as is perhaps usual, we made a poor choice to eat on the bridge at a restaurant where an eager waiter had solicited us earlier promising excellent seafood and free coffee and fruit if we come back. We should have deferred to K who knew a local restaurant nearby. The food was meager and expensive! Upon pressure, Ali sent us two small plates of sweet figs as reward for purchasing, for example, two shrimp for 20 Turkish lira, about fifteen US dollars.

IV left us to meet a young Turkish woman and a tango party leaving the five of us to walk up the hill to the pedestrian streets of the Taksim area. We aim for a lighted tower above us and climb a steep set of street-stairs, possibly three or four flights, reminding me of Urbino in Italy and Erice in Sicily where, instead of streets, broad staircases (sometimes traversed by cars) run up and down the town. At the base of the Galata Kulesi tower is a local "town square" with benches and a few small cafés surrounding the open area. We can see and hear a live group singing "Let's twist again like we did last summer. Twisting time is here."

As we wander the lively streets and soft air in pleasant companionship and conversation, we come upon a jazz club with excellent music tumbling into the street. We peek and pass, another big mistake. For the sake of group coherence, V and I continue when we should have broken the group at this moment to stay and find our own way back to the hotel somehow later. The moment passes but the regret lingers.

Instead we continue as a group to the nightly festival on the lighted pedestrian boulevard leading up to Taksim square. People watching, people pressing, passing, teeming, streaming. What are the energies that pass among us to make this flow so delightful in the exotic air? We are molecules in a fluid, vibrating individually and collectively, creating a kaleidoscope of sensation. But V and I are the old ones now, a little tired at midnight, while the 30 somethings are just ready for some dancing. For the jazz, I would have revived for another hour, but no pastry shops or disco beat could keep me now.

K guides us to a side street off the pedestrian street where he found a taxi van last night. Instead of the expected line of vans, we encounter lines of people waiting. As K asks about the destination of those on the line, timing of the taxi vans, etc., people begin to engage with us to translate, explain, and solve the situation. First in French, then English, a large, well-dressed woman, begins to get involved. She is a translator, just finished with a travel group and wanting to go home very near our hotel. She and K arrange that we three will negotiate a regular taxi for 25 Turkish Lira. She will pay 5 and we will pay 20. What a relief! We talk cordially in the taxi, and since she is sitting in the front, she also speaks Turkish with the driver. Before our hotel stop, she gets out and tells us that we have to pay 25 and that she has just paid 5 for a total of 30 Turkish Lira. "The price changed because it is night," she says. Of course, we pay the additional fare, but sense that she has just cheated us. It is the capstone of the day—being cheated by someone who spoke our own language, seemed so helpful and professional, joined with us in a long ride, earned our trust, and then reverted to some selfish impulse. Even Ali the restaurant solicitor, gave us the plates of figs as he promised. This was a more personal insult, somehow. What does "trust" mean, and does it endure after times like this? Perhaps it is mistaken on our parts to trust anyone we don't have an ongoing relationship with, like family, colleagues, and friends? Perhaps we are the mistaken ones, and she is the one more consistent with human nature?

# CHAPTER FOUR

# Auracular Spaces

*All journeys have secret destinations of which the traveler is
unaware.* —Martin Buber

## Watching Me Watching You

As I approached the Amtrak ticket window at Newark Penn
Station this morning I smiled at a woman already in the
queue. She carried a handbag and rested her other hand on a
neat black leather backpack atop her suitcase. She returned my smile.
In some strange recognition between strangers, we acknowledged each
other as equals, "Smile or Hello" answering "Smile or Hello." Almost
saying: "In a pinch, you can turn to me."

The exact same encounter happened to me at the Amtrak counter
in Boston's Back Bay station four days ago. Women recognize their
peers in age, class, and circumstances almost instantly. It's part of a
survival instinct when traveling alone. Just like instinctively noticing
where the exits and restrooms are, women will identify the peer who

will be a potential ally if danger approaches. Later that same day, as the train approached my station, a woman entered the train and seemed quite anxious. She asked if the seat next to me was free and we chatted until I got off ten minutes later. She was apprehensive about this train ride, her very first. "People in Texas don't have this opportunity," she said. I reassured her and she seemed relieved as much by my presence as by my words.

On both ticket-purchasing experiences in recent days, I observed a woman in difficulty at the counter. For the ticket agents, these may have been just samples of many long narratives that unfold during the day. In Boston, the protagonist was an international woman with minimal English trying to buy a complex ticket that might have been impossible. She was short, dark-skinned, and elderly—three strikes against her in addition to the language barrier and limited resources. She was holding a zippered coin purse at the counter and I wondered if she would pay for her ticket with small bills or possibly even with coins. The agent must have expressed doubt about the feasibility of her desired route, because the customer responded in broken English, "I go this way many time." The agent tried again and then wrote a number on a slip of paper, handed it to the woman, and asked her to wait while she sold tickets to the few of us with immanent departures. I saw the price of $148.20 on the piece of paper and then my narrative boarded a train and diverged from hers.

At Newark Penn Station this morning, the woman facing her trial at the ticket window was young, white, and blonde. She had five or six bags at her feet. Not suitcases, but canvas and plastic bags with their handles tied together. She was in an extended conversation with the agent. She told him she had just been released from rehab in a mental hospital and she needed to get home today. Her voice was urgent and highly distressed, almost panicked. She rested her cheek against the palm of her hand and pleaded with him. He asked for her name and typed it into the computer. Perhaps she had a reservation but no identification? He couldn't give her the ticket without ID. When he asked for a phone number, she quickly gave him a number and told him that her ex-husband was at that number and he could give any information needed. The agent ultimately directed her to the police, "Go around the corner and turn left." She hooked all the bag handles with her fingers and walked off. When I left the ticket counter, I was relieved to see her in conversation with a policeman. I felt some tug to get involved, but I didn't.

Meanwhile, off to my left was a row of men who may or may not have had tickets, but who were sitting along the outside wall of the waiting room on a bench marked (as they all are) "Seating for ticketed passengers." They were watching, too. They were not watching the big board for their track number to appear. They were not watching the lines at the ticket windows to pick the fastest one. They were watching out for one another as they stepped outside and then returned to the warm station and the benches. They were also watching the passengers sitting on the other benches. I wondered if they were watching to see if someone dropped something that they could pick up and use or sell, but when a package of cigarettes fell out of the pocket of a passenger opposite me, one of the watchers got up and gestured to the man until he saw his cigarettes and retrieved them.

Another of the watchers called out, "Blossom! Blossom!" and I looked to see who might respond. I was not quick enough to catch sight of any Blossom passing by.

Leaning against the information booth in the center of the waiting area and looking out over all the benches and all the people was a uniformed policeman. He scanned the room attentively. What would happen if he were not watching? And the three young soldiers in buff camouflage uniforms that I saw as I came down the escalator at the Port Authority bus station on Tuesday morning? In the universe of humans watching other humans, we may have turned the page from watching to surveillance.

# Courtyards, Porticos, Loggias, Arcades

Courtyards, porticos, loggias, arcades—these are all features that occur rarely in the US and therefore they are more appealing when we travel. These are liminal spaces, neither fully indoors or out.

I am particularly attracted to the framing of a courtyard entrance, looking through and beyond the frame to the space enclosed. I see in my vacation and travel photos a theme emerging as I have tried to capture this visual delight over and over again. Have I ever asked myself what is so appealing about this particular visual composition? And, is it just me, or is it all of us? The components of this aesthetic delight are the framing arch, the intimate enclosed space beyond it, the focal point within the enclosed space, and the quality and patterns of shade and sunlight through the arch and across the features of the space. Thinking of this particular courtyard composition in Ferrara, Italy, I was delighted by the symmetry of the interior view, a large pottery urn with greenery and flowers in the center of a white pebbled yard. At the back of the courtyard, there was a wrought iron fence and beyond the fence, a variety of trees that created a backdrop. But symmetry is not required. I recall the scene of an inner courtyard in the family home of Raphael in Urbino. I couldn't get an angle to photograph any symmetry, nor was there much symmetry to be had between doors and windows on several levels. The focal point of flowers in a corner and the slant of shadow created a diagonal dimension to the image that I find just as pleasing. Just writing this now reminds me of an academic paper I wrote called "Horticulture and Hysteria: Gardens in the Fiction of Henry James." I believe I am thinking of many of the same components he created in the enclosed spaces of his novels, seeking to express a particular condition of consciousness.

# Immersion

First of all, the landscape of Iceland looks more like a moonscape. As you view the terrain from a moving car or bus, it looks like a catastrophe struck here years ago (and of course it did). Whether it was a volcano spewing lava or a retreating glacier, there is a certain austere beauty in the devastation of the broken black landscape. We have chosen to go to the Blue Lagoon at night, but it will really be twilight. It seems we are approaching an industrial plant in the middle of nowhere, with low buildings and one or two towers giving off steam. The bus parks in a small lot surrounded by mounds of lava boulders so we have no anticipatory view of the lagoon, heightening desire and postponing satisfaction. We walk on a path through a blackened landscape and past several small pools of preternaturally blue water. The entrance to Blue Lagoon, a premier geothermal spa, is through a spa building, indicated on a map as "indoor lagoon area." The exact way is not clear, but we eventually find towels and the men's and women's locker rooms and then our separate passageways out to the actual lagoon. There is no organized way to stash your towel while you are in the water, so it's up to chance whether you find the same towel, or any towel, when you come out, but the milky turquoise water is so inviting we don't think about this quite yet. We wear our locker keys on a bracelet around the wrist. The water is amazing, filled with minerals so we are buoyant beyond our previous experience and expectations. The temperature varies from location to location in the shallow lagoon and we bob around, half floating, half paddling to feel the different currents and temperatures. There is a steam-like mist rising from the water so even body parts above the waterline feel like they are submerged. The buoyancy and the heat melt away any sensations of tightness or tension, almost melting away any sensation of having a body at all. Just jelly-fish like appendages and a mute sensibility floating through the thick primordial sea. Leaving the Blue Lagoon is like being born into a colder, harsher reality of gravity and the struggle for survival—lost towels, expensive food, tempting spa products, and a long, dark bus ride home. Two years later, I am opening the complimentary "mineral moisturizing cream" which has as long an ingredients list as any of my usual products, but thankfully no fragrance to irritate my skin and nose. I spread the small sample on my right forearm and "tennis elbow" hoping for Blue Lagoon magic from the memories and the small packet of mineral cream.

## Auracular Space #1
## London and Libraries

I remember the first time I realized that there is an invisible mist or essence around me and other people, an aura of sorts. It looks like empty space, but it is inhabited with sensory receptors and meanings.

I was sitting in one of six chairs at a heavy oak table. My work was spread out in front of me, and my molecules and meanings were also spread out, maybe eight inches all around my body, maybe even farther. It must have been farther because when another person took a seat opposite me and began to spread out his work and his molecules and meanings, mine were disrupted. I tried to continue thinking, but my processes had been punctured. I made the reasonable request that the person move to another table and he was offended. That chair was empty, the space was free. Wasn't it? No, it was most certainly occupied, though he could not see or believe that it was.

The image in my mind of what my aura looks like, if it could be seen, is something close to what we see in magnified images of zooplankton: an undulating misty gel that floats around my solid flesh and bone, spreading like a three dimensional halo with indistinct boundaries and a very delicate, sensitive skin just one scintilla thin.

That is just my personal space. There are many kinds of auracular spaces, both personal and communal; human and natural. There is also a resonance between the individual spaces and those larger spaces that are also filled with meanings and sensory experience. More than a resonance even, it is a visceral attraction, a kind of magnetic allure. We go to certain spaces—and we create certain types of spaces through architecture—that tickle and amplify the auracular sense.

In work-a-day life, the zooplankton don't register in awareness and I'm not attuned to my aura while commuting from station to station. On the other hand, in wandering time and thinking time, the aura unfolds and glows with sensitivity.

We strolled up the Strand, past the Inns of Court to St. Paul's Cathedral. It was closed, so we used the opportunity to have a bit of refreshment and conversation, and then took the tube to Westminster and enjoyed a leisurely stretch of time meandering around the tombs and chapels of the Abbey centered around the shrine of St. Edward the Confessor (c.1002-1066). Mosaics here date from 1268. Old cathedrals always evoke in me questions of sacred space: what architectural manifestations realize the worshipful thoughts of cultures and generations? What exactly were those populations worshiping, and why do we visit these spaces in awe? Sacred space may be a species of what I am calling auracular space.

And a cathedral may be a species of human enclosure that seeks to replicate the experience of awe felt in some natural spaces. In his diary of 1832, the twenty-two year old Charles Darwin speaks of the rain forest of Brazil in these terms.

> *Whilst seated on a tree, & eating my luncheon in the sublime solitude of the forest, the pleasure I experience is unspeakable ... . I can only add raptures to former raptures ... . I was led by feelings ... to the firm conviction of the existence of God, and of the immortality of the soul ... [W]hilst standing in the midst of the grandeur of a Brazilian forest, it is not possible to give an adequate idea of the higher feelings of wonder, admiration, and devotion which fill and elevate the mind. I well remember by conviction that there is more in man than the mere breath of his body.*[*]

---

[*] (http://www.pbs.org/wgbh/evolution/darwin/diary/1832.html)

Human feats of soaring; enclosed space of stone or steel and glass are attempts to replicate that experience in human settlements. St. Chapelle in Paris filters light through colored glass to achieve a related effect, not soaring height, but visually intense and stimulating space. Is the effect of a place like Stonehenge thought to be the same? Was it an attempt to evoke other senses or to evoke spirit directly?

After Westminster we search out the underground Cabinet War Rooms where Churchill and his advisers spent the most dangerous days and nights of WWII. The rooms are preserved just as they were at the end of the war. Broadcasts of Churchill encouraging the citizens of England are tremendously moving in several rooms where photographs of the effects of German bombing surround the listener. Especially after seeing *Copenhagen* the previous evening, we can't help but be awed by evidence of the devastation and extremity of war. In this space, I realize that I don't fully appreciate my father's perpetual retelling of his stories of landing on D-Day and liberating Europe with the First Infantry. This was the defining experience of his life.

Exhausted by so much concentrated viewing, listening, feeling, we take a respite in a low-ceilinged pub with another version of bitters and fish and chips and then return to our hotel for a rest and planning for the evening. By the time we get re-mobilized, a movie seems the best idea and we take a London cab (quite the luxury experience!) to see a film called *The Last September* about the final days of English imperialism in Ireland as "the troubles" were beginning to erupt. Some fine performances, but a very difficult script, confusing, gaps, etc. We walked home and found a late snack of hummus and nutty wheat bread at a local mini-mart just before closing.

We missed breakfast time at the hotel on Saturday morning, but that's vacation! We walked to the nearby British Library and in far more beautiful, indeed inspiring, surroundings, had a brunch-time snack. This library, opened within the past two years, is a sacred space of a different kind. Its modern design wants a little exploring before full appreciation dawns on the explorer. The feature that transformed it from a building into a work of art for me was the six-story glass tower of books at its center. Called "The King's Library" this collection of 65,000 volumes from George III's library is a stunningly beautiful, and yet practical, column that defines the core public space in the entire building. To be in the presence of this commitment to the history of human thought seems to me a kind of worship. I could sit here, in the fullness of this presence, and read and talk all day.

We spend deeply-felt time in the hushed and darkened manuscript room noting the qualities of documents such as the Magna Carta, the letter of King John listing the "liberties conceded by him to his subjects" in 1215, as well as many handwritten manuscripts of our favorite literary figures: Yeats, Joyce, Woolf, Auden, among others. In this room, you can put on headsets and press a button to listen to the recorded voice of many of the figures who did public broadcasts in the early years of radio. We both listened to Virginia Woolf's broadcast from April 20, 1937 of an essay called "Craftsmanship."

> *This power of suggestion is one of the most mysterious properties of words. ... Words, English words, are full of echoes, of memories, of associations. ... they are so stored with meanings, with memories ...*
>
> *[Words] hate anything that stamps them with one meaning or confines them to one attitude, for it is their nature to change. Perhaps that is their most striking peculiarity--their need of change. It is because the truth they try to catch is many-sided and they convey it by being themselves many-sided, flashing this way, then that. Thus they mean one thing to one person, another thing to another person; they are unintelligible to one generation, plain as a pikestaff to the next. And it is because of this complexity that they survive.*

We also spent some time with a real printing press and heavy metal pieces of type in another room. We are both attracted to the physical object of "book" as an experience rapidly diminishing in importance in our globalized world. What does it mean if the texture and subtleties of paper, color, and weight are no longer associated with the process of reading or learning? Does it mean anything? We have always been subject to changes in technology that have one generation lamenting the loss of their valued experiences while another embraces new modes and values. We have lost the power of memory through the printed word. Some say we gain the very fullness of association that Virginia Woolf lauds through our new web-based technology where links create a finely threaded network of meanings, echoes, memories, and potential futures. Have we lost very much as we gain this speed of technological association? I think so. It feels different to experience the associations coming via synapse firing in one's own brain than via hypertext links across the internet. Loss or gain, is anyone measuring this?

It was hard to leave the rich auracular space within that library that resonates at the same frequency as my own aura. V and I had our first date in the New York Public Library on Fifth Avenue. He was sitting outside on the steps between the stone lions waiting for me, wearing a red shirt. I approached via 41st Street and saw him first. We sat beside one another in the main reading room for hours. The compatibility established in that afternoon will last us a lifetime.

## Memorial

We are on the train from Opole to Krakow. It is a sunny day. There are light woods along the tracks. We are riding in first class with six people per cabin vs. second class with eight people. We are excited to be on our way home. The train stops at small stations, like Kedzierzyn-Kozle. Flowers grow over the tracks (tor), softening the concrete lines of the platforms (peron). Learning how to read the arrival location of your train and distinguish between platform and track is crucial!

I was reviewing my photos this morning and I was again intrigued by the street sculpture of ashen people marching into the sidewalk on one side of a busy intersection and marching out on the opposite corner. Seven figures of pewter color with dark ash faces. The ones in the back standing on top of broken sidewalk, the ones in front half way submerged as they descend through the pavement to enter the earth. A woman with baby carriage is making this transit along with a man with briefcase and workers of different professions and economic levels. What does it mean? One thought is that it was a memorial to Polish Jews begin marched off to prison camps. But also it could simply be a memorial to the quotidian tide of workers marching on the route to and from work. Their faces seem stoic-conveyed by the rigid material as well as by expression.

Other street sculptures are whimsical—two elves heaving a ball of marble; a bevy of barnyard animals casually arranged in a courtyard of art galleries. I photograph them, but they do not intrigue me. Their purpose seems whimsical, not meaningful. I realize I'm not much interested in monumental religious figures. I am intrigued by the meaningful, abstract, or unusual.

## Sacred Space: Knole

On Sunday we made an excursion via train from London's Charing Cross station to the village of Seven Oaks to visit Knole, Vita Sackville West's ancestral home and the setting for Virginia Woolf's fantasy, "Orlando". We stocked our carry-all with a baguette of "jambon fromage" reminiscent of our love affair with Paris, paid six pounds, thirty each for the ride of about 45 minutes, and then took a cab up the hill from the train station to the manor house. As we entered the grounds, the magic that both women extolled was apparent. Deeply indented hillsides with varied aspects of mowed contours, woods, magnificent trees, curved drive, and live deer fulfill the eye's and the imagination's need for texture, suspense, and the paradox of intimate vista. Entering the "outer wicket" into the Green Court was an experience akin to entering the mystical wardrobe or falling down the rabbit's hole into a world where you find yourself dressed in "olde," yet familiar, garb, understanding an antiquated language, greeting mythical figures with graceful gestures of yesteryear. We read each other the guidebook as we meandered from room to room, wanting it to continue beyond our wildest dreams, but it was all too soon over. The King's Room was gaudy, the ballroom was elegant and faded, the Great Hall echoed with majesty.

"More! I want more! Can we see everything?"

Well, of course not. Apparently some family still live in parts of the house and desire their privacy. We see photographs and drawings of the gardens and additional inner courtyards, but we are turned out after gawking (though reverently) at the "show rooms" as Vita would call them when she herself had to take family visitors on tours. Reading her biography incessantly after this visit, I now know of the many stolen kisses that delighted Vita on those tours.

The guide book to Knole contains a memorable quotation from *Orlando* describing a return to Knole:

> [U]p the curving drive between the elms and oaks through the falling turf of the park whose fall was so gentle that had it been water it would have spread the beach with a smooth green tide. Planted here and in solemn groups were beech trees and oak trees ... All this, the trees, deer and turf, she observed with the greatest satisfaction as if her mind had become fluid that flowed around things and enclosed them completely. Next time she drew up in the courtyard where, for so many hundred years, she had come, on horseback or in coach and six, with men riding before or coming after ...

Our next trip will have to include a visit to Sissinghurst, the estate that Vita and her husband, Harold Nicolson, nurtured into one of the most famous gardens in England. After this trip, I learned that my

Pennsylvania friend, MG, had lived nearby as a child and remembers visiting Sissinghurst and being shown the gardens by Vita herself!

Reluctant to leave this world we strolled back through the deer park and grounds and down to the village, looking out for a lovely spot for a Sunday afternoon repast. We stopped at Café Rouge, a French bistro with lovely dark wood, high ceilings, stained glass, assorted country chandeliers, and a family birthday party. Over a bottle of wine, we talked and read each other snippets of our books and felt ourselves in the French countryside. The bistro atmosphere is decidedly different from the English pub atmosphere. Several hours later, we took many photos trying to capture the light and playful essence of the afternoon idyll and then strolled to the train station and back to London.

## Inertia

*Sicily is the schoolroom model of Italy for beginners, with every Italian quality and defect magnified, exasperated, and brightly colored ... . Everywhere in Italy life is more or less slowed down by the exuberant intelligence of the inhabitants: in Sicily it is practically paralyzed by it.* —Luigi Barzini, *The Italians*

It is Tuesday at 5:40 p.m. My cousin, Joseph and I are in Erice, high above Trapani. Today we went to the island of Favignana which was lovely, stark and rocky. Not much to see or do, but lovely. Favignana: Ferry at 9:15 a.m., 32,500 lira ($26 one way), Siramar line, huge. We drove around the island, stopped at a beach, walked around and saw sea urchins and I got tar on my new jeans. In the village, we stopped in a tiny restaurant and had risotto fruto di mare and I wondered if this was "cous cous." We saw some caves and took the ferry back to mainland at 3:30 p.m. I sort of wanted to stay, but he wanted to move on, which, as it turns out, was the better choice. I sometimes have inertia; sometimes I don't.

# Sacred Space: Salisbury and Stonehenge

It took longer to drive to Salisbury than I had expected. The cathedral is gorgeous. It is set on wide lawns so when you see it, you see all of it. Ancient looking. Uncluttered inside, unlike Westminster. The choir was having a rehearsal and sounded beautiful. Something special happened for us in each cathedral we visited. In the round "chapter house" is the Magna Carta, one of three copies left. Also a seal of John Donne, one of my favorite poets. Salisbury is a tempting town with pretty streets and shops and teas and taverns. We rushed out to catch Old Sarum before closing time. It was the original site of Salisbury Cathedral.

"Soft verges" equals "soft shoulders" of the highway. We had break-fast at 8:15 a.m. and met a couple who had been to the Scottish high-lands. They say it is much more beautiful than England. And I thought England was beautiful! We visit Stonehenge in the foggy English mist this morning. I felt all tingly and excited as we walked toward it. Do you suppose that the power of this meeting place of centuries was still in the air? Could I feel it? I wish I could have walked among the stones, but that is prohibited and visitors can only walk the periphery.

# Auracular Space #2
# Sitting Still

*"Matter, it was discovered, can be used to tell time.*
*'A rock,' said physicist Holger Müller, 'is a clock.'"*
—Harper's Magazine, *"Findings"* March 2013

I am sitting still in a small park on a compact university campus in downtown Nanjing, Jiangsu Province, China. The temperature is in the 90's and I am inclined to remain motionless while humid currents circulate around me.

A dark-haired woman picks up a long bamboo pole and begins to swat at the plum-sized yellow fruit suspended in bunches above her head in the branches of a tree. Her companion picks up the fallen fruit and rubs it with water from a jar. She then places it on the seat of a wheelchair already occupied by a slight and immobile man in white pajamas. He may not be aware that he has become a basket for the ripe fruit.

The two women are slightly heavier and quite a bit darker in flesh than many of the other women in this city; they may be ethnic minority Chinese employed as home health aides for this elderly and seemingly incapacitated man. Three animated elderly people sit on a bench nearby eating the same fruit. The two trios are linked by the sweet ripe fruit, but nothing else.

Two school girls pass by arm in arm. Workers traverse the path just beyond the low railings with small wheelbarrows behind bicycles filled with tools and pallets of water.

The clicking sound of high heels draws my attention to a slender woman in a long-sleeved black dress with a spine overtly zippered from neck to hem.

I hear a flute somewhere behind me in the middle air.

Another wheelchair approaches the bench to my left. A young adult male pushes an older man. After transferring the older man to the bench, the younger one sits beside him and turns his full attention to his cellphone. The older man enters the park's ambiance in the role of witness.

The wooden benches are built to seat two comfortably, but they are mostly occupied one by one by one.

This park strays toward the wild side with soft low grasses that are not trimmed between the paths. The shrubs and trees are carefully randomized to present every shape, texture, and size with limbs growing horizontally, vertically, diagonally, and fractally. Greens go forth as leaves, fronds, tufts, fingertips, feathers, sprays, needles, fans, ferns, shoots, and every other possible projection and extension to form a thick and light-entrapping tent. Fallen and falling leaves become part of the appealing pattern.

Pensive notes from several flutes at a distance play hide and seek among the leaves.

This garden has many more paths of patterned tiles than necessary to pass through it in any direction. The trails criss-cross and converge at a five-pointed, off-kilter star deliberately far from the notion of center. The tiles inscribe skewed triangles and irregular four or five-sided geometric shapes. This park makes a deliberate statement about beauty and order, reminding me of the Wallace Stevens line, "The imperfect is our paradise." To rest inside this space is to pause outside the ordinary. Though all sides have low boundaries, no glance in any direction gives up the secret of its size and shape. Peripheral vision is quiet on the subject, making no guesses.

A woman with silver hair and red shoes scribbles in a notebook. Three brightly dressed girls take photos of a baby sitting on a bench. A pregnant woman listens to music through headphones.

An organic breathing space offering the privacy of intimate public rooms, this botanical sanctuary presents two objects for visual convergence. One is a bronze head on a large, slightly irregular stone block. The other is a water-pocked stone in the shape and size of two horses kneeling nose to nose. Formed of elements and momentum, the stones beckon like evidence.

I am still ...

sitting ...

and then ...

the flutes draw my themes onward.

The park takes another breath and recomposes space and time around the flight of a single white butterfly.

## Sacred Space: Two Temples in the Oven

Nanjing is known as one of the ovens of China. The students tell us that they never go outside in the summer, and this May day is a mimic of a day in the summer oven.

Our first false start is to the nearest ticket office for arrangements to Hangzhou, but even with scheduling decisions made and money on the counter, we were nowhere without our passports. The prickly heat invaded our conversations as we retreated to the hotel for the documents. We moved onward from there, confident that there would be another ticket office along our way.

Metro two stops to Xuanwu Lake stop (Xuanwumen) at Hunan Road. Our strategic student guides turned us to the right giving us a long, long stroll along the lakefront toward the gate closest to the Jinming Temple. Families and lovers camped out for the day on benches, grass, stone outcroppings, and pavilions. Many small boats on the lake. Too hot to walk along the top of Ming Dynasty wall. Too hot for much, but we kept going out of determination. I didn't faint and that was the major achievement of this segment of our day.

## Ascent

Jiming Buddhist Temple climbs stage by stage toward heavenly bliss. In my case, this was an ascent into flames. After each flight of stone steps, I anticipated a cool entry into dark chill spaces, but found yet another hot stone platform leading to a further set of steps. The only cool recesses were souvenir shops, and we lingered in the doorway of one to catch mechanically processed air for free. We also stole air and seating in the lobby of a small hotel at another level.

The temple's structure is very impressive, with small open areas leading always higher to additional areas. At each level there would have been purposeful spaces in the life of the temple inhabitants, but they are now occupied by shops and other visitor facilities. There are still small worship halls at each level, with a central altar at which were placed apples and incense and flowers. Kneeling cushions were located along the sides for appropriate obeisance and prayer.

Two symmetrical stairways led from each level up to the next. The view from each level and from the stairs was of the tiled and pointed roofs of the many rooms of the lower levels so you are always aware of your relative position along the vertical journey. You are small and individual and the journey involves many layers, each of which is specific and complex. There is plenty of elevation, but no soaring; there are small beautiful chapel-like rooms, but no opulent magnificence. It is a different sort of inspiration than the cathedrals of Europe and the mosques of Istanbul.

At one of the higher levels (but not the top), we could see monks sitting in silence on the floor around the altar in the center of a large worship room. We didn't know if they were sitting in meditation, scholarly memorization, or even in punishment. At the next level up we discovered the purpose of the incense sticks we had been given. On this scorching day, we should enter a small, stifling room where a hundred candles were already burning to light our incense sticks and then perform a ritual of devotion and blessing by bowing toward each of the four directions. The smoke and flames seemed too much to bear, but I had come this far and must take the opportunity or forever regret it. I lit my three sticks and followed our gentle guide's instructions. Bending and bowing is more than just exercising muscles; this particular motion has an actual humbling effect. I held out my hands to receive blessing, folded my hands to accept blessing, and brought my hands to heart to safeguard the blessing. It is amazing how articulate certain gestures can be. An empty hand is never an empty gesture. Extending an open hand speaks of vulnerability and supplication when it is not combined with facial expression or words for a command or demand.

This smoky level was still not at the pinnacle of the structure, but it appeared to be the highest level for visitors. The open doors and windows of a vegetarian restaurant allowed views of the city wall and lake. We could glimpse the temple's central tower or pagoda rising at least six or seven levels higher. If given the opportunity, would I have the vigor to continue beyond my exhaustion? What doorways would lead to these levels and who would be permitted to ascend? Or was this a symbolic structure to signify that there are always further levels where we cannot go? Upon reaching the very top level, would there be yet another doorway or staircase in the air? I must return on a misty cool day to see, not the view, but the meaning.

After descending quickly with only one near catapult into space, we jumped out at a taxi delivering another visitor and began the ride through crowded streets to a temple of another sort: The Confucius Temple. The streets were congested, the sidewalks even more so. A million small shops flourishing on a hot Saturday.

Upon disembarking from the taxi, I noticed a very nice looking hotel that was sure to have some lounge, tea room, or bar where we might cool off, have a beverage, and speak quietly to each other. We also spied another ticket office. First, let's be cool so that we can make the decision about travel with mental functions alert and not in distress. We entered the Mandarin hotel lounge called Firenze and were soon behind glass and grass on a continent far from the congestion and heat. While sipping cool beverages and eating ice cream, we talked about poetry and made a decision to forgo additional travel in the few remaining days of our time in China.

With renewed energy we emerged to seek the temple through the narrow labyrinthine byways of shops and visitors. Without intending to shop, we purchased two fans and four embroideries. Just imagine if we had intentions!

The Confucius Temple is a worthy destination, with historical artifacts and graceful courtyards and enclosures. In one courtyard, I paid a little extra to sound the huge bell : 2 Yuan for one swing of the mallet. In the next interior space, I paid 5 Yuan to go onto the stage and play a series of bells of different sizes. I was willing to turn around for just one photo and then my full attention was on the bells. By the time we left this temple, we were exhausted and overheated again and we decided against entering the examination hall.

All four of us were taxed and communication was strained. The ideal next move would be to sit down in a quiet, air-conditioned restaurant for simple food and conversation. How would we achieve this? It was a perplexing problem and not one of us had the experience to solve it. We took the lead from our students who led us to a shopping complex a few streets away hoping to find a restaurant there. It was crowded and loud and the food offerings seemed to be just like an American shopping mall or airport "food court" with open seating in the center of an array of booths. After another period of mutual exploring and four-way indecision-making, we entered and left two or three restaurants and finally ended up at a Japanese noodle house just before we all might have collapsed in tears and tantrum. The food was tasty and fast and quite inexpensive, just 127 Yuan (about $20.) for the four of us.

Our guides put us into a taxi with instructions to the driver. They were relieved to see us off so they could resume their young lives without us!

What will I remember from this day? The impression of heavenly ascent at Jinming Temple, the bells at Confucius Temple, and the muddles over tickets and food.

# CHAPTER FIVE

# Shopping and Collecting

*Collecting expresses a free-floating desire that attaches
and re-attaches itself—it is a succession of desires. The true
collector is in the grip not of what is collected but of collecting.*
—Susan Sontag, *The Volcano Lover*

What are we doing when we shop on an international trip? What does it MEAN? First of all, we might think "Things here are a lot cheaper than at home, so I should buy them here, even if I don't buy these things at home." Another line of reasoning is that these specific items are made here so I am getting it from the source; it is rare at home, thus it is exclusive and unique to have an X made in Y.

We also buy for status: people will see that I have this rare and unique X that I will tell them I bought in Y and that will raise my status in their opinion. Aside from these reasons, people expect gifts when a traveler returns from a big trip. I like to receive gifts when others return, and I want them to like the things I bring back for them. My usual habit is to buy a lot of things and then assign them to people when I get back. It would involve a lot of planning to purchase for specific people instead of the random buying that I do! I can't carry a lot of weight, so I must find small items that are not very fragile. Silks and other fabrics are very good—so easy to fit into the luggage and very light.

Finally, I am sometimes buying for myself beautiful things I can't resist. There are usually time limits to shopping opportunities, and making a selection is very difficult for me with time constraints. I like to think and compare, so sometimes I don't get the thing I wanted. If I'm pressured, I might not engage in the desire. Bargaining is not a skill I have much experience with so I often pay the listed price, even if bargaining is expected.

## Voodoo and Velveeta

When we saw him in Urbino, Italy, W told us not to miss the Feria São Joaquim authentic market in Salvador da Bahia, Brazil. For this you need a local guide or friend because it is wild and dirty, and not usually included in tourist itineraries. We were fortunate to have a new friend, C, who offered to drive us to special off-the-beaten-track places. It was a dry day and thus we were spared the green slime puddles described in our travel book. We entered the market in a region of fruit and grain stalls and were immediately immersed in unfamiliar and elusive scents that we learned later may come from the cashew fruits that we found stunning in their oddity.

One of the excitements and visual attractions of this market is the plenitude of offerings: piles and piles of grains and nuts, mounds of bundles of herbs for healthful bathing, and basket upon basket of handcrafted household items, like my favorite wooden spoons (5 spoons for 2 Reals).

C's student friend from Spain was seeking a particular artifact at the market on this day, a 2 foot by 2 foot plaster statue of St. George on his white horse, lit from within through lines of small holes emitting light when plugged in. We found St. George at various stalls for different prices before J made his final purchase on our way out of the market, possibly at the very first place he looked.

The main aisles of the market were thoroughfares with carts traversing among teeming stalls and slowly moving crowds. Some carts carried small goats lying on their sides with their legs tied together, chickens crammed into wooden crates, pigeons, and rabbits. In one booth, there were three or four video machines set up with young men avidly playing imaginative games in the midst of a more colorful and dramatic reality than that on the screen.

The specificity of animal body parts for sale was the most difficult sight for my eyes. A section of the market was devoted to the sale of meats, but I have never witnessed, even in my farm days when I helped slaughter cows, such a display of tongue, or liver, or snouts, or tails, or intestines, or stomach, or other organs I couldn't identify. It was possibly the grouping of so many snouts or tongues or hooves together that was disturbing. There were also stalls selling what I can only describe as "bits and pieces" of unidentified stuff, not quite meat or bone or gristle. I don't recall seeing any ice in this section to chill the meat. Unfortunately, when I decided to have a steak several nights later—for me quite an unusual choice—I couldn't separate the market sights from the meat on my plate and found I couldn't really enjoy it.

I couldn't quite guess what offerings at the market were fodder for voodoo ceremonies. Was it the baby goats? Or the beads? Or some of the herbs? I did see what appeared to me "voodoo dolls", small red stuffed figures that seemed to be exactly right for sticking pins. Although they were quite inexpensive, I didn't touch or purchase any. Just in case there really is a power in voodoo, I didn't want to mistakenly activate it and then think of someone quite casually, and then accidentally crush the voodoo doll under a book in my bag, and thus contribute to the mysterious illness or injury of anyone I know. Just in case voodoo is real. Just in case. It even seems strange to me to think this way, but there is evidence enough that some things are not to be understood in this world. For example, on another journey recently, I was two hours from home making a transition from train to bus on a very tight schedule as I approached the counter to purchase my ticket. After twelve hours on the journey, I was quite anxious to get my ticket and be on the bus for the last leg of the trip. If I missed this bus, I would have no way home that night. There were two windows open for tickets, but no attendant at the one on the left, so I waited behind a customer at the window on the right. As a woman came to the left hand window, I switched and approached to ask for my ticket. Velveeta, the clerk at the left hand window was making change for someone, but assured me she would be right with me. Of course, as soon as I abandoned the right hand window line, many other people approached and shut off my access. Velveeta came back from her errand and took my information. I handed over my money as she clicked away on her computer to print the ticket. Nothing happened. My exhaustion and anxiety nearly brought tears to my eyes and I'm sure Velveeta noticed. She told me to relax (which always makes me more anxious) as another clerk joined to assist her. Finally, the two of them were able to release the frozen machine from the power of my anxiety and allow it to print the ticket. Surely, if my anxiety vibrations can freeze the printer, we need to have respect for the power of voodoo! Another day I'll write the story of how my extreme anxiety diverted subway trains in New York City!

## Too Much Of A Good Thing

We arrived about an hour late for our last day in Krakow because of a train strike in Germany, or so we surmised. The "downstream" effect of delayed trains in Germany flowed across the border to Poland.

A very nice English-speaking man in our first class cabin pointed us in the direction of our hotel just two short blocks away on a very quiet little alley behind a church. It is a new fourteen room apartment hotel with little efficiency rooms with sink, hot plate, fridge and a few utensils and dishes, but very, very nice! A real find for 279 Sloty or about $100.

I went out almost immediately with some shopping in mind—gifts for V and assorted kids, grandkids, and friends. Mostly I shop generally and assign items to recipients later. This means I have a collection of items in my closet that have never been assigned. Sometimes this comes in handy when I need a gift on short notice because I can "shop" in my own closet. But sometimes, potential gifts languish in the closet never matched with an appropriate recipient. A pair of Venetian glass earrings that I bought years ago in Urbino are still waiting for the right match!

There isn't much appropriate for our tiny grandsons, and the Cloth Hall market is hot and crowded today. I seek the same pretzels I found the day before we left Krakow, but the three I buy are dry and stale. I try again at a different vendor's cart, but again, the pretzels aren't the same as my remembered ideal pretzel which has now assumed mythic flavor and texture! A few streets further on at the Jagellonian University gift shop I pick out my items, but as I prepare to pay with a credit card, I learn they only take cash! I retrace my steps to find a cash machine, but the first several I find do not accept my card. All the while, rock music jars the atmosphere from yet another stage erected in the middle of market square. That must be the third stage we witnessed constructed and destructed in the square in our total of five days in this city. Too much! Too much!! I'm tired now and ready to go home. I really know that my limits have been breached when I go to my favorite ice cream vendor and they have my two favorite flavors and I choose both for a special treat of a double cone! I don't enjoy a single lick of it today—too much, too much!! The flavors are flat, and the ice cream melts faster than I can enjoy it. The little children playing in a safe corner of the square where I sit on a low wall eating (but not enjoying) my ice cream like a lesson learned, are playing near an old pump fountain. They are maybe two years old, walking, but not talking much, understanding everything. They enjoy wandering to their limits along the low wall, plunking around near the water pump and fountain, a small snack from mother, and each other. Simple pleasures, simply enjoyed.

I am at a surfeit today—too much waiting, too much train, too much sitting, too much shopping, and too much ice cream. Back in our small hotel room, number nine in Apart. Hotel Maly on my narrow white bed, I feel the simple room help settle my stomach and my head. After about an hour of this austere simplicity, my senses are refreshed and re-set to zero. I'm ready to meet V and our friends for dinner.

## Confessions Of A Small Time Collector

One astrolabe with moveable parts,
Five amber bits
Wearable in silver
on fingers and ears,
Bits of blue glass with eyes,
Textile squares,
A box and two spoons,
A knot of carved wood,
A two-handled bag,
Bright cards to post,
Four tiny bracelets and
Two singing birds,
Three mini vases of deep indigo blue,
And two letter openers for the air traffic security system.

## Street Vendor

As we were finishing a light lunch at a sidewalk café/bar on our first day in Italy, we were approached by an African man who carried several plastic bags of merchandise. It was an eclectic assortment of socks, handkerchiefs, a small rug, and tea towels. He was sweating as he offered the items from table to table. We shook our heads and said "No" in our "first day in Italy" voices, probably less emphatic than we intended. We shook our heads from side to side with no facial expression. And then I made the mistake of looking up into his face. The anguish and petition were more than I could resist. I bought a set of handkerchiefs for seven Euros, about $10. If I am a fool, he will buy drugs with this money. If I was correct in linking this face with news images of starvation and political turmoil, then possibly it is a small contribution to alleviate one tiny bit of suffering. I gave up my desire for gelato to address his need. I was able to resist the three or four African vendors who approached us during and after dinner. One said he needed a cup of coffee and V gave him a Euro for that—his soft spot.

## In Your Shoes

We went shopping with Z in Cianciana, Sicily, and I bought a wallet for V for 50,000 lira. J bought gold earrings for J and C, a chess set for J and a tray for friends. Z cooked Risotto Frutti di Mare for our mid-day dinner. I rested in bed for a while because my back hurt. We had dinner this evening with R A C and her family. We talked and laughed a lot. It was difficult to leave these people who look so much like family at home and I almost cried when we said goodnight.

Z insisted that the family would present each of us with a pair of shoes so we tried on shoes. J picked a pair of hush puppies and I picked black shoes with a bow after trying on every pair in the store in my size.

## Trust

In the supermarket in Nanjing, I wanted to purchase 2 bananas. I brought them to a weighing station where a clerk was weighing produce for other shoppers. He weighed them, placed them in a sealed bag, and stuck the label on with the price. I recall a story told by a lovely Cornell University graduate about habits of students at Wegman's in Ithaca: they would weigh the item, place the sticker on the open bag and then add additional items to the bag before sealing it. I was rather shocked to hear this tale from someone I respect.

Which culture trusts its customers more or less? Which customers are trustworthy?

# Shopping Re-Education From Our Tour Guide In Suzhou

"Visitors come to China and say, 'Chinese silk is so cheap!' This is not the way you should talk about Chinese silk. I will show you how it is made and you will appreciate it more. Of course, you are thinking about quality. We have 100% pure silk and we have silk blended with synthetic fibers. I will show you how to tell the difference. When you speak of Chinese silk, it would be better for you to talk about how 100% pure Chinese silk is very high quality. When I come to New York or San Francisco, I am willing to pay a good price for American products because I know the quality is excellent."

# Purchase vs. Desire

Here is what I bought on this short trip to China, along with what I really wanted to buy.

### Purchase: Wooden Hair Comb

I really wanted two things but settled for the wooden comb. I wanted to buy several of the hair combs made of the horn of cattle. I had seen these, but didn't know what they were made of, but then we saw workers set up in the front of shops at the fishing village. They were demonstrating the craft of taking the horn and grinding it into the shape of a comb. I didn't see how they made the separate tines so evenly? Perhaps there is a machine behind the scenes somewhere? I wanted a photo of the man making the comb.

### Purchase: Small Folding Purse Mirror

I really wanted a wooden box stamped with the Nanjing University logo, but I didn't see this until my very last afternoon when my money was almost gone and I had only a little while to shop. I was also alone so I couldn't ask any questions.

### Purchase: Little Laughing Buddha Purchased At Airport (For P)

I really wanted to buy a "chop" for P, a stone carved with Chinese characters representing his name. This is then pressed on a color ink and then stamped like a signature on any document. It takes time to make one and I never felt secure that I had enough time to negotiate for and wait for this to be made. Next time!

### Purchase: Silk Scarves

This topic is a Pandora's box! Or a can of worms! Infinite variety of color, fabric, and size make this an ongoing quest. I am drawn to color and pattern first, texture second and then shape/size. Of course, price is important also. My very first purchase of a scarf was the best of all, but of course, I didn't know it at the time! It is the lightest of filmy films of deep turquoise blue with dusky darker brush strokes that form loose flower shapes. It is so thin that you can see through it and it weighs nothing at all though it is about a yard wide and three yards long. Most favorite of all ... and only 48 RMB, about $8. I should have bought more! I bought that at the Sun Yat Sen mausoleum and you can be sure I will go back there on my next trip!

My second purchase was at the touristy shops at the Confucius Temple area. Prices seemed unhinged from anything at all here. My expectations were that there would be something of a temple here where we would experience culture, and then we would add on dinner and a little shopping in the vicinity. Instead, the shopping was the central act of worship. It would be like going to South Street Seaport in NYC and expecting to learn about the history of shipping rather than shopping. The pace of shopping here was for professionals. Shop keepers were actively soliciting pedestrians into shops. Bargaining was vigorous. Not my comfort zone, but fun to accompany my more dynamic shopper friends! N found old coins to buy. In a shop where we all lingered looking at silks and other items, I pulled a couple of scarves from a table of foaming colors. These were polyester scarves, not expensive, but little whimsy items that would make little gifts. I think they were just two or three dollars each and I found five that I liked ...pink, lavender, green, purple with light filmy patterns.

Third scarf experience (with no purchase on my part) was at a downtown mall department store. This is like going to Macy's or Lord and Taylor in China. Others in the party did purchase scarves here and they were very happy with them. It didn't have quite the endorphin rush of bargaining and buying from outdoor merchants. It was satisfying in a different way, I'm sure. They had atmosphere and quality and little cute boxes. On this same expedition, we found knock-off bags on the street and I bought three little ones for just a couple of dollars each. I think the brand was "Sport Sac." I should have bought the big one, just to maintain appearances in my friends' eyes. I think they were dismissive of those of us who sought less expensive items. I did overhear a comment about someone else, but I'm sure it applied to me as well since the commenter quieted when realizing I was nearby. We are in different income categories and therefore different spending categories. Just a fact. I also don't need any more things, expensive or not, and I struggle to resist temptation.

My final silk scarf experience was at the silk factory. Was it really a silk factory or just a demonstration room in front of several huge sales rooms? After the demonstration of the silk work cycle and the making of the twisted 8-strand silk thread, we were guided into the sales room for silk quilts and blankets. Some of us found our way to the clothing area upstairs. There we all found jackets, ties, scarves, shirts, pj's and so many more items for sale. I found three or four reasonable scarves and a few tiny hankies of silk also. With a shopping basket, it was very easy to keep shopping and dropping items into the basket. I tried on a burgundy colored jacket for about $100. Then I found a gold jacket with black brocade trim that I thought was 150 RMB, a real bargain. I alerted N to the size I thought would fit her. Turns out it was 450 RMB and it was time to leave. I bought it myself, not having the time left to reconsider the burgundy jacket. I'm working at making myself feel it is exactly what I would have chosen if there were no prices listed at all. Perhaps what I really wanted was the burgundy jacket? Perhaps the one I got is exactly the one I wanted and it took a convoluted path to find me!

### Purchase: Glass Pendants With Flowers

I bought so many of these at Dr. Sun Yat Sen's mausoleum! They were two or three dollars each and so beautiful! It turns out that everyone loves this little gift from China. It can be worn with a cord and really makes a lovely gift ... small, easy to carry, not so lightweight, but since it is so small, it doesn't add up to much. Perfect! Still, I also wanted to buy those red carved flowers that probably once were made from coral or some stone. Now we think they are plastic, but the color and the fine details are just lovely. My friend B got some and next time I will too!

### Purchase: Wine Bottle Sacks

I think the first three of these I bought were at the Confucius Temple commercial area. And I did bargain for these! Each time I saw them after this, they were less expensive. I bought three the first time and two the second time I saw them. With a nice bottle of wine, this makes a good gift. No regrets!

### Purchase: NJU Tee Shirts

On the very last day, I saw C and K as we crossed in the elevator. K said they had just come from the NJU bookstore. I was on my way out for a little walk completely on my own and I asked for directions. I still didn't have any gifts for the grandkids or the men. Pendants and silk scarves were not going to serve ! I went to the small bookstore and bought three tee shirts (V, D, P) and some small ornaments with the NJU logo. Wish I had seen this store sooner! Compare this to the PSU bookstore! The U.S. is the mecca of shopping !

### Purchase: chopsticks

After our canal boat ride in Suzhou, we were met by a few "mosquito" vendors in the parking lot where we were meeting our bus. One of them had packages of chopsticks wrapped in colorful brocades. It was so easy to buy one or two. I think they were 5 RMB (less than $1 for 10) and I asked for one but gave her a 10 note. She gave me two packages and turned to the next customer. I sold one package to O-C and then regretted it and bought another one from her. When I opened the package in my room, I realized they were glued together. I had read that the largest manufacturer of wooden chopsticks is in the U.S. because of short supplies of wood in China. How ironic if these were made in the U.S. and transported via container ships to China where I would buy them to bring home to the U.S. as gifts!! Regret: not buying a higher quality of chopsticks!

### Purchase: panda bear pens and notepads

At the airport I found a shop selling "souvenirs" and quickly bought little pens and notepads for the grandkids. The only other "kid" gift I bought was little fancy umbrellas at one of the first gift shops we encountered on our first day. CG was buying one for her granddaughter and I thought I would too. I didn't buy a paper painted fan at this shop, though perhaps I wished to. I have one that I bought (for a much higher price) in Germany!

### Purchase: porcelain hand shape and tea strainer, porcelain tiny cups

M advised that this might be something to look for. When I went to the grocery store with N one day after some excursion, we passed by a tea shop and went in. I saw the porcelain hands in the window and bought two of them. The tiny cups were just 5 rmb (less than $1) and I bought 10 of them I think. Just one is out and the rest are still packed away. No regrets. Wish I could buy more! A beautiful teapot set next time. Harder to carry.

Not purchased, but desired: scroll with Chinese characters as art work to hang at home.

## Murano Glass Birds

We were up early again for our morning walk on our second day in Ravenna, Italy and discovered that the Mercado Coperto was open with fruit, fish, meat, bread, etc. We bought water and biscotti.

The clerk at the hotel desk helped us make phone calls to reserve a hotel at our next stop. We cashed traveler's checks and we went back to Basilica San Vitale and purchased an entry to five sites for E7.5 each. We managed to tour four of them by noon and get back to our room to hide out during the hottest part of the day. The mosaics created from colored glass made in Murano are beautiful. Some of the tesserae have gold surfaces. I can never hear the word tesserae without thinking of the book A Wrinkle in Time by Madeleine L'Engle where the tesseract is the wrinkle that allows a slip from one time to another, like stepping across a wrinkle in cloth.

We ventured out around 5 pm for the fifth entry in our series— Basilica di St. Appolinaire Nuovo—and more mosaics. I almost succumbed to Murano glass birds for each of our babies, but resisted at the last minute. Vacation acquisition is a problem for me. I see things I must have, but when I get home, I don't really know why. Well, not always ... I do have some treasures from trips, but also some expensive castaways, ignored earrings, and other jewelry and knick knacks. Is this part of the effort to capture and retain the pleasures of the trip?

Josephine Carubia

# Collecting

*Collections unite. Collections isolate.*
— Susan Sontag, *The Volcano Lover*

When I travel, I collect a few types of things. At the beach, I collect a few shells, beach pebbles, and glass, but cautioned by my father's massive collections of stones, shells, sticks, feathers, and dried flowers, I try to limit myself to a representative sampling each year. When we stay at hotels, I like to collect the imprinted stationery and envelopes and sometimes I even write letters using it. Currently in my collection I have Hotel Bristol, Oslo, Norway; Westpark Hotel, New York, New York; Hotel Mercure, Opole, Poland; Rantasipi Hotels & Resorts, Imatra, Finland (Valtionhotel); Hotel Europa, Ferrara, Italy; Hotel Argentario, Ravenna, Italy; and Tropical da Bahia, Salvador da Bahia, Brazil. I love the different type faces and paper textures and colors. I love the logos and text placement on the page. I love the open page itself, inviting a narrative of my time in this place!

## Be Prepared (Collecting)

Whenever I reach in my suitcase, backpack, or cosmetics bag, I come up with a little sewing kit. I have become a collector of the small kits that some hotels leave for guests along with soap, shampoo, and hand lotion. Some are labeled; some are not. One is labeled "SET COUTURE NÄHETUI" on one side of the package and has six additional languages on the back of the wrapper. I have no idea where I picked up this one!

Fortunately, the little kits are usually carefully wrapped or I would have pincushion fingers from rummaging for my tweezers or socks and getting stuck with a needle that I might need someday. Inside each tiny packet, smaller than a book of matches, I have found quite similar items: small safety pins, two or three small buttons, wrapped pieces of thread in several colors, and a couple of needles and pins. This is a nearly universal language of clothing crisis and repair. The real trick is having a kit available at the exact moment and in the exact place that you need it.

Being prepared can be an obsession; possibly, my habit of collecting sewing kits is a symptom of this obsession.

CHAPTER SIX

# Pleasure on the Tongue

*Life is a journey, not a destination.*
>—Petite Rue des Bouchers,
>*Street of the Butchers, Brussels*

We did it again! We barely stepped onto the narrow street of restaurants and began to look at menus and the beautiful displays of seafood on outdoor carts when a young man persuaded us to come in by the fire and have our first drink free! We said we would be back ... just strolling ... just starting out. He said we would find nothing else this good, this fresh and this plentiful, this warm on a chilly night.

We entered and joined the guests already seated inside. I joked with V that they paid or offered free food to their friends to come in and fill a table or two. No joke!! It was certainly a deciding factor for us to see someone inside an attractive space rather than just empty tables. The wait staff was very chummy with the young folks having wine and coffee at a table visible from outside. Not long after we were seated and one or two other tables were filled, the young people left and went home to their dinners.

We were seated (not by the fire) but further back to give some depth of field to the restaurant's image from the street, beside a pleasant—if artificial—garden open to a second floor gallery. The prime table by the fire (and the front windows) was soon filled by two young women. We could hear their demanding American voices from our table ..."Give me garlic! I want to choke on garlic!" V surmised they were from New York ... perhaps.

At first I felt we had failed in a familiar way yet again—succumbing to the ultimate tourist trap restaurant come-on. But as soon as we asked to see the menu that was displayed outside instead of the very expensive a la carte menu we were offered inside, things got better.

The first-drink-free offer was soon revealed to be a small aperitif glass of sweet white wine, sharper than my taste buds could appreciate. After that, everything was great. We each had a three-course meal for eighteen Euro. I had fish soup as a starter and V's appetizer was fresh whole shrimp in garlic sauce, fortunately, not enough to choke on. We both had grilled salmon and a just-right dab of chocolate mousse for dessert. We enjoyed three beers, one light, one medium, and one brune. The food was excellent. We've had this same experience in many cities, drawn in by the eyes and nose (and an experienced hawker) on a crowded street of restaurants (Paris, Istanbul, Krakow, Copenhagen, etc.). This was one of the best meals resulting from our continuing naiveté.

## Letting Go

We had a perfect dinner in Ferrara at L'Osteria Cucina & Vino, Palazzo Montecatino, Via De' Romei, 51, Ferrara, Italia. We wandered around checking menus and ambiance, and I left the final decision to V. He tends to select the higher end, nicer places, while I am always trying to find the hidden gem, inexpensive, intimate, local ambiance, intriguing menu, i.e. someplace that doesn't really exist.

V's selection was perfect! We were welcomed with a small tasting of champagne or sparkling wine and proscuitto bread on the table. We ordered one appetizer—warm octopus salad with vegetables and white sauce—delectable! S-o-o tender—reminded me of watching the fishermen in Bari flinging their catch of octopus against the rocks again and again to tenderize them. V had black linguine with calamari and I had amazing gnocci with some hunks of shellfish, possibly shrimp or small lobsters. These were crusty delectable bits that required both hands to eat. I'm glad to be Italian and willing to put gusto into food! V ordered a perfect soave wine to go with the meal. Again, I was leaning toward red and let go for him to order and it was perfect. We strolled for another hour after dinner.

## Recreate Perfection

The drive to Ravenna, Italy on a secondary road was lovely and sometimes hair-raising—trucks speeding around turns coming towards us—no shoulders on the roads. We decided to stay two nights instead of one and to find our next stop for two nights again. Less driving, more relaxing!

We slept for most of our first afternoon in Ravenna although our room's air conditioner wasn't working yet. It was HOT!! We just scoped out the city on the first day, getting our bearings. We had dinner at Gardela, a restaurant recommended by our hotel clerk. It was very good and reasonable. I wanted to recreate a remembered fish dish from years ago at a Fordham philosophy department Christmas banquet at Dominick's restaurant in Little Italy in the Bronx. It was an incredibly delicate flounder, breaded and fried in a lemon sauce. Amazing! I took our waiter's recommendation at Gardela for a whole fish that he would debone for me at the table. It was wonderful. Maybe even as good as the distant memory!

I finally had my first gelato in Italy tonight—one scoop of pistachio and one of ginger. Again, I was trying to recreate a wonderful memory of ice cream from the dairy near M's house in Groton, MA. This gelato also met and possibly exceeded the memory! This is a very rare occurrence since memory is without the little imperfections of reality and therefore so difficult to match.

On our second night in Ravenna, we encountered another of the recommended restaurants—Il Melarancio—and had another octopus delight. It was chilled in aspic with fruit and salad—amazing combination of flavors! I had risotto and V had ravioli stuffed with pumpkin and leeks. Both were excellent. Il Melarancio seems partly German and we drank beer. We ended with a big salad each and had no room for dessert or gelato.

## Capim Santo

We waited only briefly for a table at the loveliest restaurant in our neighborhood—which happens to be right next to our hotel—for a typical Sunday buffet in Sao Paulo. It is Father's Day here in Brazil, and families with small and medium children, even adult children, are gathered for the holiday buffet. We wait with a caiperinha and glass of wine in the first courtyard of the restaurant under beautiful palm trees beside a water pool for the shortest 30 minutes ever, watching families. Our table is in this courtyard and the buffet is just inside the restaurant and before the second courtyard. We could see salmon and salads on plates as we waited, and of course, we looked to find both as we approached the buffet. There were several lettuce salads, fresh olives, nuts, farfalle, zucchini, cucumber salads, mozzarella and tomatoes, and hunks of parmesan. The hot plates included chicken and beef, and even other meats that we couldn't identify. A waiter who spoke English was very happy to help us at every turn. After two plates each of main course and salads, we approached the dessert tables for fruit and chantilly (whipped cream) along with briggaderio of pistachio, m-m-m. The nut bowl had been replenished with cashews and raisins so we sprinkled these on top.

The image I wanted to capture from this meal is V and I talking to our English-speaking waiter with our plates heaped high with wonderful Brazilian foods under the palm trees. I was also thinking about how I would love to serve a buffet with some of these foods for those of our friends who appreciate savory variety.

CHAPTER SEVEN

# Transformations

*The first great joy of traveling is simply the luxury of leaving all my beliefs and certainties at home, and seeing everything I thought I knew in a different light and from a crooked angle.*
—Pico Iyer

## Mediterranean Kitchen Colors

Our two days and nights in Fano, Italy were the calm before the storm of the seminar in Urbino. We sat in the "libre" area of the beach on the first afternoon and then splurged for two shade beds and an umbrella at Spiaggia Peppe for our full day in Fano. Spiaggia Peppe has the most beautiful umbrellas of all the commerciale beaches. They are a starburst pattern of deep yellow and orange with loose flaps around the edges. Imagine the beautiful contrast between the umbrella and sky, the umbrella and sea! These are the colors of Italy! I should take these colors and recreate our kitchen! With terracotta floor tiles and shades of blue and yellow paint, it could happen ... lighting, countertops, structural changes to come later. On the wall, an enlargement of one of my photographs of the Fano beach day.

# The Shape of Your Head

On our recent vacation in London, my husband asked me two intriguing questions: first, he asked what I think is the purpose of a vacation, and maybe a day or so later, he asked me how I view the experience of travel. Suspecting that he had already reflected on his own views before asking me, I took some time to think before answering.

"Vacations are for spiritual renewal," I responded. Every subsequent statement I made seemed to be an example or a further clarification of that initial statement: To separate one's mind and senses from the habitual to make room for new insights, experiences, thoughts, feelings. To be reminded of deep, abiding affinities that one tends to forget or neglect in the press of daily obligations. To set aside schedules in order to rediscover the rhythms of one's body, one's curiosity ... to follow inclination only. To re-learn the serendipitous efficiency of spontaneity. Travel and vacations make space for surprises, for growth, for experiencing side by side the strange and foreign along with the familiar (even in thought), often providing impetus for change.

V's core view on the subject is that vacations are for sheer pleasure, but part of their pleasure is intellectual, for the best vacations are always processes of discovery and insight. For him, they provide opportunities and inducements not only to encounter new things but to clarify (even re-discover) what is all too familiar. Familiar things, persons, and activities tend to become transparent: we look through them, not seeing them in their richness of texture and relationships. A vacation is – or should be – an instance of schooling in its original Greek sense (skolia was the Greek word for leisure that came to be used to designate a place and time carved out from the workaday world for the purpose of joyful growth). What vacations provide for V are opportunities for truly self-directed activities, not inactivity. Such activities in turn provide opportunities for self-clarification, for becoming clearer about what he has actually been about during the workaday year and, of greater importance, what he would more like to be about when he returns to his everyday doings. For vacations remind us that the point of life – the point of our lives – is to live them on our terms, in the most intense and playful manner possible. What the demands and constraints of our workaday lives tend to blur, the leisure and openness of vacations assist us in clarifying; life lived intensely, vibrantly, playfully but intelligently needs no justification or support but itself. Such at least are the leisurely musings of one vacationing philosopher.

Charles Darwin hardly thought of the voyage of the Beagle as a vacation, but he did reflect on how this travel changed him:

> *The voyage of the Beagle has been by far the most important event in my life, and has determined my whole career ... . I discovered, though unconsciously and insensibly, that the pleasure of observing and reasoning was a much higher one than that of skill and sport[i.e. hunting]. That my mind became developed through my pursuits during the voyage is rendered probable by a remark made by my father ... for on first seeing me after the voyage, he turned round to my sisters, and exclaimed, "Why, the shape of his head is quite altered." (28, 29)*

Do "travel" and "vacation" convey the same quality of experience? Not if we look at the core meanings of the root words! And perhaps neither adequately conveys the reflective self-transformation that I seem to be talking about here. "Vacation" derives ultimately from the Latin vacare "to be empty, be free" (The American Heritage Dictionary of the English Language). Freed from one's "daily grind" seems about right, but emptiness does not seem to suggest the wash of observations, feelings, and insights that I have been associating with vacation or travel. The word "travel" appears to derive from Old French travailler meaning "to travail" through Old English travailen, "to toil, make a (toilsome) journey." Many of us will define these words and describe the experiences still named by these words in very different terms. Thus the point of V's questions.

# Being Careful

"Be careful !" must have been the last words out of my mother's mouth as I left the house each day because they are burned into my soul. I fight it, but there it is, carved in stone, the tendency to take care, watch out for danger, stay safe. I've learned to weigh options by asking myself, "Would I be willing to die for this?"

"Yes!" to flying, sailing in the open ocean, skinny-dipping at midnight, diving headfirst into a labyrinthine cave, and walking across bridges.

"No!" to hang gliding, para-sailing, bungie jumping, and skiing on the diamond slopes. But those are just the obvious choices that come along once a year or once a lifetime. What about the small, ordinary occasions of being careful in life? What kind of soul is always careful? I have been observing myself and a few others in the past day or two on this matter of being careful with choices involving money. We are currently with a group of varying backgrounds, nationality, ages, and incomes. I come from a modest home where eating out was extremely rare. Although we ate well at home, I love to eat in restaurants. I love to sit at an outdoor café with a beverage and to read or chat with friends. I love, most of all, not to always be careful about the cost of such experiences. I found myself observing the care of others, and how difficult it is to manage social occasions when you are the one with least resources. Joining a group and behaving carelessly can consume today's, tomorrow's, and next week's budget. How tempting to throw caution to the winds and just live in the moment! I notice several of our group choosing not to join in for a meal, but leaving and rejoining us later. I notice the careful selection of menu items and leaving exact change for one's share. My inner voice was activated at a recent gathering and I was unable to order a second drink and contemplated leaving before dinner to save the cost of my meal. I could have crackers and nuts in my room. I don't know the answer to this. It is simply not fair that some people have the resources to live carelessly while others have to be careful constantly. I am fortunate to worry less than many and fortunate to have a partner who is generous all the time.

## Simplicity

*All I want is a room somewhere, far away from the cold night air, with one enormous chair, and wouldn't it be loverly."*
—Eliza Doolittle

I love the simplicity of hotel rooms. In general, the hotel room has few of the distractions and complications of house and home. There is no attic waiting to be organized, no kitchen stove to be cleaned, and no small leak in the ceiling to be explored. Or, if there is a leak, it is someone else's responsibility to fix, not mine. There are not so many things to fidget with: couch cushions to straighten, dishwasher to empty, plants to water, junk mail to sort into recycling bins. And there is no garden or yard attached to my hotel room. If there is a garden, it is groomed for my pleasure, not claiming my pleasure for its grooming.

My own possessions in a hotel room are also simplified. Even if I unpack into drawers or shelves, the choices of what to wear are simplified to what I've brought with me. Each garment has far more potential in a hotel room than at home, among so many other choices. And all the little things that I've collected that fill my desk drawers and bathroom drawers and baskets at home: all these things are not here. I have culled the collection to the necessaries that fit in my travel cosmetics bag and the small zippered pockets in my carry-on and purse. If forced to evacuate with just one backpack or tote bag, I imagine I could reduce this load even further.

This hotel room, #405 at the Conti Hotel on Brusseler Strasse in Cologne, Germany, is a particular pleasure in its simplicity. It is quite small with a built in double mattress bed of light wood matching the doors and the armoire. A small shelf with drawer hangs on either side of the bed and above that is a reading light. Opposite the bed, with clearance of only about 3 feet, is the armoire flanked by a suitcase shelf on one side and a small curved desk shelf on the other. Above the desk area, is a corner shelf attached to the armoire. A very small TV sits on this shelf. It's screen is only about the size of my travel laptop computer. Another wall lamp is above the desk.

The room has two large windows on Brusseler Strasse. These are those amazing windows that swing open from one side into the room when you twist the handle one way and that tip open from the top about 6 inches when you twist the handle further. Why they don't just fall out with all this flexibility is a mystery. The building across the way has the same kind of windows, but they also have a narrow balcony of perhaps 18 inches where plants and a few benches are placed. Brussler Strasse is quite narrow. We all have lightweight opaque drapes over the windows to allow light but not vision, for privacy, and heavier drapes to close at night to allow us to sleep in the morning.

Even the bed dressings are simple. There is a bottom-sheet on each mattress, but I believe it is a flat sheet carefully and tightly tucked, rather than a special fitted sheet. On top of this is a down comforter in a white case. That's all. At night, each person has options with his or her cover: lie on top, wrap up, stretch out under, partly under, partly out, etc. This is quite different from our bed at home, with its one set of top sheet, blanket tucked in at bottom and quilt on top of all.

Imagine if we could have the actual option of having our "home away from home." This would be a huge disadvantage, despite my thoughts of how there would be no packing problems in this case. A big part of the pleasure of travel is to have imposed this simplicity of reduced baggage and spare surroundings. This necessity is part of the reason why we are free to think more when traveling. We are not so busy grooming our possessions.

# CHAPTER EIGHT

# Same and Different

*Travel is more than the seeing of sights; it is a change that goes on, deep and permanent, in the ideas of living.*

—Miriam Beard

*If a train is large and comfortable you don't even need a destination; a corner seat is enough, and you can be one of those travelers who stay in motion ... and never arrive.*

—Paul Theroux

## Driving Through Italy

The seaside community of Fano was described as a "sleepy little town" in our guide book, but we found it to be fairly large with energetic crowds of vacationers and vigorous street life. In fact, from our room at Hotel Roma, Viale Dante Alighieri, we were immersed in street life for about twenty hours a day! Just as we thought things were calming down around 3 a.m. on our first night, there was a horrendous metallic crash just outside our window. We were surprised not to hear shouting from the drivers involved (a crash sound is always followed by shouting in our experience). Litter from the event and a crumpled guard rail remained as evidence of the nocturnal collision in the morning. On our second day we were sitting at an outdoor café less than a block away when we witnessed another accident on the same corner. Needless to say, our departure from the hotel in a rented car was rather stressful given the record of one accident per day on that corner!!

After a long morning walk north along the waterfront of Fano, we departed with vague directions for reaching Urbino. Driving in Italy before cell phones required quick decisions based on sketchy information. Everyone else knows where they are going, and there are far too many traffic circles! We are used to 4-way stop signs or traffic lights. Even though I know that traffic circles are demonstrably safer than, say left turns against oncoming traffic, I still prefer the full stop to the ambiguous glide. It seems to me that traffic circles bring on a collective, and very literal, agoraphobia.

Highways in Italy are kind to the landscape. They are built with many bridges and tunnels in order to accommodate the hills and valleys. These roads seem soft, unlike those where a bulldozer rearranges the earth to make a straight new thoroughfare.

Urbino's signature is "Emozioni in forma di città," and we learned it the hard way. The drive from Fano to Urbino seemed quick compared with the time it took us to locate the conference site once we arrived! We quickly found the location of the "Seven Deadly Sins" meeting we had attended eleven years before at the **Università degli Studi di Urbino Carlo Bo**, but that entire campus is now under construction. That didn't hinder people from sending us to three or four buildings based entirely on rumors. An hour later, when two recommendations converged on the fact that we needed to go to another campus 5 km out of town, we were not surprised, but were disappointed that we would not be within walking distance of central Urbino.

The Sogesta campus is isolated from any village by 5 km of very steep, curvy, narrow roads. Even after we found the main building, it was difficult to find the registration desk for the conference. On the other hand we were able to register for our room right away and discovered that it was air conditioned!! We both remembered a torrid room facing the afternoon sun at the main campus.

I had a wonderful pranzo in the cafeteria (chicken, vegetables, salad, fruit, wine) and then took a nap. I hope to do the same every day! Being isolated on this campus all day was frustrating, so we decided to take an excursion to Fermignano, reportedly closer than Urbino. As we approached a stop sign just outside the town, I shouted to V to stop, and so he did, causing the car behind to hit us, rather hard I thought.

The driver got out and began shouting at us in Italian. When V got out of our car, looking a little dazed and confused, the other driver got progressively more and more angry at my husband's silence. Finally, after two long minutes of this shouting and pointing, I regained the presence of mind to say, "No capisce Italiano." The formerly aggressive driver shifted his tone and began to apologize (I think). V and I were both shaken by this episode although neither car was damaged at all. We tried to go to a grocery store in Fermignano, which, of course, was closed, so we cautiously drove right back to the campus parking lot and went to our room to compose ourselves before dinner. I felt a little like a character in the short story, "The Appointment in Samarra" by Somerset Maugham. After all of our efforts to avoid the "crash-a-day" we witnessed in Fano, "fate" followed us all the way to Urbino, and came close enough to give us a fright!

We had a very nice dinner on campus with our friends, and found a ride into Urbino for a nightcap afterwards. V offered to drive, but fortunately someone else won that joust. We sat outside a café in the Piazza de la Republica, drinking Campari while water sparkled from the fountain like a curtain of jewels.

# Work-a-day Worlds Apart

We watched stonemasons renovating a brick wall opposite the outdoor tables of a small restaurant called Vitae (Life) on "our" street in Venice. I had been watching work sites for days as we drove from town to town in northern Italy. I noticed that there were more men on an Italian work site than I would expect to see in the U.S.

It seems to me that in Italy work is performed on a human scale; you can actually see the manpower involved in transforming a landscape. V added to my reflection by commenting that the difference is also a cultural/social philosophy about the meaning and purpose of work. In the U.S. it seems that the purpose of work is to efficiently finish the job. What we were seeing in Italy seems to have more to do with human efficacy, that is, work as an expression of human worth. People deserve meaningful work and social systems have a responsibility to allow this to happen. Eliminating human workers for efficiency's sake and replacing them with huge machines is not necessarily a social good. It may produce wealth for a small number of people but at the cost of a livelihood and well-being for larger numbers.

I suspect what I observed is the source of the cruel ethnic joke, "How many Italians does it take to change a light bulb?" In the "clash of cultures" through immigration, it must have seemed wasteful for three people to attend to a single light bulb. In another light, we might find that it is wasteful of human dignity to hold efficiency as the higher value.

# Plumbing Tour of the World

So comfortable are we with our own faucets, flushing, flows, and fabrics, that sometimes these facilities are magnified in our travel experiences as quite significant, perhaps even of utmost significance. For some of us, based on our conversations, you might think we had just returned from a plumbing tour of France or Turkey. From the view of pipes and drains, did the trip deliver the experience we expected or not?

We only came to appreciate a vigorous shower drain after we experienced the slow drain at our hotel in Istanbul. What microbes living in the drain floated up to our feet and even ankles as we showered? We learned to run the shower only to rinse and turn it off while soaping up or the water would overflow the barrier between shower and bathroom.

I had only one experience of the "footprints-stand-up" toilet on this trip. As we crossed borders from Turkey back to Bulgaria, we stopped after the last Turkish border check to spend what money we had left in that currency. I couldn't wait for another stop so I paid my small coins and used the toilet off to the side of the concrete expanse. I never know whether to face the back or the front of the stall.

## Porcupine City

Sao Paulo is a porcupine city. Each of the myriad skyscrapers is an individual spine sticking straight out of the curving earth in a perpendicular line. Each has a unique shape to permit the maximum of sun and utility for its occupants. Some are shaped like a U, some are oval, some are rectangles with huge granite outcroppings along the sides. What an opportunity for architects here! Unlike other cities, where a building's shape is determined by its fit within the space between two or three other buildings, here, each building rises in its own space, set back from the street and within a footprint that may include a curved driveway, gated entrance, back gardens, etc. Often, there is a fence surrounding the property and even a small gatehouse for the security guard. The main entrance door is often locked with another security guard within the building. Many of the buildings have outdoor terraces on every floor and even a pool or garden on the roof. Our building has an enclosed pool on the roof. The poolroom ceiling can withdraw to open the pool to the sky or remain closed for a muted skylight effect. The view over rooftops is quite different here than in NYC or London or Paris because of the individual buildings existing in their own space. Spider Man would have a more difficult time negotiating the airways in Sao Paulo than in those other cities.

On the ground in our neighborhood of Jardims, this is a city of hills, sometimes quite steep ones. Our street, Alameda Ministro Rocha Azevedo, goes uphill toward Paulista, one of the main avenues of the city, and steeply downhill toward Rua Oscar Freire, a renowned shopping street with many exclusive shops. The sidewalk is a staircase for two or three blocks down toward Oscar Freire. On streets with a gentler slope and many private garages under buildings, driveways allow residents to drive over sidewalks and gutters to enter and exit. For pedestrians, the city landscape of slopes, steps, curbs, driveways, and broken pavement stones can be treacherous! I wondered how children perceive this fractured landscape. What does life feel like to a three-year old who lives in this neighborhood? He or she must be lifted from apartment to car to playground, but not be able to walk hand-in-hand with parents along the streets of her/his city until the age of six or seven. I was a small child in the Bronx and my memory is of endless walls with very few doors that allowed any entry. Those doors were impregnable to me, so they were frightening as well. One could pound a small fist against a door endlessly before an adult would hear and respond, opening the way inside. The doors all seemed the same to me, so part of the anxiety would be trying to determine if it was the correct door. How am I permanently fixed with that fear of never finding the correct door and if I do find it, never even gaining entry at all? How are the children of Sao Paulo growing with the steep steps of their walking ways and the gates of all the buildings? I remember one of my friends in NYC telling me that her daughter was afraid to walk on grass because she lived in a land of sidewalks and grass feels very odd to a small child who only walks on concrete.

## Trash Arts

I'm just noting that the seats and litter baskets in this airport are "art." In NYC design seems to favor function, i.e. comfort in seating and commodiousness in litter baskets. The litter receptacles here in Milan, Italy are cones tipped over an oval base with the narrow end of the cone at the bottom. The rows of seats are set into granite eggs. Or is it that we notice our surroundings more carefully when they are expected to be different?

## Weird but Polite

At London's Buckingham Mews we saw a horse carriage pulling out into the street. On the back there was a sign, "Horses in Training." Like student drivers, I guess!

There is very little graffiti anywhere. A man sweeping near the side gates of Buckingham Palace used a broom made of sticks.

The play began on time and was very funny. Sort of slapstick or farce, but funny. It was a good choice. The ushers sold programs and chocolates before the play and ice cream and juice at the intervals which were short and crisp.

People are not so much afraid of each other here as they are in the U.S. How do they keep it that way? Younger people and older people talk to one another. How do they preserve that friendly respect?

The play ran from 7:45 to 10:10 pm. I wanted to go home with my slight headache and sore feet. We had a hard time finding a bus stop and the correct route to get back. I ended up jumping off the bus while it was still moving because the ticket fellow said "Here!" and we thought he meant "Right here!" but the bus wasn't quite at the stop, only a pause. We survived and got to our room at 11 pm. I slept well.

Not everything is rosy when traveling. I leave out the annoyances, blamings, mistakes, and frustrations. Is traveling easier for new lovers or for long familiar partners? Hmm.....

On Bus 24 to Victoria Station: The kids here look weird, but they are super polite. A girl in tight jeans, roman gladiator sandals, and with a semi-shaved haircut around the ears and pink hair on top going left, right, left, and full bright lips moved her seat and then converses politely with an elderly woman. The ticket man on the bus calls older ladies, and me, too, "Darling." He says "Cheerio" when he checks bus passes of the elderly.

Civilized does not necessarily mean reserved.

We are on the Gatwick Express on our way to pick up a rental car at the airport. I hope all goes well. It seems we've been away from home for ages already. I want to take pictures of everything because it is all so-o picturesque!

No one has collected our tickets yet. The fellow went through selling tickets for Brighton, but said he would trust everyone for tickets to Gatwick!

You need your ticket to get off the train.

The politeness must begin with automobiles yielding right of way to pedestrians.

Houses have names here: Sandydown Cottage, Fairview Farm. We see taverns with flowers and outdoor tables everywhere. No need for McDonald's. No shopping centers or billboards. Public toilets in every town. Grass and trees right up to the roadside. They say caravans instead of trailers. Mews, petrol, roundabout, give way, row (pronounced "r-a-oo"), and ring road for beltway.

Soft verges means the highway shoulders.

On a back road we saw a sign that said "No tipping." I couldn't figure out what it meant, Who was not getting a tip here? I finally guessed that it means no dumping.

Corn is oats. Our corn is maize for these speakers of the English English language.

## Apparent Prosperity

Traveling from country to country in Europe reveals many differences in relative prosperity. What makes prosperity apparent? The level of transportation services and maintenance of public spaces, for example, trash services. We don't think about this much because it is invisible when it is done well, but when it is a "work in progress" we notice trash and litter. The grounds-keeping of public landscapes is another invisible service unless it is still growing into its full capacity. Ragged roadsides and public parks are something we are not accustomed to. In Bulgaria we saw workers using scythes, not lawn mowers, to cut the grass. In a restaurant courtyard, a woman followed the scythe worker with a pair of scissors to trim what he could not bring to her standard. Sorting out who maintains the sidewalks and spaces between buildings is another aspect of community living that needs to be negotiated, but is often taken for granted in countries where this was decided long ago. When you see piles of earth, scraggly trees, and mud outside the main entrance of an apartment building, you learn something about the complexity of community planning and organization. How does the system of allocating responsibility and resources to create a functioning community happen? It is all taken for granted unless it isn't happening at all.

It seemed to me that each place we visited has a percentage of urban space in stable condition, a percentage deteriorating, and a percentage under construction. In Sofia, Bulgaria it might be one-third in each condition. It is new and old at the same time. I told the story of my father saying that when he was with the First Infantry "liberating" Europe at the end of WWII, the American army could have marched all the way to Moscow, but they stopped and waited for the Russians to march across Eastern Europe. I said I was very sorry and Kristian said, "We are even more sorry!" We see a country with just a handful of years of growth after decades of communism and then chaos and inflation. One of our friends estimated it has just been in the past seven years that Bulgaria has been moving steadily forward with its economy. Another young friend said, "You would have to try hard not to get a job because there are so many new, exciting start-up businesses, especially in technology."

Sizes of cars might be an indicator of relative prosperity as well. In Poland, I notice there are larger cars than in Bulgaria.

Texture of commerce is another indicator: size of enterprises, number of small shops owned and run by individuals vs. larger establishments vs. chains and foreign commerce. Bulgaria was literally awash in small enterprise! Every doorway in a building that had room for a few products was a tiny shop, many selling exactly the same selection as the garage, front room, stall next door and the one after that. Some sold home cooked food, some all beverages and packaged snacks. It seemed that apothecary business was the only one that was more organized and official and institutional looking.

In Poland—in Krakow at least—there is less and less of this. In fact, there is an English language weekly paper that reported a "Clamp down on 'wild traders.'" The stores in the Market Square area seem to be well established businesses, as they did in central Sofia and Budapest. Outside the center, though, Sofia still has the feeling of excitement at the concept of private enterprise.

## Similarities/Differences List: Bulgaria

### *Differences*

+ Size of cars
+ Common foods
+ Eating time and habits
+ Shaking head side to side for yes (looks like "No")
+ Tiny stores
+ Dilapidated things
+ Park benches with awnings
+ Liquor sold everywhere
+ No drinking age
+ Dogs not on leash; dogs not aggressive at all
+ Posters of the dead in public places
+ Cars parked on the sidewalks

- Alphabet
- Local fast food is not chains
- Informal gatherings in cafes

### *Similarities*

- Cherish children
- Street food
- Technology invading daily life?
- Young love
- Flowers

# Fathers Everywhere

Perhaps being a father is different in Germany? Fathers and small children seem to be everywhere. I saw a father carrying a small child in his arms in the evening. Another father and small child are out for a walk on Saturday morning. Another child is in a phone booth and the father is outside with his cell phone. They are trying to connect, quite comically! The empty stroller waits for a resumption of the role and the walk. On Saturday afternoon, I see a father on a bike with one small child in a seat just behind him and another in a small buggy pulled behind the bike. A small dog trots beside the child buggy stopping precisely and patiently when the procession halts for traffic lights. There is no leash on this obedient dog.

# CHAPTER NINE

# Language and Conversation

*In traveling to a truly foreign place, we inevitably travel to moods and states of mind and hidden inward passages that we'd otherwise seldom have cause to visit.*   —Pico Iyer

## "Travel Conversations"

Last night V and I had dinner with NH and TS. After an extended and vigorous political debate, T asked N about the beginnings of his critical positions. N took a deep breath and began at the beginning with the Weekly Reader of his childhood classrooms. He took us back to his early convictions formed in the early 1960's that the U.S. is good and Russia is bad, and then to the cracks in this belief when he first realized that there were lies and deceptions in the stories he was being told. He challenged his teacher on one of the Weekly Reader stories, something about whether communist parents loved their children. The teacher was angry with him for raising such a question and thus challenging the pervasive evils of communism and the Soviet Union. That was the beginning of his doubts about the stories he heard in school and from the government. I asked him whether he could similarly pinpoint his loss of faith in God, since he had told us he was an atheist. In contrast to political debate, this probing recollection of early transformative experiences was fascinating. To recollect the moment of questioning your 100% conviction about anything is intriguing. This conversation caused me to ask myself if I ever believed in God. I don't think so. While N told us of making a deal directly with God to give his father a place in Heaven—N's own place—I perceived myself as believing in a system of rules when I prayed every night for a year to give Aunt Fanny enough credits to get out of Purgatory and into Heaven. In a busy restaurant, these conversations take place in a hushed bubble. I almost hold my breath not to disturb the atmosphere of intimate revelation. The heated political debate seemed to throw down sharp splints, stiff-arming the three men in rigid positions apart from one another. This soft conversation wove an elastic fabric among the four of us, drawing us closer.

## Family Tree

It is now 9:30 p.m. Cianciana, Sicily time, which is 3:30 a.m. NY time, I think. It is wonderful here. I keep thinking, "V will love this!" We explored a bit before heading for the family's home. I was pleased to learn that my cousin Joseph does like to wander and see what is around the next bend or corner. We have been happily "lost" several times already.

I'm in a 2nd floor bedroom over the Carubia family's store on the main street, Corso Vittorio Emmanuele, in Cianciana. I'm conversing in a mixture of Italian, Spanish, English, and gestures. Doing well, I think. I was a bit shy at first (I always am, at first). We were having a three course dinner when we heard drumming outside, so we all went out into the street to watch the candlelight procession of church people carrying San Francisco and singing. Saint Francis – today is his feast day. It was so real. That sounds like a stupid thing to say! What I mean is that it feels so genuine, so full. Later we had a tour of the whole of this building owned by my father's uncle and his family: basement print shop, street level store plus living and sleeping rooms, 2nd floor me, 3rd floor Joseph, and 4th floor, a terrace! Again, as soon as I stepped out there, I was thinking: "V would love this !" We could take that top level bedroom and sit out on the terrace sipping Sambucca until late, or just lean over the banister railing and watch vibrant life flowing up and down the street.

I fell asleep exhausted on Saturday night and slept until 11 am Sunday. We went for a stroll around the town after a bowl of hearty vegetable soup that my parents called "minaestra." Was this lunch or dinner? Spectacular views on all sides of this town. We are on a hill.

We visited my mother's side of the family. The oral tradition is so lively. We relate over and over who we are and who our families are and then others narrate their family lines. The threads connecting us are reinforced with each telling. Earlier I met a young woman named Josephine Caltagirone who was born in England and speaks English and Italian. This afternoon while tracing the Alessi family (my mother's) I (we) discovered that she is related to us! V, you will love this! I think we, you and I, should learn Italian together to prepare for when we come here together. This town looks like a movie set, or a theater. It might be playing Romeo and Juliet or old Italian westerns. I want you here with me to "read" the semiotics of village life—architecture, streets, balconies, shutters, beaded doorways, and on and on.

I mentioned Umberto Eco, G. di Lampedusa, and L. Pirandello tonight and they were all known. Pirandello's home in Agrigento was recommended for a visit. Two or three of the cousins knew the titles of his works. A number of relatives are teachers in elementary schools. The laughter and language are joyous.

Through a misunderstanding of the word "farm," we ended up

at the marble factory of Benedetto Carubia again today. Apparently, "farma" means factory, and although we had wanted to see the family homestead farm that our parents knew as children in this town, we ended up at the factory again instead. This is an example of language yielding an unintended experience, and I hope that my disappointment was not too obvious.

## Us and Them

We arrived in Sofia, Bulgaria over four hours delayed from our scheduled arrival. We hoped to see someone waiting for us holding up a card with our names on it. Unfortunately, we did not find our names, but an entrepreneurial driver found us. We must have been an easy target.

We paid 15 Euro for a ride that should have cost maybe 5 Euro, "tuition" as V says for learning (yet again) that when we are tired and disoriented, we are vulnerable to such persuasion.

The hotel is a true refuge, with modern rooms and convenient bathroom and the all important shower. In just an hour, we felt refreshed and ready to join a small group for dinner at the home of MP.

KB picked us up and we drove to her apartment. K pulled his little blue car into a space on the sidewalk between two metal posts scarcely as wide as an armspan. The buildings are visibly old and decrepit, but the people are vibrant and very intellectually engaged. MP's husband, P, came to the building door to let us in. K went to the staircase and we went into the elevator with P. It was an experience in itself: a small box, entirely dark, rising from the ground floor to the sixth floor.

The apartment was a comfortable home with artworks, books, music, and a round table already set for our dinner. M and P were having cocktails with two colleagues from Greece. The seven of us sat down for a congenial meal of conversation and typical Bulgarian food: tomato and cucumber salad, sliced cold meats and cheese, a baked cheese and filo dish and Kentucky Fried Chicken! I thought I recognized the chicken pieces, but no, it couldn't be ... . Yes, it was! KFC take-out!

We talked about common friends, many of our accidental travel experiences where one or another of us was "lost" for hours or days, the several academic meetings we will participate in over the next weeks, and so on. A topic that caught my attention in particular was about the cultural group called "gypsy," but more accurately known as the "Roma" people. Around the table there seemed to be deep agreement that the Roma are essentially different and inassimilable in mainstream culture, that they are characteristically dishonest, disposed to use "welfare" for support rather than traditional work, and that they are almost all musically talented. I was surprised by the firmness of this stereotype. Not living in these countries or knowing these people, I could not challenge the views, but what is the basic starting point for our beliefs about other ethnic groups? I am probably very sensitive to this because of my own experience as an identifiable "ethnic" growing up in a very WASP area. The stereotypes of dirty, stupid, criminal Italians, especially true of Sicilians, always shocked me! Was I those things? It didn't feel like it to me. But somehow I may have absorbed some of those views, never feeling quite at home in some groups. I should have challenged the expressed stereotype of Roma people that evening. Speaking up might have helped dispel lingering effects of the stereotype assigned to me.

## Problem and Problém

Our friend K says that the word "problém" is a common introduction to a conversation in Bulgaria and, as we learned, also in Turkey. K was driving in Istanbul and he had made a very judicious, but illegal, U-turn. A policeman on a motorcycle appeared out of nowhere. K got out of the car and the first word the policeman uttered was "Problém."

K is not only patient, but extremely diplomatic. He knew that the right approach was to admit his error, try to explain politely, and promise never to do this again. It worked, and we were soon on our way, at least that one problem behind us.

That very evening, however, K found himself facing another problem as he tried to get back to our hotel in a taxi-van which takes many passengers and drops them off one by one. K had negotiated a set price for his stop at the hotel, but it was 2 am and he fell asleep. The driver let him rest until after all the others had been dropped off and then demanded that he get out. K repeated the name of our stop and the driver repeated the word "Problém," until they began to approach each other with talk of hard cash. The negotiation settled at 5 lira from a high of ten and low of three. K told us the story at breakfast seven hours later, shaking his head slowly as he impersonated the driver who seemed to possess only two phrases: "Get out!" and "Problém!"

K takes a calculated risk and makes a prohibited U-turn to correct the problem and from nowhere a policeman on motorcycle appears and motions us to the side of the road. Diplomat as he is, K is back in the car in a minute, a long minute as the three of us separately and quietly contemplate "Prob-lem" says the policeman, the universal introduction punting the ball back to the offender. What is the response? K is limited to sign language and gestures to acknowledge the illegal move, apologize sincerely, and express our intended destination to the Istanbul Kultural University "SEMIO" congress. He is successful and the policeman gestures him to be off.

## Strangers in Conversation

Do we reveal more about ourselves to strangers? On two flights today—London to Bucharest, Romania and then Bucharest to Sofia, Bulgaria—I had interesting seat partners, both total strangers.

On the first flight, a young Romanian woman who lives in Miami was traveling home to visit her family. We bonded immediately over two things: the shrieks of a small child two rows ahead of us and the lack of information from British Airways regarding luggage restrictions for travelers through Heathrow airport in London. For her, from Miami, and for us, from Philadelphia, there was no advance notice that we could not board our connecting flights in Heathrow with more than one piece of cabin luggage. She had enough time to exit and check her luggage, but we missed our connecting flight entirely. I don't typically talk to people seated beside me on flights anymore, but this woman and I made immediate contact on those two points.

On the flight from Bucharest to Sofia I was seated next to a gentleman from Hong Kong on his way to Sofia for his company, a shipping logistics enterprise. We had a lively conversation about globalization. He thought a common language would be the factor most likely to make globalization a success. A common currency would also be helpful, we concluded. Already, in the shipping business, large Asian and European companies are buying American companies, and these behemoths are the only competitive entities in the business anymore. He knew a lot about US ports and shipping, even the ones we see in New Jersey with containers stacked almost as far as the eye can see. English, in his view, will be the global language.

Even though I no longer engage quite this much with traveling strangers, I remember other times of speaking more freely with strangers met on a plane or train than with my own circle of acquaintances, friends, and family. Perhaps in those days I was not as comfortable in my own skin, in my own life, as I am now. I was still seeking myself, and I would speak into the potential future when I would be in the right life, the right fit. It felt like there were no consequences of speaking myself, no checks on the veracity of my sentences. I needed these encounters to help me grow into the self I am now. By making statements about myself, sometimes to my own surprise, I learned who I was growing to be. In conversation with strangers, I heard a new voice that I sometimes liked and sometimes did not like. Frequently, I was the one asking questions, probing the other's life experiences as if I were an empty vessel seeking the other's experiences to fill, or at least inform, my emptiness. Occasionally, I would hear myself speak of goals and potential paths forward. Experiencing my own emerging voice helped to crystallize the aspirational self that I had only dreamed before.

CHAPTER TEN

# Savoring Now

*Two or three hours' walking will carry me to as strange a country as I expect ever to see.* —Henry David Thoreau

## Paris Chronology and Reflections

Saturday: We arrived at Orly airport at 9:00 a.m. and bumped into BF not long after V said we would meet someone we know, and I said this would not be possible. We took a bus, train, and metro to Les Halle stop and decided to surface and take a cab, but we got lost inside a shopping mall. When we finally came out, I snapped up a cab and we gave the address of our hotel. The driver had to look it up on a map! Was this his ignorance? No, it was the obscurity of rue Claude Tellier! Our room is small but clean and we are off the beaten track, but only a few steps from the Metro and it is a very quiet neighborhood. We checked in and went right back out for coffee, tea, and a baguette. We picked up some water and collapsed for three hours of sleep. Refreshed, we went back out at 4:00

pm and headed for St. Germain des Pres for drinks and jazz outdoors. With time to make a new plan, we found Café de le Petit Prince for dinner. Very nice appetizer of mushrooms and artichoke, rabbit and fish main courses and desserts out of this world—raspberry crepe and pear with chocolate sauce and ice cream. Strolling and one more drink and home by midnight.

Sunday: Continental breakfast at the hotel was very good. We went out at around 11 am. Museum pass, walk in Marais. We slip into the Picasso museum as it begins to rain. Very comfortable museum with white underground galleries with occasional cut-out peepholes from one room to another. Picasso was accomplished in many forms, both traditional and in his own distinctive vision.

We walked from Marais through Tuileries, Champs Elysees, and Arc de Triumphe, and I vowed never to order eau Minerale in a café again! It cost $8 each for two glasses of water. We went to the Latin Quarter for dinner at a Greek restaurant and had a mixed seafood grill. It was quite good. Back to our hotel by 8:30 pm to watch World cup finals between Italy and Brazil.

Monday: Louvre (it leaks in the rain). Deux Magots café. Dinner in St. Germaine des Pres on rue Christine. Shrimp. Concert in Church of St. Germaine des Pres.

Tuesday: Heavy Rain: Musee d'Orsay. Café on the corner of rue Jacob and Bonaparte. Movie: Roseaux Sauvage. Pizza dinner on foot.

Wednesday: Tour Eiffel. Musee Rodin. Search for sewer tour. Café with Mozart for lunch. Sewer tour. Montmartre. Sacre Coeur. Café. Dinner at Restaurant Durer. Jazz Club "Duc."

Thursday: No rain! Café. Pompidou Centre. Walk to left bank. Shakespeare and Co. Dinner in St. Germaine at Procope: wonderful oysters for me; V had a whole fish! Crazy Horse live show. Walked along Champs Elysee for tiramisu ice cream at a Café.

Friday: Two sandwiches jamon fromage. Montmartre. Café rue des Abbesses. Walking tour: Bateau Louise, Moulin Rouge, Van Gogh. Up to Butte to café—beer. Shop. Café Beer and Salade oceans (mmmm). Piano. Marais for dinner, Café Du Impasse. Warm goat cheese salad. Cold seafood salad with best tomato.

Reflections on Paris Chronology thirteen years later: How much I didn't capture in those sketchy notes on our days in Paris! I didn't write about our massive luggage and the struggle to carry it through the city that first morning and how V got hit in both arms by the gates closing as we exited the shopping mall or Metro. Boom! He had suitcases in both hands and was hit from both sides as the gates withdrew for a normal passenger and then snapped back right on this burdened traveler.

I didn't write about the show at the Crazy Horse live revue. Beautiful tall girls in just a few lines of sparkles here and there and high-heeled shoes, and maybe some feathers. Dancing in formations and up, down, and around poles on the stage.

I didn't write about waiting on line for the Musee d'Orsay in the rain along with every other tourist in Paris for a refuge out of the rain! Now I can also see that the Greek restaurant with mixed seafood grill is one of a long line of tourist restaurants. Open to the street, enticing display and always someone out front to call out to you that this is the most amazing food at the best prices anywhere. Thirteen years later we are still susceptible to this display! Our bridge restaurant in Istanbul was just the Turkish version of this genre. It still works!!

We look so young in the photos from this trip. I've given away most of the clothes I was wearing then, but I see one favorite shirt of V's that still comes out on special summer days. Photos help prod my memory: what is this blanket and what looks like a handful of colored fabric and cotton? Oh, yes, the Metro puppet theater! A young man would quickly hang up the blanket and begin a puppet show between stops on the train!

My favorite photo of myself: Taken on the balcony of the Pompidou Centre. It is a close up of me with my sunglasses pushed up on my head holding my hair back wearing a black scooped neck, sleeveless shell. Behind me is the view over rooftops of Paris. My hair is long and

I look young. I try to recreate this scene on many trips and ask V to take my photo. I wonder if he knows what I'm up to, reenacting this moment of perfection on our first trip to Paris?

There is V sitting at Café Chez Plumeau. I think we spent several hours there in the perfect air reading and absorbing the selves we are in Paris.

Rodin's hand sculptures amazed me then and continue to delight me now, even in my amateur photographs. I love the large size of hands and feet on his sculpted figures, as if they are rooted in materiality of their bodies, of their weight and their work. As my own feet spread to a larger size in adulthood and as a NYC walker, I imagined myself growing into a Rodin figure with those amazingly expressive hands and feet full of purpose and substantial to the challenges of the world. These two photos of hands that I photographed are different, but both are amazingly graceful and in extraordinary poses evocative of sensitivity beyond words. The tingling nerve ends of these hands are almost visible as they barely touch each other, but lean toward the touch with vulnerability and sensuous openness. Rodin is worth a pilgrimage to sculpture sites in any city. I've not been able to resist touching in NYC, Palo Alto, and Paris, and I hope more to come. My hands are drawn to the strength and flow of these stone and metal figures.

## Water City; Water Day

After arriving in Helsinki, Finland, yesterday, we spent the afternoon walking in downtown, locating the university, getting oriented to main streets, tram stops, markets, restaurants, train station, etc. We happened upon a parade of the samba schools of Helsinki, quite a surprise so far from Brazil! After much inactivity in Bulgaria, being driven around in traffic, this liberation into a pedestrian city where water views open through every third street, feels wonderful. Expensive, however. We had a long afternoon nap after playtime, and woke at 8 pm to go out for a light meal in the long, long twilight.

Today we wake up in Helsinki and V is working, writing the paper he will give at the conference that begins here tomorrow. I bring him coffee and set out to walk in our hotel neighborhood. I go in the opposite direction from the familiar tram stop and intend to try to walk along the water if possible. Our current home in central Pennsylvania feels far from water and I miss it a lot. In New York City, in Montgomery, and in Marlboro, my life could always be oriented in relation to the water: rivers, ponds, reservoir, ocean. I am in Helsinki making new memories that will form layers of experience over those still vibrant within me.

Manhattan, between the Hudson River and the East River, is very much a slender island. The beautiful east/west light flowing through a cross street from river to river always seemed half water/half light to me. I knew uptown and downtown by alignment between the rivers. Crossing the slender Hendrick Hudson bridge at the tip top northern end of the island always feels like a momentous event, transition from solid earth to a floating island; from black and white to full color.

Montgomery, on a smaller scale, held for my growing years of adventure and dreams, three ponds and a small lively river. We had a pond, probably man-made, but wild to us kids, beyond the end of our property, across a broad field and through a small woods. In summer, it was a place for hearing frogs, feeling the buzz of heat and light among growing fecund nature, even to the mud that seemed alive. On special summer evenings, our father would organize a fishing expedition to the Creamery pond or to the Wallkill River. It would begin when he told one of us to "dig worms." We would be excited and get the digging fork from the dark crawlspace under the house and seek damp spots to dig for nightcrawlers. The fishing gear would be next—our poles with reels, dobbers, hooks and sinkers. The box of extra everything along with pliers and an old knife. Juggling poles, a pail, and a can of worms, three of us and Dad would get in the car to coax small sunfish (pond) or catfish (river) to bite our hooks and end up in a pail of water. Watching the captured fish swim feebly in our pail was hypnotizing. We actually brought home and cleaned some of these tiny fish for our mother to cook for dinner.

Later that same river was a highway to growing up as my sweetheart and I canoed upstream and floated down on many afternoons imagining that life would be exactly this simple.

The third pond was probably a classic rural "swimming hole," but to us it was the center of the summer universe in early adolescence. With the "little raft" on the near side and the "big raft" on the far side, Dunn's Pond stratified growing up quite safely and clearly.

In winter, the wild pond far behind our houses was our skating pond during the short afternoons. I would wait till everyone left and continue skating alone in twilight, singing the "I'm flying" song from Peter Pan at the top of my lungs and choreographing an ice dance that I hoped would lift me up off the ice into the dusky air.

The early adult years I lived in Marlboro were oriented in relation to the Hudson River and to a small reservoir that was part of my everyday view of life.

So, water as part of everyday life is familiar, almost a necessity that I crave constantly in central Pennsylvania. Helsinki more than meets this desire!

> "We do have a tuning fork in us that continues to vibrate to the ocean's susurrations and contrapuntal thump—to the seashore's scented swell, with birdcall ebullience and the amphibious chiming in."*

The most enchanting aspect of my day was serendipity—all of my discoveries and delights following the pull of water were entirely accidental: just following a path or other sojourners led me to an accidental itinerary of delight: cafés, museums, fanciful fountains,

---

\* Edward Hoagland, "Endgame: Meditations on a Diminishing World", Harper's Magazine, June 2007, page 37

sculpture, parks, bridges, antiquities, shady benches, English-speaking tour guide, sunshine, boats, sea views, and much more.

Why is it that when we are seeking so hard to have a special experience, it seems so difficult to come by? When we let go into the rhythms of the day and the flow of surroundings, sometimes the gifts pour down in abundance!

This used to happen to me all the time in NYC. I love New York! I am a native born Manhattanite who was exiled to "upstate" for my adolescence and young adulthood, but who found a way back to myself as "city person" at the age of thirty-eight.

On a day when the complexities of being a divorced mom of two teenagers and a minimalist budgeted graduate student were pressuring me to produce a positive experience for my county-born kids in my new city habitat, everything would go wrong! I am convinced that my anxiety alone re-routed the number 1 train from the Bronx to the opposite side of Manhattan just so the kids would have to walk further with their disappointing and weird mother to reach whatever strange destination she had in mind for their forced visit.

On one of my better days when we floated through the city with a very loose agenda, the streets and parks seemed to open for us like magnolia blossoms in May. We would turn a corner and discover a hologram museum or a street vendor of exactly the treat we'd been craving. We arrived at every mode of transportation to find no lines and a train, bus, ferry just waiting for us. We found the Wall Street bull, a window table high above the hubbub with a view, and a friendly waiter who understood shared drinks and plentiful peanuts! Street theater and free music would anticipate our arrival on park paths and my memory even released Edna St. Millay's phrases back to the Staten Island Ferry: "We were very tired; we were very merry; we rode back and forth all night on the ferry." I don't know exactly how this happens that rigid planning sometimes yields less than open meandering, but it does happen to me. How about you?

# CHAPTER ELEVEN

# Borders and Identities: The Familiar Strange

*It may be that when we no longer know what to do, we have come to our real work, and that when we no longer know which way to go, we have begun our real journey.*

—Wendell Berry

*All my life I have loved traveling at night, with a companion, each of us discussing and sharing the known and familiar behavior of the other.* —Michael Ondaatje

## Poem from Lecture

The poetry of our lives forms a
Matrix ... evolving, and always turning
Toward illuminations
Near and far.
Nourished on

Surprise and delight; growth
Grows along a continuum
Both ends of which draw
Us closer together.
Precision and profundity;
Chaos and culture;
Vagueness and indeterminacy yield
The meaning of continuity.
The universe grows by chance, and love,
Though imperfect, is elemental.

## Aroma

The beautifully matched pairs of horses pulling ornate carriages on Rynek Glowny in Stare Miasto of Krakow, Poland, are missing something this year. There is no smell; no rich aroma of horse dung while sitting outside in the many cafes drinking Okocim, Zywiec, or Tyskie beer. How nice, and yet something is missing. Dorozki is plural and dorozka is just one in Polish, but what about the horse dung? I seem to recall that horses wore baskets below their tails the last time we were in Krakow three years ago. This time, no baskets and no dung. Where is it?

## Objects vs. Experience

I stake a good deal of my present identify on the question of which to prioritize in life, things or experiences. I am in favor of experiences—of course—but my categories may cause some questions to arise. For example, a tree can be an experience, books are most certainly experiences. A scarf is so close to being an experience that it might as well weigh nothing instead of next-to-nothing. I put on the experience of Copenhagen's walking streets with my most treasured scarf. My husband's love blossoms on my shoulder with a thick square of silk. Even a whisper of fabric can transport me to a street vendor in Paris or remind me of my mother who wore this scarf or my dear friend who selected that one. A garden is certainly an experience not thing. What about a sculpture garden or a painting of a garden? I am beginning to think that all art falls into my broad category of experience? Music certainly does.

In my twenties and thirties I lived in a constant debate between things and experiences. It took me years to even begin to articulate the terms of the debate, but I know that one of the founding legends of my world view came from Helen Boyd.

Helen and Ray Boyd came to live in the little white house on one-eighth of an acre that complete our seven-eighths when he (they) retired. I wasn't much interested in Ray and I don't even know what he did for a living in NYC before they moved north to our small community in Orange County, or "upstate," as people say.

I was more interested in Helen. Even then, I suppose, I was seeking role models of mature women to teach me how to grow up. Helen was very different from the Sicilian-born women in my family. She had pink skin and white hair, while my women were olive-skinned and tended toward steely grey hair. The only person Helen resembled in my extended family was Aunt Nettie, married to my mother's brother Steve, who also seemed different to us. Aunt Nettie and Helen Boyd were from a different class. They had crystal and china and fur coats. They had style!

Helen Boyd and my mother visited back and forth between their small, quiet cottage and our noisy household of five children. I'm sure that each received something precious in the exchange. My mother glimpsed a more refined lifestyle less constrained by constant child care. The Boyds had only one grown child, Rob. Helen may have enjoyed the liveliness of youngsters and conversation with my mother's daughters, i.e. my sister and me.

I remember this story that Helen told as aimed just for me. I may have been in my early twenties, just married, pregnant or already a mother. The occasion may have been a visit to talk about buying the Boyds' crystal and china. Helen and Ray were moving into assisted living and couldn't take all their possessions with them.

Helen had service for twelve of both crystal and china. We had neither. I loved the idea of having these delicate pieces along with their history of elaborate dinner parties in Brooklyn. There were twelve tiny aperitif stemware and matching fluted wine glasses in two sizes. There were slender parfait glasses and broader sorbet glasses. The china was similarly tuned to elegance with plates of many sizes for exotic courses I could only imagine.

I think Helen was very happy to have all these objects go to me. I paid very little for them. The real medium of exchange was my youth and enthusiasm for her vivid memories: the memory of a glittering table set with four or five glasses per person alongside the delicate shapes and colors of fine china; the sounds of the elegant guests, delicate tinkling and ringing as jeweled hands touched crystal or a fork touched china; all the voices, the ladies dressed up and the men in suits and aftershave. I never touch a piece without activating this image.

Around this negotiation and the packing of boxes, I may have been telling Helen about my dreams of travel. She and Ray had always wanted to travel, too. They had saved their money and were about to reserve a trip to Europe when they were offered a house for sale at just the amount of money they had saved. You know how this ends, of course. They bought the house thinking that they could save again and travel another time. Life intervened and they never took that trip. As Helen said, "One thing leads to another."

Helen told me that she always wished for that trip. She longed to have the memories of that trip now, as she got old, far beyond the usefulness of a house and all her other possessions. She urged me to take the trip whenever I would face such a decision.

Helen's story bolstered my own inclination to seek the experience not the objects. I am vulnerable, like everyone else, to temptations all around. I try to stay out of stores. I try to remember that most souvenirs don't accomplish for us what we wish ... to return us to that time and place where we felt so alive. Experiences fit better into your luggage and are easily refreshed by an evocative color, sound, smell, or other link right back to the vibrant experience itself.

# Three Questions With Many Answers

### *"What are you doing?"*

. . . just taking up space. Just thinking. Just writing. Just listening. Just looking. Just nibbling. Just sipping. Just waiting. Just hanging out. Just between. Just noticing. Just scribbling. Just brainstorming. Just me. Just now. Just casual. Just drizzling. Just wondering. Just imagining. Just strolling. Just daydreaming. Just standing. Just playing. Just whispering. Just pointing. Just reading. Just saying. Just wishing. Just doodling. Just browsing. Just eavesdropping. Just being. Just holding on. Just biding time. Just peeking. Just playing. Just remembering. Just whistling in the dark. Just watching.

### *"Why are you here?"*

. . . to see. To feel. To touch. To be touched. To experience. To learn. To handle. To marvel. To buy. To converse. To share. To watch. To explore. To satisfy. To taste. To know. To be stimulated. To wonder. To be. To test. To interact. To go forth. To be challenged. To try. To climb. To stroll. To savor. To renew. To be surprised. To change. To make memories. To think. To sense. To refresh. To recreate. To meet. To intensify. To deepen. To expand. To exchange. To have stories. To build. To acquire. To make memories. To cultivate. To be inspired.

### *"What are you seeking?"*

Seeking water. Seeking color. Seeking complexity. Seeking shade. Seeking speed. Seeking solitude. Seeking a breeze. Seeking diversity. Seeking company. Seeking quiet. Seeking sharp taste. Seeking motives. Seeking plenitude. Seeking simplicity. Seeking space. Seeking beauty.

Seeking harmony. Seeking comfort. Seeking challenge. Seeking stimulus. Seeking balance. Seeking a question. Seeking help. Seeking a view. Seeking antiquity. Seeking expanse. Seeking cozy. Seeking unique. Seeking direction. Seeking perspective. Seeking mystery. Seeking authenticity. Seeking familiar. Seeking strange. Seeking the only. Seeking transcendence. Seeking epiphany. Seeking you. Seeking a sign. Seeking illumination. Seeking insight. Seeking convergence. Seeking the nexus. Seeking a word. Seeking surcease of sorrow. Seeking a snack. Seeking a drink. Seeking advice. Seeking transportation. Seeking style. Seeking a calling. Seeking faith. Seeking a deal. Seeking more. Simply seeking. Seeking wonder. Seeking touch. Seeking news. Seeking symmetry. Seeking solace. Seeking roots. Seeking a seeker.

# Captain Blood: Getting in Touch with Your Inner Pirate

*Captain Blood: His Odyssey* by Raphael Sabatini
Houghton Mifflin Company, Boston and New York, 1922

Let me introduce you to someone near and dear to my heart. This persona lived with me for many years, and in many ways, lives with me still. He shaped a voice inside my head that still speaks to me. At times, I was his beautiful, young aristocratic mistress, but most of the time, I wore his own boots, wielded his own mighty sword, and spoke in his exotic Irish accent. The very words, "Captain Blood by Raphael Sabatini," when repeated, become an elixir to transport me back to the days of my most vivid (imaginary) adventures.

- Peter Blood, Irish, medical degree at Trinity College, Dublin, both parents dead, about 30 years old, already veteran of many military conflicts for several countries.
- Approximate date: 1685

Captain Blood was the embodiment of three qualities for me:

+ The courage to take risks in experiencing the world.
+ Tenderness and patience in love combined with passion and vigor.
+ A sense of justice that transcended laws and rules.

Now, in my own life and persona, what would it mean to adopt any one of these? If I were to take the first and apply it in my life, it would mean saying "Yes," to more opportunities without allowing fears and cautions to guide so many decisions. It would mean embracing new foods, welcoming strangers to my community and home, venturing into unfamiliar neighborhoods, exhibits, events, etc. It would mean allowing myself to be in situations where I don't know the outcome, where I might be uncomfortable, but where I will learn something new about the world or myself in the process. It isn't just the big things like signing up for a trip to China, but also in the little things like inviting a student from Bahrain to my home to meet my family or even saying "Yes!" to a challenging new committee assignment. That's what Captain Blood would do!

*The world is a book and those who do not travel read only one page.*                                   —St. Augustine

## Borders, Boundaries, Tectonic Plates

The threat of rain was just a threat and we are in sun and the breezes of the Bosphorus right now. Well, I always sit in the shade, but I'm appreciating the sun. This is a spectacular restaurant on the straits of the Bosporus with a view of the bridge between Europe and Asia. Istanbul, Turkey is the ONLY city that spans two continents.

Sitting there at the border of continents reminded me of Iceland several years ago where we visited the conjunction of the tectonic plates of Europe and North America. I am attracted to such places where two entities meet. Is it a universal attraction? Is it about wanting to see what can't be seen, what is essentially mysterious? There are often tourist attractions around such places. Do they remind us of the literal transition experiences of birth and death where the mystery is across time and spirit and cannot be viewed over and over except in memory, and we don't effectively remember either one? Are we intrigued by boundaries as puny efforts to keep disorder and chaos at bay? Or do we simply like to marvel at the juxtapositions of one thing and another?

I am content not to know and to continue seeking and enjoying momentous juxtapositions in space and/or time.

## No-Man's Land

We have just crossed the border from Bulgaria into Turkey and are on our way to Istanbul. We expected delays from thirty minutes to two hours, but we were through in about twenty minutes. Sounds easy? The border was a series of six heavily guarded kiosks where our friend and driver, K handed over all four passports and other required documents. We rolled down all our windows so the officials could peer into the car and verify that our faces matched the passport photos. Three kiosks were on each side of the border and presumably each was verifying one set of documents or managing one set of regulations. Each was set in a field of concrete barriers. There was no running away from your car without the proverbial hail of bullets, or so I imagined from seeing too many spy films.

Guards motioned us to pull over at one kiosk on the Turkish side and eventually we had to open one suitcase for a cursory examination. We were all a bit nervous. Guards are armed and the atmosphere is not focused on service to clients, but of extreme suspicion of any and all wrong doings. Don't we all feel guilty when anyone, especially an armed guard, looks at us with suspicion?

The countryside on the Turkish side of the border looks similar to Bulgaria in geographic features, but is more intensively cultivated. Similar orange tile roofs. As we pass the first town after the border, K points out the mosques. They are easily spotted with their high minarets and round domes. I didn't know that the number of minarets signifies the level of its sponsor: one for a common local mosque, two for a more distinguished local sponsor, three is for a relative of the sultan, and four minarets indicates that the mosque is sponsored by the sultan himself.

## The Longest Line

As we approach the Turkish border driving from Istanbul to Bulgaria, we drive alongside hundreds of stationary tractor-trailers for over ten kilometers. They are stopped in a long, long, long line waiting for any movement to reach them in the process of inching across that border. An industry of local folks ride small vehicles alongside, selling food and water. We are told that the wait can be up to a week. Perhaps there is a strike? This long a line is not ordinary, but a wait of two or three days is ordinary. I am so relieved that we four travelers are in K's little blue car and that we are traveling with great luck through three sets of border gates on each side; three in Turkey and three in Bulgaria, each one checking us for some official business, but moving quickly and letting us pass.

CHAPTER TWELVE

# Solitude

*To awaken alone in a strange town is one of the pleasantest sensations in the world.*                    —Freya Stark

## Making Meaning

My flash drive isn't functioning. I may have inadvertently caused it to malfunction by packing it together with my new iPod. Did the battery of the iPod erase the flash drive? I don't think there will be any serious consequences.

This loss does bring my thoughts to the article I read about Gordon Bell, a leading figure in the computer industry who is making a complete archive of his life and trying to develop some marketable product for Microsoft to persuade the rest of us to need.

What is the value of a complete life archive? I can see the point of converting all of our paper files to electronic files, but why every image of every day, the history of every eyeblink and heartbeat? AND how would anyone access the information in an orderly way? The article only superficially explores how we make meaning in our lives from our quotidian minutia. AND since technology changes dramatically every ten years, we might be holding the equivalent of vinyl recordings in ten years with no turntables to retrieve our beautiful symphonies. And the delicacy of my flash drive is another reminder of why some of us like "hard copy" for backup.

*"Remember This?: A project to record everything we do in life."*
Alec Wilkinson. *The New Yorker*, May 28, 2007, 38-44.

## Raveling and Unraveling of Mind

I am sitting on a bench in a park overlooking a panoramic view and Piazza Mercantile, Bari, Italy, thinking, thinking. I am always fearful that my time of being an impostor is almost over. An imposter of an intelligent and lively mind. At what age will the inevitable decline become noticeable and will my husband and children talk to me about it or just become frustrated.

I watched this process with my grandmother, mother, and aunts. Sometimes a stroke is the dramatic onset of a precipitous decline as for my mother's mother and her older daughter, my Aunt Rose. For my mother, it was a slower, much more subtle decline over five or so years until it was no longer safe for her to be home alone with my father. I remember a Sunday afternoon when she drove me to the train in Beacon. We stopped at a diner for lunch. As we read our menus, she had some sort of episode—a seizure or other event. Her eyes went unfocused and she did not hear me or respond. It was a "far away look." It lasted a very short time, but it alarmed me, and I insisted on driving her home again.

My sister-in-law C said that the slow decline was a fortunate means for us to get used to life without her—our time of learning to let go.

Every slip (saying lira instead of Euro yesterday) is a terrifying preview of the unraveling of my own mind. I think of the play/movie "Proof" where the senile mathematics genius goes to his study every day and produces gibberish-filled notebooks. What if someone picks up this notebook and sees that my pen has been scribbling nonsense?

So, I make plans to ravel up the unraveling—learning and training my mind while it unravels, hoping that the balance of accounts will at least reduce the overall decline.

## Morning Browse

On the 17th and 18th I went into Urbino, Italy for the morning to browse, walk, absorb, read, write, view, photograph, and otherwise "be" alone with the city. My daily gelato here was straciatella and pistaccio.

What is the value of time alone when traveling? Is the experience different from touring in a pair/couple or in a group? Yes, certainly! I had to figure out everything myself—how to pay for parking, finding a bathroom, whether/what to purchase, using a bank machine to get Euro, etc. etc. I often do much of the talking with merchants when we travel in Italy, so that was not too different. The experience of meandering is different depending on whether you are alone or with others. When I was much younger, I enjoyed traveling alone, perhaps more than now. As a woman of mature years with silver hair, I sense that I have a different advantage than when I was younger. Possibly, there is a level of respect for elders that becomes an advantage in some places. I did notice that no one beeped at me when I was driving in second gear all the way from the campus into Urbino.

## Born Traveler

My friend AH, reflecting on her feelings about traveling, commented, "I guess I'm just not a born traveler!" I think she was implying that I am a born traveler, but of course it doesn't always feel like that to me, although I do really like to set off on a journey, open a new book or a new, blank journal, and face a day without knowing what it will hold. I can even recall wishing, in the middle of routine weeks at work, that something would disrupt our function in such a way that we would be challenged to perform in unanticipated ways. Hmmm, what is that urge?

Thinking about what makes a "born traveler" reminds me of a past life regression experience I sought out in my early twenties when routine was settling over me as a young married mother of two angel children. I'm thinking of this as ultimate travel or else as complete farce. I had met this kind of alternative/mystical woman somewhere, either on a trip or locally, waiting on a line for something. We had plenty of these alternative/mystical folks near where I lived in the 70's and early 80's, not all that far from Woodstock the village and Woodstock the festival (two different locations).

This woman and I struck up a conversation which meandered to past life regression. She claimed to be a facilitator of such encounters. Being curious and a bit of an explorer at heart, I decided to experience this for myself. The session was held at her woodsy home within an hour's drive of my traditional home, and the minimal cost of the session was worth its value in strangeness alone.

First she guided me into relaxation and then into two experiences. It's rather vague to me now years later, but I conjured up two images with her guidance. The first identity I sensed was an old prospector figure, a cliché from some film—beard, dusty clothes, hat, old boots. I don't remember the second figure as well, but it was a person guilty of some theft. If I were to believe this was one of my past lives, it would explain my low-level anxiety that store clerks will think I'm shop-lifting. I don't much believe that I was a dusty old prospector, but I'm glad I tried this experience. I only went for one regression session, but on another occasion I had a sort of flashback.

I was on a crazy sailing trip alone with a man I'd met in Café La Fortuna on the Upper East Side of Manhattan on a Sunday afternoon as I read The New Yorker and sipped cappuccino. C owned a sailboat that he wanted to deliver to Florida for winter rentals from its current location on Long Island Sound. He wanted a companion along for safety, for company, and for additional finances. I nearly quit my job for this trip, but at the last minute listened to a wise friend who said this was not the situation for which to make such a sacrifice. I ended up taking one week's vacation and the two weekends to meet C and the boat at Wrightsville Beach, North Carolina. We mostly putt-putted through the intercoastal waterway, slowly but relatively safely, with only one experienced sailor aboard. I was such a novice and perhaps he was reckless. We managed to drop a beam on my head on the very first day. It was like Thor pounded me with his hammer on the top of my head to drive me through the deck like a nail ! C told me afterwards that he instantly thought I was gravely injured, but somehow I wasn't, although someday I may reap the consequences.

After several days of placid and cautious sailing, we took the boat into the open ocean for some speed and adventure. I remember vividly the moment when, sitting at the extreme front end of the boat, I realized that I could see only ocean in every direction! I was Columbus! Sailing in the wrong direction, perhaps, but it was a magnificent sight and emotionally stunning.

I was not aware of any fear, although I should have been terrorized with the possibility that one of us could fall off, and in either case, I would be doomed ! I thought in that moment that my past life must have been as an explorer because the sight was so exciting in the way of returning to a remembered bliss. That day ended with an unexpectedly sudden storm, Coast Guard officers boarding our boat to search for drugs (because only crazy people and drug dealers are out in such weather), and then gratefully and meekly following them into the port of Charlestown, South Carolina. Even today, many years later, the exhilaration of being a speck at the center of a complete 360-degree disc of ocean is vivid and feels just right.

So, if I'm not a born traveler or a direct descendent of Christopher Columbus or one of his crew, there may be some cluster of travel dispositions embedded in my identity somewhere. Despite loving my home and family to extremes of Italian passion, I am often ready to set off into the (relative) unknown with only a minimal agenda and carry-on luggage for another excursion both outward and inward.

## Passagiata

In Sicily I loved the concept and the reality of the vital street life and passagiata in the small towns. All day long, kitchen chairs were carried to the doorstep and small groups congregated to watch the day unfold. In the evening, the older people lined the streets where the young and youthful parade in small groups, breaking off to greet and cheer their elder family members and then rejoining the flow with a new cluster. Each small chair beside a doorway is an orchestra seat to the living drama unfolding through time and space with dimensions of operatic grandiosity as well as intimate pas-de-deux. The street/stage evokes a metaphor of history and flux as all ages gather, dissolve, and coalesce, all the while meandering along.

## Down-time Day

It is 10:30 a.m. in Sofia, Bulgaria and I am lingering over tea in the lobby/breakfast area of our hotel inhaling at least a week's worth of second-hand smoke. Suddenly, I notice that I am the only woman here! There are three additional occupied tables among the fifteen or so in this hotel lobby area. Three men sit at each of two tables, and at the larger table to my right, five men are reading newspapers and talking vigorously. These seem like local men gathering here for a routine morning coffee or other beverage. I don't understand a word, but catch the bonhomie of the conversation. I hear the word "American." Are they noticing me or commenting on the visit of President Bush anticipated next week?

The three men to my right look younger, certainly working age.

What is their schedule that brings them here mid-morning? The five older men make me feel sad for my own father who sits alone every morning and every afternoon instead of meeting a group of comfortable cronies at the local park or hotel lobby, not that there is any hotel in his town. I hope that as I age I will live somewhere that allows me to mingle with other women to talk over the day's news, local gossip, the appearance of a stranger, the weather, our children's lives, books, films, and our memories.

From the hotel window, I see a man drinking from a bottle while several scavenging dogs make their rounds of a small park. The grass in the park is over a foot high; the streets are rough as though under construction (or destruction) as are many of the buildings. K. says we are having an anachronistic experience of Soviet-style socialism in this hotel, one of the chain constructed in each town during communism as the sole facility for any visitors.

Some days here are intensely packed with activity and purpose; some are very loosely structured. Do we feel we are missing the most important experience of the county when we have a downtime day of strolling, reading, observing and breathing the local air? We may be missing a church, museum, library, or monument. But perhaps the usual itinerary is reversed and we are missing the real experience when we enter only the destinations listed in guide books instead of entering the quotidian consciousness of the place? In this dusty, shabby suburb, we may be seeing and having Bulgaria in a more intense way than by marching from public site to public site through the city center. We are witnessing the ebb and flow of commuting workers, children with family elders in the ragged park, food offered in small cafés far from tourist areas, lawn trimming with a pair of scissors, and the one ancient computer in the hotel's office. This is the experience of Bulgaria as much as the beautiful Alexander Nevski Memorial Cathedral.

# CHAPTER THIRTEEN

# Liminal Time, Meantime

*No matter where you go, there you are.* —Unknown

## Interlude

Just being here, now
Vision gradually settles down to
Noticing the smaller and smaller aspects of life.
Attention moves
From objects the size of the Blue Mosque
To noticing
The color of ripening apricots,
The patterns of clay tiles moving rain
Quite simply down the roof.
No clocks or watch:
Time is different by the sea.
When I finally put a watch on,
I didn't look at it.
When I looked at it,
It made no sense.

# Lost Day

We arrived in Urbino on Sunday after a few hours confusion related to directions of which campus was the location of our conference. Was this a lost day or a transition of mind-set day? Mostly the latter. I should know by now that it takes time to shift from immersion in one setting and consciousness to another. We were in full vacation mode in Fano, but here in Urbino, we are immersed in social networking and academic dynamics. Especially for V, this is a dramatic shift—he is now "on stage" in his professional persona with the additional challenge of speaking only one language, English.

# No-Agenda Day

The days just go by ... breakfast ... . reading ... walking ... a swim. ...exploring another area of the neighborhood ... market for water ... dinner and done.

It is more than a little disconcerting to feel the days and hours glide by so quickly.

I want to peg down a morning and keep it fresh until a decisive task is complete.

And then unroll a long, wide ribbon of afternoon with blocks of colorful activity stretching around the corner into a leisurely pool of twilight.

This is going to take some practice!

# What Time Is It?

It is Thursday at midnight in Imatra, Finland on the border with Russia when I have an email from my daughter who is living Thursday afternoon in Groton, Massachusetts. She is unpacking from a whirlwind business trip to Beijing. Time feels like an artificial convenience to keep humans organized on a spinning globe so we don't all crash into each other.

# Postcards

It is 2:00 a.m.. I'm tired but wide awake. So much on my mind. Sometimes it is very difficult to separate what we want to do from what we feel is expected or what we ought to do, for example, postcards. I have written 30 postcards this week to family, friends, and authors! I wrote to all who have sent me cards in the past or who said: "Send me a postcard."

Please exempt yourself from this – clearly, I want to be writing to you! If you were here, we would be talking tonight, not writing postcards.

# Reading Lincoln in Sofia

*"What makes Lincoln still seem noble, to use an old-fashioned word, is that he had not a guilty sense of remorse but a tragic sense of responsibility ... . Lincoln exemplifies the problem of liberal violence: the disjunction between the purity of our motives (as they appear to the liberal) and the force of our violence (as it is experienced by the victim)"*\*

Gopnik uses a discrepancy between two recollections of words spoken at the moment of Lincoln's death to reflect on the processes of history. Today, reading this in the breakfast room of the RAI Hotel at #6 Ak. Nikola Obreshkov Str., 1113 Sofia, Bulgaria, I am also watching a CNN documentary on the TV suspended above plates of cheese, meat, fruit, and sweets. The broadcast is about the civilian deaths in Iraq in January 2006. The skyline of Baghdad looks like the Istanbul skyline I enjoyed yesterday. The women screaming are wearing black burkas, but they sound like all the women I know would sound upon finding their children dead in the street.

---

\*  "Angles and Ages: Lincoln's language and its legacy" by Adam Gopnik, *The New Yorker*, May 28, 2007, 30-37.

A parent rushing to safety cradles a blond girl perhaps 3 or 4 years old, the age of my own granddaughters, whose lives I would protect with my own. Do Americans know that small girls in Baghdad may have blond hair and trust their parents and grandparents to lift them to safety? These images should be playing on the "jumbotron" in Times Square instead of breasts and buttocks, and on the Lincoln memorial in Washington and on the screens of drive-in movie theaters all across the countryside.

The irony is that our current President does not have the "charismatic ethical intelligence" that Gopnik attributes to Lincoln (36), but was elected twice by force of empty charisma (like empty calories) and full coffers. It is more difficult to be a traveler with an American passport than ever before.

## Dilly-Dally

I can really dilly-dally for literally hours! I woke at 6:00 am and left the room at 9:00 am.. What on earth did I do for three hours!! Linger in bed, organize, shower, chose clothes, write, wash hair, change clothes, repack my purse and backpack, count my money, file receipts, look out the window ... What is going on here with this lingering? My mind is spreading out and slowing down.

## Café Serendipity, Imatra, Finland

After our last scheduled event today, we went directly to the train station to purchase our tickets for tomorrow and then walked the three kilometers back to our hotel. The walking path followed the river and was just delightful in the mixed sun and shade, heat and cool breeze. We had a sense of "What could be nicer than this?" reminding us of the quotation from Kurt Vonnegut at the banquet earlier in the week.

The last of our companions diverged from us at the hotels and we looked for a café table in the sun/shade to enjoy a beer marking closure of the forced itinerary and the beginning of several days of unstructured time on our own.

We found a table at "Martina" on a corner across from a small public stage where a troupe of young performers were entertaining children with a sophisticated puppet show. One performer had white sleeves from elbow to shoulders and bare lower arms and hands to create the legs of an ostrich with fluffy white feathered thighs and skinny skin-and-bones shins and feet. A second performer wrapped a feather boa around one hand, and then positioned her/his second arm and hand to be the neck and head of the ostrich. Very difficult to describe in words, but it worked!

In the skit, the ostrich finds a balloon and explores its properties, passing it from beak to foot, from foot to foot, and so on. The ostrich tries and learns to balance standing on the balloon, but soon, the bird accidentally bursts the balloon and then begins to improvise with the bright red elastic remnant to create a bow tie around the top of its long, skinny ostrich neck. With the rest of the human bodies dressed in black in front of a black curtain, the illusion was really magical. It took only a 17% suspension of disbelief (and a full glass of beer) to actually see an ostrich playing with a balloon. The children managed with far less suspension and also without the beer!

How much suspension of disbelief are you capable of on short notice? Do you see horses galloping in the cumulus clouds? Or dolphins playing in fountains? Can you connect the dots to see full figures when a sculptor gives you only hints? Or imagine hunters by the fire, and druids dancing, and Hesperus at his forge with sparks flying every which way?

Half (well, ok, 48%) of the magic of travel is the willing suspension of disbelief in hearing the bold sketches of history and filling in the blanks with real people in terror fleeing or hiding or laughing. I learned in Bulgaria that Thrace was an actual location in the mountains of Bulgaria. Thrace was the home of Orpheus, the character of myth who played the lyre to bring his wife back from Hades. The deal was that he could not turn around while leading her all the way out. At the last moment, he hears her stumble, turns around, and loses her forever. So, finally, the experience of a country is not about the numbers (population, industries, gross national product, length of rivers that I learned in grade school and high school) but about the stories of real people with complicated family alliances who are half blind with emotions and flaws, and yet making decisions they live to celebrate or regret or who don't live and others celebrate or regret.

## Higgledy Piggledy London

After we left the academy, we walked over to Shepard's Market at the recommendation of Penny Blasko, the charming photographer who recently photographed D and Y for their engagement gift. I was very glad of the recommendation as I might not have discovered this little charming nook of narrow streets and sidewalk cafes. We shared a bottle of wine and a warm goat cheese salad. We then walked over to Green Park and I was exactly in the mood to sit on a park bench and observe the passersby, drop my eyes and read, and do some writing in between. V headed off to look for tickets for our last evening and we made a plan to meet at the Covent Garden market where we had heard a lively classical street quartet earlier in the week. I wanted to stay on that bench in the glow of the wine, absorbing the "higgledy piggledy" energy of the city. Virginia Woolf describes it like this in "The London Scene"

> "The mind becomes a glutinous slab that takes impressions and Oxford Street rolls off upon it a perpetual ribbon of changing sights, sounds and movement. Parcels slap and hit; motor omnibuses graze the kerb; ... Buses, vans, cars, barrows stream past like the fragments of a picture puzzle; the white arm sinks, and away it streams again, streaked, twisted, higgledy-piggledy, in perpetual race and disorder. The puzzle never fits itself together, however long we look" (18).

# Reading with Virginia Woolf

*These are the soul's changes. I don't believe in ageing. I believe
in forever altering one's aspect to the sun. Hence my optimism.*
— Virginia Woolf

Reading is an important component of travel and vacations for
me. My parents, siblings, and friends might add that it is an important
component of all aspects of life for me, but vacations are special: I
can read without interruption, greedily, for the sheer pleasure of it.
Reading in public places is a very particular kind of pleasure, perhaps
because I can lift my eyes from the teeming world of the imagination
to the equally fascinating, multiple fluidities of the airport terminal,
public park, or café.

This inner/outer and visual/auditory stimulation simulates
the traffic flow of chemical/electrical energy in the brain and I find
myself quickly needing a pencil and paper to record thoughts. Virginia Woolf suggests that the first part of reading is to "open the
mind wide to the fast flocking of innumerable impressions," and that
we should read "to refresh and exercise our own creative powers"
("How Should One Read a Book" Second Common Reader, 239,
243). She suggests we intermittently read and look up and out:
"How stimulating the scene is, in its unconsciousness, its irrele-
vance, its perpetual movement -- the colts galloping round the field,
the woman filling her pail at the well, the donkey throwing back his
head and emitting his long, acrid moan" (239). She suggests that to
understand what authors do in the books we read, that we ourselves
"write ... make ... experiments with the dangers and difficulties of
words" (235).

# Thanksgiving Letter

Dear L,

Happy Thanksgiving! I hope you are enjoying a lovely holiday weekend visit with your family. (I think you said you were going to your parents for Thanksgiving.)

We are in Cologne, Germany and we had a very nice day on Thanksgiving, but, of course, missed our families, too!

I finished reading *The Needle's Eye* by Margaret Drabble, and I want to write to you now as I think I'll leave this book here for someone else to find and adopt. This is necessary purely from a weight perspective as I have acquired a few mementos that weigh about the same as a book, perhaps even a bit more! I may have to leave my clothes here as well!

I found myself frustrated for about the first half of the book. I felt mired down in minutiae and wondering where it was going. Did you notice how often a character is described as bored, mentions being bored, or discourses on boredom? Perhaps this is part of the point: life is full of these tiny details and we struggle to find a motivated relationship to our own set of details. On the theme of boredom, I even noticed that the dogs were bored (418) at one point!! It was curious, as well, that Christopher is the only character who is described as "know[ing] how to stave off boredom" (384). I suppose that is why he is necessary to all the others!

Round about pages 197-199 (pretty close to exact middle) I felt something change. Simon says about his mother, "If she had not aspired she would have sunk or died." And there is that beautiful passage on 199 about illumination and how man "creates for himself an ordered darkness, an equality of misery, a justice in the sharing of the darkness." Right around there I started to become more interested. I thought perhaps that Rose was some kind of "saint" or "angel spirit" to lift the others out of their darkness. In the end though, I decided this was not the case. She was just as flawed as the others. But if she is not some illuminating path, then what does she represent in the novel and in Simon's life? Perhaps that is what you are also wondering?

I enjoyed the character of Emily, Rose's friend. She grows more beautiful with age. On page 257 there is this description of their friendship: "the natural flowing of a resilient, indestructible personal joy."

One of the questions the book asks is the same question Christopher raises on page 268: "how absolutely wicked and selfish people are when they get hold of this idea of being good ... They end up in a burning desert." Is this what the book is about, rather than some concept of redeeming grace?

I'm now reading John Berger's *Here is Where We Meet*. V bought it for me for my birthday and he has already finished it this week. It is a beautiful book. If you haven't ever read him, you should start here! I can't find the passage now, but I think I came across a sentence that echoes the quote from Christopher above. I don't know if that means anything, but I do notice things like that.

Anyway, I'm glad I read the Drabble, but there were some moments when I was about to give up on it. I look forward to hearing your thoughts!!

Love,

Jo

# CHAPTER FOURTEEN

# Sounds of Place ("Musicking")

*Two of the greatest gifts we can give our children are roots and wings.* —Hodding Carter

## Musica Antica

After dinner in the dining hall, we took the shuttle into Urbino, Italy with W, L, and S to meet up with M, A, F, and C for a concert in the Musica Antica series. It was relocated from a courtyard in the Palazzo Ducale to a church, and out of disappointment we almost didn't go. But we did and it was amazing, particularly after having read *An Equal Music* by Vikram Seth so recently.

The performance was by a group of ten musicians on lute, harp, violin, flute, and pianoforte, but the voices were the most spectacular instruments! The women, in particular, seemed to project their sound vibrations to a convergence point within their semicircle from whence it emanated to the audience. At the convergence of voices, one could feel a numinous, multi-dimensional, sound-energy field. With our modern imaginative capacities nurtured on special effects, I could almost see a milky opalescent globe of sound created by the merging voices. I felt suspended in the air by the force of voices. In concerts like this, my brain/mind feels activated in new ways and contemplations or reflections are touched off by the sounds. I used to think I was supposed to focus intently on the sounds, but now I think the phenomenon of aura elicited is the most significant effect of the performance.

# Tango Evening

We gathered in front of our hotel in Imatra, Finland at 8:30 pm to wait for the bus that would take us to our Tango Evening. I had been looking forward to this for over a week as I patiently sat in a variety of conference session rooms that seemed the same in some essential ways. Even though I limited my participation to three hours max per day, I was ready for an active, unscripted evening.

I took some time thinking through the contents of my small suitcase to find my tango clothes and tango shoes. Not much in there that qualified. As each person joined the group waiting for the bus, I saw that some of us had packed with more purpose than I had. There were actual dance shoes, and many kinds of dress shoes. There were short flirty skirts, colorful fringed scarves, flowered dresses and black dresses, and even some men had packed dancing clothes. I stole a few minutes to run back upstairs to change out of my day skirt and sandals into a long black skirt and my flat red shoes, the best I could come up with from my mix and match, carry-on wardrobe.

The bus was full, but our friends N and A were not among those who entered. We wondered if they had decided to forego the tango evening because they were disappointed by the plenary lecture on Finish tango earlier in the evening.

The bus traveled on a highway at first and then diverged onto a small road through woods for another ten minutes or so. We passed a huge factory processing logs into paper—huge! There didn't seem to be any other buildings at all: no villages or clusters of houses. Where do the workers live? During our travel time, R was composing clever riffs on "tango." For example, "Shampoo that gets rid of tangos (tangles)." and "A condensation of dance for astronauts: tang-o."

Finally, we pulled into a parking lot where two other buses were already parked. We crossed a small bridge between two modest lakes to a square wooden building open to the evening. One small room was a bar area; a second slightly larger room had tables, benches, and a food counter with home-prepared food by local women. It looked like the food offered at a social event, where an organization turns member contributions into fundraising. There were small open sandwiches, strawberry pretzel-like pastries, and soft drinks. Outside there was a small separate building where someone was selling sausages that people were holding like ice cream cones in napkins.

Aside from the small food and drink areas, the rest of the main building was a huge dance floor surrounded by rows of chairs along the walls and, at one end, a large stage. The whole establishment seemed like something from the Catskills years ago: a simple wooden building with openings rather than windows. Shutters swing up or down to close the building to the elements, but open to the summer air in season. The bathrooms are under the dance floor and you get there by going outside and around the building. A said this was the first time he was "doing his business" while 5 or 6 mosquitoes attacked him about the head! The band was already on stage preparing to begin our evening of tango. Our friends had boarded another bus from a nearby hotel where they had been having dinner. Our enjoyment was multiplied by the laughter of our friends.

When the Finish tango began, I didn't even notice it. The rhythm of the music sounded vaguely tango-like, but the couple dancing (clearly with experience and purpose as well as grace) seemed to be doing a waltz. After much observation and conversation we learned that the Finish tango is much more like a waltz than like the traditional Argentinean tango. I was fortunate that one of our friends seems to love to dance as much as I do, so we tried not to embarrass ourselves on the floor with a one-two-three step to the music of several songs. I feel so strongly that if I just let go, I can dance to the music without hindrance, but I never quite let go. I try to match my steps to the partner, to others I observe, to my idea of the dance. (I'm listening to a talk on pre-natal music as I'm writing—just the parts that break through my concentration. A speaker from Lagos, Nigeria is responding to a theory of scholars who are also in the room, that music sensibility is developed in a fetus before birth. "Physiological semiotic perceptions")

The band engaged ten couples or so for the formal dancing, but when they switched to rock and roll and "wedding music" later in the evening, they had maybe 50 or 60 people on the floor. I feel sure it was a "bunny hop" that motivated the largest number of people to get up in a sort of snake with feet tapping, hips swaying, and a lot of hopping. I hold myself back from this, although everyone is having such fun! I did get out and twist and dance "freestyle" with V and our friend for several dances each. The organizer's wife told me that this is the first time they've included a tango evening. Previously, they have had a sauna evening. Hmm, I've tried to imagine that! Tango evening was a lot of fun, but I wish they had included a lesson of a few simple steps. After all, we had a professional dancer and dance teacher among us. V said he would be willing for us to take lessons at home, but suggested that we find a way to have different partners for the learning process. Good idea! I must act on this! Now my list of things to learn when we return home is French, Spanish, Italian, tango, samba (for our next trip to Brazil), and some instrument (oboe?).

## Sounds of Place: Budapest Keleti Station

The train station called Keleti in Budapest, Hungary is gigantic and beautiful. We are inside the confusing, hot, and crowded Keleti Station today waiting for an overnight train to Krakow, Poland. I have loved train stations for a long time because of the vibrant aura of travelers setting off on a journey or arriving at a destination. Grand Central Station in New York City is a very special train station for me. It represents my claim on my own life, starting a new existence right there at the center of the universe!

Centered in this station, between tracks and ticket booths, there are two old-fashioned "big boards" with metal cards clicking over to display the times of arrival and departure of the trains along with the origin or destination, notes we can't understand, any delays and how long, and finally, the datum that completes each line, the track number.

Every couple of minutes, the board begins to transform itself, molecule by molecule. One by one, beginning at the top, each element of the line of information will begin rotating to repeat, momentarily, the line below it. For just a blink of an eye, the two lines are identical, and then the elements of the second line begin to flip to bring up the train just below it. This movement is nearly constant as track numbers and other information is updated. At any moment, some element is flipping through all of the small metal cards with all of its potential readings to stop at the exact right one.

The "big board" entertains us in anticipation of the track posting which will catapult us into action towards the arriving train. The sound of all that clicking mesmerizes us, rivets our attention.

This sound is like prayer beads clicking, like many fast, small marbles snapping against one another, like thick, flexible plastic cards shuffling, like heavy dry leaves rustling in the wind in October. It is similar and yet unlike any of these. If the mechanical big board holds still and silent, for even a moment, everyone watching it is still; we all stop breathing for an instant, for a heartbeat, until the rapid flipping begins again.

I tried to figure out who or what is behind this hypnotic system, but can't quite imagine! This system predates computers, but is it computerized now? Of course, the next iteration of big boards is digital readouts: practical, but not at all dynamic or interesting to watch.

In addition to this repetitive, resonant sound locking on a brain frequency that immobilizes us, we are also enchanted with the names of destinations that flip through our sights each time a line moves up the board.

Potential destinations from this spot in Budapest flip over each other, revealing and concealing jewels and tapestries, markets and minarets, rich aromas and strange twisting cries. Today we are not going to Nagykáta, Zűrich, Sopron, Hatva, Moszkva, Szolnok, Sűlysáp, Košice, Pëcs, Graz, Berlin, Zagreb, Hamburg, Belgrade, Thessalonika, Dormond, or Bratislava, or any of the places with names so complex I couldn't capture them from the short glimpse on the big board.

Our train finally appears at the bottom of the big board as the departure time of 18:30 takes the bottom line below 18:25. Before we are assigned a track number and achieve the top line, I am already nostalgic for the sound of the big board at Keleti Station in Budapest, Hungary.

## Around the World with Jazz

One summer we pursued jazz in a number of countries, and found many rewards along with a lost opportunity in Istanbul, perhaps the most evocative jazz of all! In Sofia, Bulgaria we happened to notice the Social Jazz Club as we scampered out of the rain with our young friends K and P. If you want to find it, the touchpoint landmark is the book fair in downtown Sofia. It is very near this location that everyone knows. I bought a child's alphabet book from one of the outdoor table merchants and subsequently realized it would have to be for me since it would confuse any of my young friends who are just learning one alphabet and don't need a backwards "K" to add any further confusion. Later in the week, we returned and heard a wonderful jazz singer at Social Jazz Club, a woman named Belaslava. It is her first name, but also her entire professional name. She is well known with a big following. The place quickly filled up and she entertained with her voice and sensuous movements. Her percussionist was an African woman who was very good.

Our next find was Jazz Garden in Budapest, Hungary. On our

ramblings during the day we had passed a barge in the Danube with a big sign for jazz. Our guidebook also mentioned a place called Fat Mo's. We inquired at our hotel and were given excellent advice to ignore both of these and look for Jazz Garden. As we set out seeking both food and music, we turned left out the door of Hotel Anna and zig-zagged our way to a neighborhood we had not yet explored to find Jazz Garden. It was early, so we meandered in search of dinner and returned for a competent opening set of familiar tunes from three young men on piano, bass, and drums. The bass player was constantly caressing and wiping down his voluptuous companion with a soft cloth, especially during the drum solo when he could let his mind and hands wander sensuously over the curves to waves of sound.

In Krakow, Poland, we sought out a place V recalled from an earlier visit. First we descended to Indigo on Florianska Street. It was a deep set of small caverns with tables and a bar but no music. Further along the street toward the market square we came upon U Muniaka, also a deep cavern, but this one promised jazz every night. We paid the cover charge and sat down to watch the group set up.

On our ramble through the Jewish district, Kazimierz, we spotted another jazz venue called Plastik (our memory of the name). We returned to this area for dinner and then came to this underground club for music. The group was very young as was the crowd. Apparently, the market square clubs attract tourists, but perhaps this was a more local crowd of students, or so it seemed.

After stepping briefly into a den of smoke and fiddles at Harry's Piano Bar, we returned to U Muniaka with friends several nights later and heard a different small jazz combo. About a week later, also on a Sunday night, we headed for this same spot to find it closed. V had done some scouting earlier in the day and we went around the corner to another place, The Piano Room, and descended to yet another cavern, this time decorated with deep tones of fabric, small fringed lamps, and plushy sofas to look more like a bordello than a jazz club. All the other jazz caverns had mostly bare brick walls with art, sometimes in a jazz theme. The group playing here was an all-girl trio. The bass guitar player was singing when we walked in, and her voice was very appealing. The next song went to the percussionist who had a different style, perhaps even more appealing. During that set the lead guitar player, less flashy but more proficient than her partners, was silent except for her fingers. In the second set she belted out a song that convinced us of her talent in voice as well as guitar.

# Tracy

We disembarked from the train at Waterloo station on the South side of the Thames to explore the cultural center there and see if there might be any tickets returned for the Tracy Chapman concert in Royal Festival Hall that evening.

V's confidence that there would be tickets returned kept him on line for over two hours while I strolled along the river, browsed at a used book fair and took turns on line while he did the same. We did get phenomenal tickets as did thirty other people in the final minutes before the performance began.

We needn't have rushed in on time for the "warm up" act, not memorable in the least. But Tracy Chapman was intense. She has such personal presence and her lyrics and rhythms are so moving that everyone was electrified for the entire concert. She sang every one of her old songs and I suppose every one of her new songs as well.

A cappella is probably the most stunning mode of all with her muscular voice and visceral lyrics. Her band distracted me; the mix seemed to cover her voice more than it should. She sang "Rollin on the River" as her second encore; clearly a new one for the band. The audience was up out of their seats at the stage. At the end, she jumped at least 6 feet up from the stage to punctuate the final chords and with that as her final gesture, left the stage. It was worth the wait and more.

We walked across the river on the footbridge and joined the late crowds taking the last trains home, a very particular energy that NYC will never have because the subways run all night. Should a "city never sleep"? Hmmm, I think not. There is a gentleness to a city that does sleep. The argument in NYC is that many people work shifts that require them to travel home during the hours that trains sleep in London. What if a mayor someday proclaimed that quality of life was so important that we wanted everyone home with their families at night? London, of course, has a fleet of taxi cabs and "gypsy cabs" to take the late night crowds home well after the tube is closed.

## Monterey Pier Grunt Suite

Waves asymmetrically toning awash
    schugch ... schugch ... .
Spanking ropes of sailboats on
    tall hollow bells,
Slapping feet on warm wood,
    buffed and polished by flesh,
Timpani seagulls punctuate time,
and a bass fiddle ferry pumps distance in mind.
The frozen sun-worship of skin soaking in
    a sensory surfeit on the rim of good-bye.

## Follow... Follow

Follow ... Follow ... the sound of the flute ...

A young man is testing the sounds of many flutes and two older men are watching and discussing as he plays a brief melody or scales on each one. A young girl is watching. Stones and vines surround and entwine with the notes here in Nanjing, China.

Long flutes and short flutes, each protected by a long, narrow cloth bag more like skin than like a coat.

An elderly woman is doing exercise stretching to one long slow note. She and I smile at one another and she approaches to ask me what I am writing. I say that I only speak English and we smile more and each say good day.

Is this the music department area of campus? In between flute melodies, I hear a piano.

Two flutes play a duet and a mother and child play peek-a-boo.

Some people manage to busy right by.

Evocative notes, lyrical, longing, questioning and suddenly an answering flute from somewhere else! I hear strings. The pace picks up. Is this recorded music or just a flute jam session?

The young man packs his flute family in a shoulder case and leaves. Suddenly the entertainment ceases. And then his duet partner, an older man, begins to play a duet with the recorded music, and the notes elevate the leaves and also my heart. Was this an interlude repeated every day, every week, or just today, just for me?

On the path just beyond the music I see a woman pushing a wheelchair, then another, and another. Women push babies in strollers on the same path. Babies and old men in baskets taking the afternoon air.

# CHAPTER FIFTEEN

# Eyes to See

*Our happiest moments as tourists always seem to come when*
*we stumble upon one thing while in pursuit of something else.*

—Lawrence Block

## No Photo Day

Is this a day when I simply stay away from picturesque sights distracting me from real experience? Or is it the day I just forgot my camera in my backpack at the B&B? Is it the day I decide to rely on my descriptive abilities rather than the wordless framing of an image? Or is it simply a day when the battery in my camera needs to be charged?

Just ordinary streets, buildings, automobiles, trees, sidewalks.

The river even seems ordinary. Perhaps I'm wearing my wrong eyes today. What was I expecting that makes everything seem so ordinary? It's not the city; it's me. Well, it is partly something about the landscape. Let's take the river for example ...

On my no photo day stroll, I wandered off from the B&B as V

worked on his presentation. I set out in the opposite direction from where we went the afternoon before towards a neighborhood the B&B host had pointed out on our map as having cafes and nightlife. I approached the back of the museum of art and then went right by it toward the river. Drawn to water as always, seeking what? Remember the river flowing through Krakow? Through Budapest? And rivers through Toledo OH, Florence IT, Providence RI, Montgomery NY, London UK, Harrisburg PA, San Antonio TX, Pittsburgh PA with its three rivers, and of course, my home town with two rivers, New York City.

This stretch of river in Antwerp, Belgium was rather like a version of the humble Wallkill River, middling in size with brushy banks. Along the riverbanks were decrepit buildings, concrete lots with weeds growing, a few cars, a warehouse, and reeds or low brushy growth and sparse but tall grasses. I hazarded across the busy highway to walk toward something that was labeled a miniature city model or diorama of Antwerp. Did I really want to walk around the back of a warehouse where men were smoking, just on the chance of finding an entrance facing the river? It didn't look promising and I didn't want to be hidden from view of the drivers even though they were speeding by without looking at me.

Instead, I re-crossed the highway and strolled through a different grid of streets heading in the general direction of the B&B. I saw several attractive cafes in this neighborhood of streets adjacent to the art museum. I picked one, ordered a decaf espresso, and settled in to study my guide book and jot a few notes.

Johnny Cash (or Roger Miller?) was singing. "When I was a little bitty baby, my Momma would rock me in my cradle, in them o-o-old cotton fields back home. When those cotton fields got rotten, you can't pick very much cotton, in them o-o-old cotton fields back home!"

When I signaled the young waiter for the bill, he approached my table by the window and asked if I was a traveler just walking around the city. I said yes and he pointed out a street running diagonally away from the street we were on that was another route towards the center of the city. Along this street, he told me, there are many antique shops. "You will like taking this street!" He mentioned the museum of photography and I asked him about the museum of shipping and the printing museum. My thoughts were thus diverted from the river and the cotton fields toward richer pastures!

## Morning Views

This hotel/castle was a leisure destination of Russian czars who would come to relax and enjoy the "Imatra surge" which I guess is a waterfall and rapids through a gorge (Imatra, Finland). I haven't seen it yet, but I took a secluded table by the window at the very back of the hotel dining room for my breakfast alone this morning and just outside I saw a rock gorge with paths along both sides and what may be spotlights or speakers on poles along the banks. Apparently, the flow of water has been dammed up for some time and some purpose, but I hear that on some days, the flood is released for the pleasure and refreshment of visitors in a compromise between utility and pleasure.

After breakfast the sun comes out and I walk behind the hotel to see what there is to see in the gorge. There is a sign pointing to rock carvings and a long flight of wooden steps down to a viewing platform on the gorge. Beautiful ! I can look up to the left and see the dam that holds the water back; look down to see thick, jagged slabs of granite and just a trickle of water in the channel; and look right to where there appears to be a small lake in the sunshine surrounded by green, green fir trees. I feel happy just to see all this deeply textured landscape!

## Photo strolling

I went out for a photo stroll. I had in mind a store window within the vaulted Galeries Royales de Saint-Hubert. One of the many famed chocolate shops in Bruxelles, Belgium had caught my eye. On the wall to the left of the entrance was a wall of shelves filled with bright tin boxes in the shape of the narrow and beautiful houses in the city. Each box, presumably, was filled, or could be filled, with chocolates. I wanted to explore more in this neighborhood; find out prices, fill my eyes and my lens with this exquisitely detailed display. Unfortunately, I was out early; too early on a Monday morning for much commerce. I had to satisfy myself with a photo through the window of the shop. The glare of being outside looking in will remind me to capture sights when they first catch my attention and not to count on returning tomorrow for a more leisurely shot.

My stroll meandered in and out of the Grand Place, exploring the side streets that lead off in six or eight different directions. Usually in a block or two, the magic of a medieval city rubs off and the modern metropolis-at-work emerges. Brussels is a modern city, the seat of the European Union's Parliament and economic engines. Some of my photo strolls in other cities have brought me to further delightful neighborhoods and off-the-beaten-track sights, sounds, experiences. Perhaps it was just the limitations of the day, needing to get back in an hour or so for a train, but I didn't make any discoveries on this particular stroll.

The Manneken Pis doesn't count as a discovery although I did happen upon his corner by accident. I was circumnavigating the Grand Place at a distance of two or three blocks from the actual square when I noticed some other early morning strollers with cameras gathered at a corner. How odd on such an ordinary corner. They were taking photos of the small fountain statue of a boy peeing. So, I took a photo, too. I have to admit that one of my goals on this morning stroll was to browse the souvenir shops for a small replica of this statue. What was I thinking? A gift for someone? Who? I recognize that I make bad decisions when faced with rows and rows of small replicas of famous landmarks. I try to compensate by looking and never entering the decision making process of which item to buy, but staying only in an observational mode, or a photo mode. Almost slipped this time. I managed to escape with four postcards, my default option if purchasing something seems inevitable.

Manneken-Pis seems of a genre with the little mermaid in Copenhagen and other distinctive public sculptures of children in cities around the world. I have a photo of V with another of these in Budapest.

## Seeing Too Much or Too Little

The tall Black girl in the departure lounge,
    wearing school sweatpants;
The two water fountains, side by side,
    one lower than the other;
The small spotlights set into the high ceiling,
    and one burnt out. How do they change this bulb?
I am grateful for the brown horse
    standing in the frosted field.
I am grateful for the eyes to see.
I am grateful for all the backyard gardens
    that go by, page by page;
    an illustrated book of everyday life.
When I lived by woods, I was a poet.
When I lived in tight neighborhoods and tall vistas,
    I was a scholar.
When I lived on shady streets, I was a leader.
If I lived by water, I would be a prophet.
I am grateful for tall trees in a hedgerow beside cows.
I am grateful for small birds landing and taking off
    in detritus by the side of railroad tracks.
I am grateful for three hawks circling on pillows
    of air, making the sign of infinity.
I am grateful for the old-fashioned caboose
    just sitting alone on the railroad tracks.
I am grateful for the child on a commuter train
    laughing.

# Venice Snapshot

We left Urbino, Italy around 7:30 am for the drive to Venice and arrived around noon. The final approach to Venice and returning the car were quite harrowing, but finally over. We took a vaporetto to the Rialto stop as instructed and walked just a few blocks to our Bed and Breakfast on the 3rd floor of a residence on a small dead end street. A neighborhood restaurant and a brick-wall restoration project shared the street with us giving it a lively "our neighborhood" feel as we came and went.

Venice is simply breathtaking in every way, almost too much to decipher. Every few steps reveal another framed view that I wanted to capture. Here's one that I wanted but missed because my camera batteries simply gave out from all the beauty.

On the street called Loredan, facing toward the Grand Canal: two walls of buildings on either side are approximately eight to ten feet separated. The dark buildings frame a rectangle of light that includes, from bottom to top—the fundament (canal sidewalk), the canal itself reflecting sunlight, several boats moored on the opposite bank, two or three buildings of terracotta colors with windows framed by shutters, balconies, and flower filled window boxes, and above them the perfect sky of a blue with the knowledge that it caps la Serenissima. The detail that clinches the view for me is the double lantern suspended between the buildings at the canal end of Loredan street. The symmetry of the lantern's globes in the light foreground between the dark framing walls is the spice, the feature that defines the view and makes it a view. The globes suspended in air between near and far, left and right, bottom and top are the spirit of a traveler in Venice.

I didn't know that V had always wanted to see Piazza San Marco since he was a small boy. We went there three or four times, but did not wait on the long lines to enter the church or palace. This was a trip to visit the city itself. Another time we'll come off season for the art and atmosphere inside the buildings. In his fascinating book, *Invisible*

*Cities*, Italo Calvino imagines that Venice is the subject of the description of every city that Marco Polo gives to the Kublai Khan.

Both nights in Venice we ended up in the area called Fundamente Zattere allo Spirito Santo on the Canale della Guidecca for dinner—once at a pizzeria recommended by our B&B hostess and the second time at a restaurant called La Piscina—located in a hotel where John Ruskin and Rainer Maria Rilke had stayed. We enjoyed both very much. After dinner we wandered to San Marco for gelato. Venice is for walking, more and more walking!

## Toque, Toque Grande

We leave Sao Paolo, Brazil at 10:30 am with W and L to go to Toque Toque Grande to L's brother's beach house. It is a rather long journey of 3+ hours, but we stop for groceries at a huge supermarket, then stop for lunch at a wonderful restaurant in a small beach town along the way. Three of us have squid stuffed with pumpkin and I have shrimp in champagne sauce. All exquisite dishes, but the mixed fruit caiperinhas with kiwi, strawberries and grapes are the very best part of the meal! Our mood is very, very merry!

The beach house is like being inside an art gallery or "House Beautiful" photo spread. It is entirely white: floors, furniture, bedding, dishes and pots, sculptures, and light fixtures all white. In fact, the light fixtures ARE sculptures. A pool transcends the glass wall of the house facing the sea. With a little dip under the two-story glass wall with metal frame in geometrical shapes, you can swim from inside to outside.

The master bedroom and two guest suites each have full private baths and unique window features. Ours has a skylight that throws organic shapes on the ceiling at night and the sound of a river rushing by all night long. The wind and rain outside make the dwelling experience even more dramatic. The wind ruffling the outdoor pool causes a rippling effect indoors as well. We are separated yet fully connected to the forces of nature.

We eat and drink, read, nap, talk, watch movies, and in between rain showers, go for a long walk on a wild, deserted beach.

## Travel Kiss

65 degrees F. in London. We're still at 37,000 feet over Ireland. We're on Pan Am, our third flight assignment with this charter. I'm glad actually. The first two were rather small rinky dinks. We left NY almost two hours late. We had snack, then dinner, then movie, then breakfast. All in 5 hours. There are ten seats across in this plane. A lot of babies in this section. Big romance one row up, A and B 32. I think they just met. Two good-looking guys and one lively girl. The guy sitting next to her is busy kissing her. His friend is reading a magazine. What if their seats had been reversed? Is the friend just as likely to be kissing her? What if her seat had been in the middle? No, the friends got seats together. Will they ever meet again? Will they remain together when we get off the plane and spend the night together?

My eyes would like to be asleep.

## Gate 17A

Look around you! What is everyone doing while we wait here for our boarding call? Lots of us are reading; at least one woman is writing. I see a woman doing needlework and a young man fussing with his iPod. I see a lot of brand new sneakers, some last minute phone calls on cell phones. The phone stalls are occupied but no one in them is using the phone. One fellow is eating sushi, one is on his laptop, and one woman is sitting in the booth while chatting on her cell phone.

Some of us study our boarding passes and passports, reviewing the data for a potential test at the security desk. Some study their traveling companion as if wondering who could this be seated beside me here, and where exactly am I?

A boarding lounge could be anywhere in the world. If you dose off, you risk waking with vertigo, not sure if you are in Kalamazoo or Caracas. Many of us clutch water bottles for this is an era of safe water scarcity ever since potential terrorists have made all liquids into combustible artifacts prohibited to passengers unless purchased inside security gates. Some days, I buy and discard several bottles of water at increasing prices between first level and inner security gates. If you were a terrorist, couldn't you figure out how to thwart these measures?

A phalanx of youth in brown tee-shirts with blue organizational logos march by. Not at all like the brown-shirts of Mussolini.

Some of us waiting at Gate 17A stretch our legs before the seven-hour flight from Philadelphia to London. One man studies a world map. Lots of blue jeans traveling today. One crying baby reminds me of D and how difficult it can be to travel with a young child. I used to be relieved when I saw infants on my flight; I felt sure we were safe in the air with such innocent lives aboard. I'm not so sure now.

V dozes a little—good for him; I'm here to remind him where we are when he awakens. Did the young robust girl just meet the two young men with iPods? Will the red cowboy boots beside me meet someone new in the seat next to her? When I was young, I always chatted with my seat partners. Now, I so love the solitude of travel, that I rarely talk at all.

I try to be aware of people needing help. Oh, is that a lie? Last time I was flying, a very young woman with a two-year old in a stroller and at least one suitcase was waiting for the shuttle bus from one terminal to another at the same time as me. I consciously avoided her (what was up with me that day?), but she knew there was a better self buried not too deeply inside me and she sought me out for assistance to board the bus. As a result of her trust, I lingered to help her get off the bus and kind of kept an eye on them in the terminal. What possessed me to try to avoid her?

# Outdoor Sculpture

As we drove through Sofia, Bulgaria, I noticed very unusual outdoor sculptures. I'll try to get photographs another day. Stones sculptured to look like ancient artifacts and forms suggestive of modern technology. For example, a horizontal bar made of about 6 roughly cubed or spherical shapes held up at two points by supporting frames. Like a weapon swung by primitive people, or a scepter wielded by an emperor, or like a pure symbol of law, power, and technology. Some of the pieces were reminiscent of Stonehenge and probably other artifacts I may not be aware of. Another monumental piece was two, rough-hewn, light color, broken corner shapes with a contrasting smooth dark cube suspended on a diagonal between them. Juxtaposition between old and new? Between the decaying and the new, indestructible forms?

Another shape was two huge spiral staircases dancing with a standing stone. It was like a wall curved up into space. Two broken egg shells of stone about one meter across made another grouping. Fragments of columns lay in the grass fallen from far off temples of long ago gods. A millstone formed of different textures of pie-shaped fragments pieced together witnessed the slow traffic of Bulgarians and one curious American woman peering out of a small blue car every day for a week.

K noted, as we drove, that the old socialist buildings have flat roofs, but that many of the new buildings have creative shapes at the top. He told us that even for homes this holds true. New home owners may engage with the design process to create a uniquely shaped top floor even though the main floors are traditional.

# Sunshine in Gornya Banya

After 2 grey, rainy days, we woke up to sunshine this morning for our last day in Sofia, Bulgaria. I sat out in the sun for an hour just soaking up the heat, hoping to heal my tennis elbow.

On my walk today, I noticed a woman coming up the stairs from what I thought was a work site at the side of a church. As I looked closer, I saw it was a public water source. I wonder if the ornate building that I thought was a church, was in fact an old bathhouse? Someone told us this district, Gornya Banya, was the site of natural springs and that they bottle mineral water here in the factory-looking building adjacent to this ornate church. Seven or eight people were filling large plastic jugs with water from the 4 or 5 spigots in the side of the building.

Despite the trash, ragged roadsides, broken sidewalks, and wandering dogs, this is an area of luxury homes behind gates and fences. Some are very blocky buildings with multiple balconies. I might have mistaken these for apartment buildings. I think now that they are individual homes—large and protected with views of the lush mountains when eyes are lifted above the ragged streets. It's almost impossible to discern the luxury, so hidden is it. I saw more SUV's and other larger cars here than in the neighborhood of our previous hotel closer to city center.

I see nasturtiums in the flower boxes of this restaurant's garden. Nasturtiums always remind me of PK and the early 70's when we were young married women, girls really, together in our two apartments on Prospect Street, Marlboro, New York. I had never heard of nasturtiums, but she introduced me. They didn't catch my interest and I never planted them again, but they do always remind me of PK. I haven't heard anything about her or her children for 15 or twenty years.

## Vignette

From the taxi on our way to the airport, I see a young man putting down his backpack to assist an elderly woman up off the ground at a bus stop where she has fallen. He helps her up and hands her the packages she dropped. They exchange a few words, "Are you ok?"

"Yes, yes...it's nothing...thank you." He picks up his own bag and walks away. I feel a rush of emotion in my throat, like when you hear the first strains of the wedding march or the graduation march. I am reminded of research that shows how three people benefit from an act of kindness: the giver, the recipient, and the observer.

I have received this gift in a short vignette this morning while just passing by. In a movie or TV show, this action would be followed by a shift of scene to me as I assist someone at the airport, and then that recipient will pass along the gift by stopping to help another person in need and so on. I will try to play my role and be alert for any opportunity to give a gift of kindness.

## Camera Lens

I had a discussion several days ago with a young couple about taking photos of people who appear to be "picturesque" in some way. For example, on the day of this conversation, V and I had walked by a railroad construction site in Sofia, Bulgaria as we were exploring the neighborhood surrounding our hotel. The workers were in small groups attending to various specific tasks at a short distance from each other. Each small group had a beach umbrella set up to shade their work area. The umbrellas were a delightful and incongruous splash of color and whimsy in a rather grim railroad scene. Imagine a turquoise umbrella imprinted with a ring of palm trees shading a pair of grime-covered workers in a grey and black railroad bed.

I took out my camera and intended to point at one of the scenes, but I couldn't do it. If I couldn't ask their permission, I couldn't bring myself to make them into a photograph of themselves. In Sofia we also occasionally saw horse-drawn carts (as described in our travel guide pages) carrying loads of hay. One in particular stands out for me, a father and son riding smartly through the street in front of our hotel. I might have been quick enough to get my camera out, but stopped myself. What are the circumstances in which I would take a photo of unwitting subjects? Far enough that they don't see me; if I can ask first; if they are part of a public spectacle anyway. The women dancing in the samba school parade in Helsinki were clearly prepared to be watched and photographed!

My feelings about this were confirmed more than a week after this conversation when I found myself at the other end of the camera lens. On our bus from the hotel to a Tango Evening organized through our conference, one of the participants took candid shots from his seat opposite ours. He shot down the aisle, between the seats in front of him, behind him at the last rows of the bus, and across the aisle at us. After the first two clicks aimed my way, I realized that he was still pointing at me and taking shot after shot. He would sometimes wait, pointing at me as I turned to talk to R behind us, or was partly hidden by my husband who sat in the aisle seat. He would wait, take a shot and then look at the screen to check whether he liked the results.

I was flattered at first, but it wasn't long before it felt threatening in a vague and confusing way. After we arrived and walked from the bus to the dancing hall, he was still focusing that lens on me. I told my husband that I was going to go up to him and ask him to stop, but my discomfort may have been apparent enough for him to notice and turn away to other subjects. I began to wonder what he might do with all those images of me (10 or more). Why was he doing this? Whatever his motive, I was confirmed that pointing a lens at someone is not innocent. An image of a human person is not free. After the first couple of images, I began to feel he was stealing something from me. My image belongs to me. We tend to chuckle at the primitive notion that a camera is stealing a spirit from the subject of the image. Well, it is worthwhile to think about the truth inherent in this belief. I love candid shots of people absorbed in their ordinary days and works. They are often so contemplative. A lot has been written about this, but experiencing the objectification of that lens pointing at you is more powerful even than reading about it.

# No Photos

I didn't take any photos in the Grand Bazaar or in the Spice Bazaar in Istanbul. My eyes were so full of sights that I could not divert them to look for my camera. Besides, I've taken these photos before and they never show what I'm seeing! I am seeing "myriad incessant motion," a phrase I have used for many years to describe the motion of leaves on trees in the breeze, so many leaves one could never count them, so many trees they form a canopy, so much motion of individual parts that there is a sussuration of sound. The Bazaar sound is more like a roar with distinct trumpeting over and beyond the general growl.

The Spice Bazaar is small and simple compared with the Grand Bazaar with its labyrinth of passages like a convoluted cave following dozens of streams down rocky beds to the branchings of lower streams. The streams are made of flowing people tightly packed like water molecules navigating among the shoals of jewelry, tapestry, pottery, and silks. My eyes flow over colors and textures swiftly, pausing for fingers to pick up and assess the commitment on both sides to an exchange. At first I need our friend to ask prices and to negotiate for me. Then I warm up to the task, making my own decisions about what an item might be worth to me by its quality in my own eyes and by comparison with others of its kind that I have seen previously.

The greeters at each small shop stand in the stream trying to divert attention first, but more importantly, to divert bodies into postures of gradually increasing interest. "Let me help you spend your money." "I am your brother of carpets!" "Come! Come here!"

The scene gradually shifts from a tourist based economy inside the covered bazaar to a local economy in the lanes outside. The canyons are still lined with small shops, but now the goods are domestic products: men's, children's, and women's clothing, from underwear to the long coats worn everywhere by women with their heads covered. Many shops sell headscarves. The variety seems endless with solid colors, stripes, and patterns of every kind. The fabric varies from light silks and cotton to synthetic fabrics and heavy pashmina. Walking is difficult and the three of us find it difficult to stay together. Frequent baby strollers seem to create pockets of congestion with thick slow divergence around them.

We orient ourselves by the slope of the narrow alleys, heading downward, ever downward toward the shore and finally to the Galata bridge. We emerge from the Grand Bazaar and almost immediately enter the Spice Bazaar for a slightly different version of the same. Here many of the stalls display heaps of brightly colored spices in a row across the front of the space: oranges and greens are beautiful even beyond the fragrances and on into the spectrum of smell simultaneously with light.

# Photos Sans Camera

### Nanjing, China

- Workers sweeping with willow branch brooms
- Confucius temple boats, water ripples in reflected red and yellow from boats and dragons, men fishing from banks of river
- The red lantern and ribbons hang down, the willows hang down, the fishing poles bend down too; long seed blossoms from riverbank trees hang down, clothing drying along balconies hang down, square wooden bird cages hang down.
- Two women in costumes arrayed on blanket beside a tree on campus. What occasion?
- Fish brought to our table live for our approval and price check before cooking.

Josephine Carubia

# Tin Man

Today the tin man standing at the window directly across the narrow street from our hotel room is holding a bowl of fruit in his right hand. I can't tell if it is ripe fruit, plastic fruit, wooden fruit, or tin fruit. He is wearing sunglasses, perhaps a disguise. I can't tell what he is holding in his left hand. It could be a camera he will use later to photograph us.

# CHAPTER SIXTEEN

# Turbulence
# (Weathering The Storms)

*Why not turn this mishap into an adventure?*
—Alice Steinbach

## Dark and Thundering

We caught the # 82 vaporetto from Rialto to Piazzelle Roma and then the bus #5 to Marco Polo airport. Our flight from Venice to Philadelphia was fine although we were not seated together. I didn't sleep at all. We were lucky to be able to land in Philly when we did because thunderstorms were moving in simultaneously to our arrival. We managed to pick the wrong line in customs with an official who was really taking his job very seriously, having extended conversations with each person. As we were traversing the airport to our concourse for the connecting flight home, we kept hearing that nothing was coming in or going out. Still, on the monitor, our flight seemed to be on time. Crazy enough, we believed it ! We stopped along the way for a beer and finally strolled to our gate where a nightmare was being enacted by Americans in minor distress behaving as though the employees of the airlines at this gate were intentionally thwarting their travel arrangements and the downstream effects of cancelled flights.

The mostly white travelers were harassing the mostly Black or Hispanic workers. They wanted—rather, demanded—to be scheduled on flights, routed through other cities, given vouchers for airport meals or hotels. Meanwhile, the entire airport was bombarded by wave after wave of lightning, thunder, and torrential rain. The impatient travelers would prefer to force an on-time scheduled flight than to assure their own safety! Like spoiled children, they badgered authority figures.

It seems to me that even on occasions when professional Americans are on leisure travel, they ramp up their aggressive skills learned to succeed in the push and shove marketplace of business competition. They (we) have fewer skills of accommodation to events out of our control, of kindness, of communal flourishing.

## Airport Emotions

My name went in the book! There were several bombings in London and Scotland a day or two ago and security is heightened. We have a very complex flight itinerary and I expected an easy start with frustrations and delays later, but it hit us right in the face before 6 am. Our luggage cannot be checked through (Paris, London) from Krakow to Philadelphia. We can only check it as far as London. That puts us in the same situation as on our way here plus all the heightened security in London. We decide to take our luggage in Paris instead and then re-enter for the flights on British Airways, hopefully checking in there all the way to Philadelphia. If need be, we've already decided to abandon our luggage and go on without it. OK, we got through that—postponing the real frustration to Paris where we have (if everything is on time) about 3.5 hours.

Next challenge comes almost immediately as I realize I've

purchased a gift that will not be allowed to pass through security. No it's not a gun or a bottle of plastic explosives disguised as shampoo! I bought two letter openers for about $15 each at the Jagellonian University yesterday. What was I thinking? I pulled them out of my backpack and put them in the bin so the guards wouldn't think I was hiding them. Of course, they noticed and called me over. After examining the sharp metal points, they said I could not carry them on, but could go back out and put them in my suitcase. Right!! Who knows where that suitcase is now ... on its way to oblivion! I say to just throw them away and they pull out a big clear plastic bin. Apparently, I must put the items in myself voluntarily, so I do. Then another guard takes my passport and boarding pass out of my hand and walks away to a small desk nearby. He first headed to a doorway and I had a moment of panic. Would V see me following him? At the small desk, the guard pulled out a ledger and wrote my name and passport number and some other information I couldn't read in Polish. So, I am now inscribed in the big book of airport security offenses in Krakow, Poland. If asked someday about my record, do I have to confess this?

## Following the Raven

We had a slightly bumpy takeoff this evening. At first there was the sense of wellbeing, of resting inside a gentle beast lumbering along and then up, up, and away. Then we felt shudder after shudder as the craft crossed layers of turbulent air. My mind turns in several directions for distraction and comfort. First I turn to fragments of poetry that I have memorized over the years, many years. From the poems of my adolescence, defensive against lost love, to e e cummings' mind challenges and Robert Frost's comforting, deceptively simple short verses. I recite lines in my mind trying to occupy all the brain cells and neurons that would otherwise be firing with fear.

Tonight one of the fragments that comes to me is the beginning of Edgar Allen Poe's "The Raven." I love the phrase, "the silken sad uncertain rustling of each curtain thrilled me, filled me ..." Tonight, in addition, I think about the joy of working in my garden. I've always loved talking to the earth, getting my hands into it, smelling it. I am often talking to the weeds that creatively mimic the exact plant that I've decided to grow in a particular spot. How do they know what these plants look like!!

I also try to breathe as I've learned in yoga, focusing on the exhale phase and recalling that I read that the exhale cools and calms the mind. I visualize a stream of molecules as I inhale and exhale. I'm always open to learning new strategies to try during turbulence in the air. Without any strategy, I'm likely to focus on various scenes from movies and books where all the luggage falls out of the overhead compartments, the food carts (and loose passengers) careen and pile up at the front or rear of the plane, all the oxygen masks drop down, and everyone is screaming. I wonder whether we will be conscious for the many long seconds while the plane disintegrates or otherwise pulverizes us. See, poetry is so much better!!

## Rainy Days on the Road

Rainy days on the road: I wasn't too successful following my own advice to keep the sunshine inside and forge ahead with plans despite the weather. I was tired and lethargic, possibly also from an attack of intestinal distress the night before.

## How We Cope

It's bound to happen; even when we hope against hope that it will not! Something will go wrong. For us, this time, it was the decision to carry on our suitcases along with a backpack each. We pride ourselves on traveling with one "carry-on" sized suitcase each and one backpack each. It's not easy to fit six weeks into these dimensions, but we try to avoid one disruption—lost luggage—by this means.

This time our efforts were entirely counterproductive. When we reached Heathrow and began the process of transferring from our overnight flight to our connecting flight to Sophia, we were informed of the rule that only one piece of cabin luggage is allowed per person traveling through Heathrow; no exceptions!! We had to exit the transfer area, through passport control (lines) and then get on another line to check our luggage for the connecting flight. By the time we got to the check-in desk, we had missed our flight. We were directed to the ticket counter to be re-scheduled to our destination. After at least four more obstacles (lines), two more flights, one additional country, and seven more hours, we arrived in Sophia.

The fact of this disruption is very likely familiar to everyone! It is more interesting perhaps to reflect on the range of possible responses to such disruptions.

Emotional Responses

Rage: one potential response is anger at the airline, its policies and procedures, and possibly even personnel. As we learned at Heathrow, it is appropriate also to be angry with the airport personnel as distinct from the airlines who diverted our anger in this direction, with the national safety bureaucracy, and with developing nations around the world.

Frustration with traveling partners. Someone must be making poor decisions about travel planning to land the group in this situation. Even if it's the travel agent who delivered an itinerary with 23 minutes between flights, one of us must have selected this agent and agreed to this itinerary.

Blame: someone must be responsible for this inconvenience and we need to pin the anger we feel on this person and hear them accept the responsibility to apologize and help us deal with the consequences, including offering free flights, hotels, food vouchers, and their first born daughters. We have on occasion, during violent thunderstorms, sat in a departure lounge with rabid travelers berating gate attendants for delaying or canceling flights and insisting on instant accommodation of rebooking or car rentals or hotels. The worst part of this is to notice that most of the travelers are white and most of the attendants receiving their vituperation are people of color.

Zen of Travel : if we can achieve this response to disruptions, we have reached the highest level of travel commendation! With the "Zen of Travel" response, we disconnect from the surface events and focus on the ultimate purpose of life.

Pragmatic Response: Hopefully one traveler in your party is pragmatic. This person will be thinking about what decisions need to be made and which decision leaves you with the best range of opportunities. "What do I have to do now?" is the stance of this person who quickly moves the travelers to next best options.

Disruptions range from missed flight connections, lost luggage, lost family members, weather delays up to three days (Denver during snow storms!), lost documents, theft of cars and money, and many more! It is small consolation to realize that the more dramatic the disruption, the better your story will be afterwards.

## Academic Disruption

On this five-week trip, V has been giving lectures every few days. He came with several early lectures prepared and has written the rest along the way. This morning he delivered the final talk of the trip in Opole, Poland, quite a miraculous achievement given the events of the past twelve hours.

Last night we left the very congenial dinner party thinking that others were staying for dessert. We got back to the hotel around 10:30 pm and V immediately set about organizing the notes he has been writing for days on yellow notepads gathered in his small black briefcase that was a participant gift at the Semio meeting in Istanbul. The briefcase was not on the chair, not on the desk, not on the bed, nor under the covers, not even under the bed or in the bathroom. Not believing that it was actually not in the room, we searched in our suitcases, laundry bags, window sills. I didn't think to search in the mini-bar fridge, but if I had thought of it, I would have looked there, too! We were both completely distraught—all that work and now nothing! How could he prepare for a lecture delivery at 9 am ?

We divided up the necessary tasks: V began to work on his PowerPoint presentation. At least he could complete this and keep himself focused on the presentation rather than dispersing brain energy on the loss and search. I went downstairs to the reception desk to ask if anyone had turned in a briefcase and also to ask them to call the restaurant we had just left. No briefcase at the desk nor at the restaurant, but they took our hotel name and room number to call if it should be found. I went back to report on this and we thought next of looking in the computer room, so I went downstairs again. One of our colleagues was using the computer for his email and he helped me search the room, under the desk, under and behind all the chairs and equipment. Back upstairs with empty hands again.

I felt this loss deep in my gut as I've been writing a lot in my notebooks and the thought of losing one of them before I've entered it in the computer and made several back-up copies is devastating. V is sure he did not leave it at the restaurant where he and G had lunch. He had it when he came back to the hotel for a few minutes rest before the plenary lecture and then dinner. It must be under his chair in the lecture hall, locked and secure for the night.

I determined to call the conference organizer who might be able to get access to the room early in the morning and then bring the briefcase to us. By now it is at least 11 pm and I am fairly sure I'd be waking him up. Nonetheless, I ask the desk clerk to help me again, finding the number and making the call. C answers the phone and agrees to stop at the lecture hall on his way to the hotel in the morning. Still, empty-handed, but at least some action will happen, even if 8 hours from now.

V is showing enormous control in persisting to work on the presentation, crafting a set of slides with images and texts that will guide his talk if we don't find the yellow sheets of detailed notes and paragraphs already written. I go to bed with my iPod and recorded books, but sleep only from about 3am to 6am after listening to parts of two books and a "deep peace" music CD, and taking a melatonin capsule.

I hesitate to ask in the morning if V is ready to present even without the discovery of his briefcase. I go to breakfast alone and sit with L and W who share their similar story of a lost manuscript thirty minutes before the presentation! No time to rewrite anything! "What could I do? Improvise!" says L in her own special way with a gesture reinforcing the inevitability of that solution as the only possible one.

Soon after I return from breakfast with a carafe of coffee for the worker, our phone rings. It is C downstairs with the briefcase! V quickly reconciled his versions, and off we went to the Villa Academica for the morning session. It was a very successful presentation, provocative and suggestive with a strong core thesis. V talked the presentation, a refreshing alternative to most of the other papers which were read. The means was a reflection of the meaning, many small humorous moments lifted the spirit in the room!

## Strike

Siracusa: The Sicils were here in Ortygia before the Corinthians arrived around 734 BC. Rome took this part of Sicily (Siracusa) around 212 BC. We arrived at 8 p.m. on an October evening and secured a room in a hotel listed in one of our guidebooks in the old part of the city still called Ortygia.

We had been traveling for much of the day and we went out to eat almost immediately only to find that everything was closed! Not one restaurant, pizzeria, trattoria, bar, or gas station was open. This is very, very strange in Italy at 8 o'clock at night. Driving from one dark façade in a dark neighborhood to yet another darkened café or shop, we began to question even our basic assumptions like days of the week, time of day/night, and where we were. It was disorienting to the point of making us feel as though we were living an episode of The Twilight Zone, transported to a place of tornado-green sky and immanent catastrophe.

We finally came upon a lone roadside food cart that was open along the highway. We ordered sausage sandwiches and asked the vendor what was going on. He said all the businesses were closed to protest the collection by organized crime of protection money from local proprietors. Every business in a very large city was closed and dark on this night. It was extremely disturbing to arrive hungry in Siracusa in the midst of this strike. We had been expecting the exuberant passeggiata of colorful strollers, illuminated storefronts, abundant food and beverages, and good cheer we had experienced in other parts of Sicily. We took our sandwiches back to the hotel and stayed in our room, eating quietly and wondering about the wisdom of coming here.

The next morning Siracusa was transformed into a bustling city in contrast to the ominous cemetery it had seemed the night before. Inside the cathedral we saw the remains of a Doric Temple to Athena built in the 5th century BC. We went to a market where vendors displayed and sold fish, fruit, and vegetables and where men were singing out their prices in a wonderful, full-voiced street opera! We visited the archeological site and saw the Ear of Dionysius, the Greek and Roman Amphitheaters, and the Neapolis.

The deepest impression of all, however, was our experience of the dark and deserted city, silently protesting against organized force.

## What If?

+ As I scheduled a taxi to pick us up at 2:30 p.m. at 330 E. Irvin Street, I thought, "**What if** the taxi comes to 230 E. Irvin Ave. at 3:30 p.m.?" I kept the phone number on the kitchen table just in case.
+ As I stepped out a side door of the airport terminal to mail a thank-you note to my friend B for the fabrics she brought me

from Ghana, I thought, "**What if** the 'entrance' door is locked and I'm stuck outside?" I pictured myself walking the long way around the terminal to the front of the building where there are multiple entrances.

+ As our plane rose through the cloud layer and we were wrapped in opaque space, I thought, "**What if** we collide suddenly with another airplane?"

+ As I relaxed in my seat, I thought, "**What if** I forget my coat and scarf in the overhead bin?"

+ As I left the hotel alone in a strange city, I thought, "**What if** I get hit by a tram and no one knows who I am?"

+ As I observed from the sidelines of a classroom while both instructors were out of the room, I thought, "**What if** I were to stand up and begin teaching this class?"

+ What if...

+ What if...

+ What if...

CHAPTER SEVENTEEN

# Chance

*Destination no longer ruled. My only map was that of free association: I would follow each street only as long as it interested me and then, on a whim, choose a new direction.*

—Alice Steinbach

## Serendipity Day; Serendipity Life

*Move in the direction of your passion.* —JC

Of course, I did massive planning to get to the point of waking up in the Kalajastorpa Hilton in Helsinki, Finland. Of course, there were web searches, consultations, reservations, complications, visas, trains, planes, buses, taxis, etc. etc. But that morning was clear; in fact, the whole day was clear: no plans, no agenda, no companion (my husband was reading and writing in preparation for meetings beginning later in the week), no guide .... just .... clear sailing through the open air for the day.

191

So far, all that I knew of our neighborhood was the hotel grounds, view over a body of water, short walk down the hill to the tram stop, and a little sea-side café we could see from the hotel restaurant balcony. The water attracted me; water always does. This was a large, lake-like body of water, surely connected to the rest of Finnish seas I had marveled at from the air. The terrain looked more like a sprinkle of cocoa, parsley, and oatmeal on a bucket of water than like a solid country!

I set out with intentions of seeking water-side walking although I had to begin in the opposite direction to get there. Instead of heading down the hill from the hotel cul-de-sac, I turned right and walked down a lovely residential block shaded by huge trees. At the end of the block, I estimated that if I turned right, it should bring me toward the body of water, and soon I was crossing a bit of park and several lanes of quiet roadway to a path along the water. This was definitely a day of being pulled by glimpses further on, the enchanted horizon, the mystery around the bend.

The hotel was along the shoreline to my right, so I headed left. Besides, there was a small bridge to the left that I could cross and there were small boats, and other pedestrians seemed to be headed purposefully along a path on the other shore across that bridge, so I followed my curiosity in that direction. Meanwhile, I am dropping mental crumbs along my way so that I can retrace my steps back to the hotel.

After I crossed the bridge, I had to choose again. Straight ahead was a paved road and to my right, along the shore was a pedestrian path. I selected the path and descended from the elevated bridge level to the shore level among trees. I came upon a sculpture that was a metal beam shaped like the central form of a ship's hull, a beautiful curve that held the sky in and the water out. I tried to frame the small boats inside that curve through my camera lens. I also tried sitting for awhile on a bench nearby, but the unknown further on was intriguing me beyond the lure of calm contemplation of the graceful curve.

Further on rewarded me almost immediately with yet another sculpture, this one set up a small incline to the left within the woods and adjacent to the side of a building that faced the street beyond. More intriguing and complex than the simple sculptural form, this was a metal tea set on a metal table. The intruiging aspect was that this was a fountain and water poured out of the samovar into a cup poised daintily on its saucer in mid air. Water flowed like a smooth, clear cloth covering the table and spilling over the four sides in sheets. No one else seemed to notice this delightful setting on this beautiful day! Was I dreaming?

Reluctant to leave my personal delight, I was still being pulled along by the mystery of the path. I continued on and along. Thinking that a Finnish pastry and cup of tea would be nice, I imagined for myself a tiny rustic place with outdoor tables overlooking the water. Yes, that would be just over this little hill. Café Adjutant would open in just a few minutes and so would the main house, now a museum open for tours. The Tamminiemi home of Finland's president from 1956 to 1982, Urho Kekkonen, was a small house by today's presidential standards. I had a private tour in English. Kekkonen was a modest man, living a simple personal life and taking responsibility for complex international balancing acts. Finland was part of Russia, then part of Sweden until less than 100 years ago. It is a very new country! Hekkonen was known for "sauna diplomacy" between the Soviet Union and the west, although the guide explained that western diplomats didn't really enjoy the sauna. After describing each room of the house, my guide took me to the sauna building right on the water, and we walked through the lovely wooden rooms with a pool and steam rooms. What could be better than this personal history lesson?!

I left the Kekkonen house by a different path, the high road rather than the low road along the shoreline. Again, following the trajectory of other pedestrians, I was intrigued by a tiny yellow structure on a sharp hill within the park grounds. It looked like a child's play house or a woman's summer reading refuge. I moved away only because there seemed to be more to see beyond. There, yet further beyond, another forest café with tables set in a wooded, shaded area. I went in to scout out future possibility and bought a bottle of water to carry away with me. I'll be back.

By now I've reached another roadway seeming to end in a parking lot. If people are parking here and walking on further, there must be another attraction nearby because there was scarcely anyone at the Kekkonen house. Where are they all going? I see another little bridge at the further end of the parking lot. A foot bridge this time, even better! And an ice cream wagon just at the entrance to the bridge! Fortified with an ice cream cone, I am delighted to cross the footbridge to what seems to be an island museum of some sort.

I soon learned that Seurasaari Island is a "plein air" museum of Finnish cultural history. I purchased a descriptive map and enjoyed the beautiful setting with rustic cottages, church, windmill, etc. from the countryside gathered together for our pleasure on a beautiful Sunday in late spring. Meandering with my map through the open air of Seurasaari Island, I was enchanted by the tiny wooden cottages. Imagine living in one of these? Possibly not so enchanting to share an abode with a pig or goat. So picturesque, but is the picturesque ever quite comfortable? After several hours of rustic sights and taking photos from every angle, I reluctantly crossed the footbridge in the opposite direction and sought out another small snack and a shady table at the forest café.

I started to retrace my steps and head in the general direction of my first bridge crossing and our hotel. This time I stayed on the road rather than the shore path. Here were more surprises: the building that was just a blank backdrop for the delightful flowing tea sculpture fountain was an art museum from the front. I explored briefly and hoped to return. As the road approached the final bridge, I was unable to resist entering another cottage with an inviting outdoor seating area. It was a buffet restaurant with a magnificent table of Finnish foods and pastries offered cafeteria style. My mind was already returning homeward so I didn't linger for yet another snack, but again, intended to return.

As I crossed the final bridge and repeated in reverse my morning's trajectory, I was eager to tell V all about the day filled with gifts, charms, and gems as if falling from the Finnish sky.

Today, exactly six months later, to the day, I awoke at 3:30 a.m. in our own home in State College, Pennsylvania. For some reason, the serendipity day in Helsinki was in my mind and it slowly unfolded again to reveal a new dimension as a snow-globe miniature of my life. My resume documents the highlights of over thirty years of moving on to the next enticing career vista around a corner, over a hill, or across a bridge. Storm King Mountain, The George Washington Bridge, and the Delaware Water Gap each beckoned with glimpses of new challenges and magnificent views of waterways, skyscrapers, and whimsical sculptures. Each stop on my Finnish meander represented one of my career episodes: an ice-cream cone as a freelance journalist, forest café sweets in publishing, a graceful sculpture in graduate school, a parking lot in the legal industry, a "plein air" island in education, and so on.

I've been fascinated with bridges for a long, long time. I love the very idea of bridges and the fear-tinged exhilaration of height and trembling! I've walked across many bridges: Thousand Islands Bridge, Golden Gate Bridge, Brooklyn Bridge, Newburgh-Beacon Bridge, a (not THE) London bridge, and many more. The two bridges I crossed in Helsinki on my serendipity day were not extraordinary among bridges, but were quite ordinary. Perhaps that was the point. I am a bridge myself, doing the same work as other bridges, always vulnerable to the resonant frequency that may vibrate my bones far beyond their ordinary structure.

I felt touched by magic that June day in Helsinki, as if all I had to do was activate my senses and my curiosity. As a result, the world would lead me on a wizard's tour of a fanciful landscape. The most enchanting aspect of my day was serendipity—all of my discoveries were entirely accidental: just following a path or other sojourners put me on a fortuitous itinerary of delight! This book is filled with similar episodes as I continue journeying towards glimpses of magical landscapes further on.

## The Queen's Day

After a culinary excursion in London's Soho District, we reboard the bus for the rest of the tour. At this moment, the Queen's day intersects with ours as she is helped from her beautiful car by a surprisingly handsome Prince Philip. She smiles and waves to all of us and extends her hands to those in the front row of the crowd.

She must be coming for the opening of Lord Snowden's exhibit of photographs in the National Gallery. Snowden is the husband of her younger sister, Margaret.

Virginia Woolf has captured this scene far in advance of our arrival. On Clarissa Dalloway's morning errand to the flower shop, she becomes part of a similar scene:

"a motor car ... had drawn to the side of the pavement precisely opposite Mulberry's shop window. Passers-by who, of course, stopped and stared, had just time to see a face of the very greatest importance... yet rumours were at once in circulation...The motor car with its blinds drawn and an air of inscrutable reserve proceeded towards Piccadilly, still gazed at, still ruffling the faces on both sides of the street with the same dark breath of veneration whether for Queen, Prince, or Prime Minister...there could be no doubt that greatness was seated within; greatness was passing...removed only by a hand's-breath from ordinary people who might now, for the first and last time, be within speaking distance of the majesty of England, of the enduring symbol of the state...It is probably the Queen, thought Mrs. Dalloway" (21-23).

Living a parallel existence to Mrs. Dalloway, the WWI shell-shocked Septimus Smith perceived the "accumulated traffic" as the result of his "blocking the way."

Septimus was as out of sync with the circumstances in front of him as the young man in ragged black leather and pins who perceived the crowd we stood in, the gathered Bobbies, and the barricades as NOT blocking HIS way. On this, and at least one additional occasion, we two New Yorkers were reassured to recall that in Great Britain, city police do not carry guns.

## Alive

We started our last day in London with a stroll to a classic jazz store called "Moles." V was able to find some unique CD's and I didn't mind just absorbing the atmosphere.

From there it wasn't far to 37 Mecklenberg Square, location of the Woolf's Hogarth Press and their home from 1939-1940. From there we tubed to Anthony Goodman's recommendation of the National Academy of Fine Arts for the Chardin (1699-1779) exhibit. We hadn't thought to go here since neither one of us really appreciates graphic depictions of dead rabbits nor ducks hung on the wall over the dinner table. Yes, that Chardin. Anyway, it was expensive and crowded, but wait, there was a compensation for this out-of-the-way effort.

There was an exhibit called "Alive" of life drawings by secondary school students under the guidance of Academy artists. This was fabulous and rich! Young people drawing the nude human form with discussion and reflection on themes such as imagination, motion, form, and interpretation. Their words were excerpted to accompany the charcoal sketches. One that particularly caught my attention, because I had just been reading Marion Wright Edelman's book, *Lanterns*, was on imagination: "Once the mind has been expanded, it cannot go back to its original dimension." Would young students in the puritanical U.S. be encouraged to draw from live nude models? What is lost by that prohibition?

## Momentum

As we step out of our room in Istanbul with our luggage at noon, I see the origin of the buzzsaw sound. It is a biplane doing high aerobatics over the Sea of Marmara! The plane roars straight up and seems to be suspended motionless for long moments, and then the tiny dragonfly twists and dives trailing a long, loose, curling ribbon. Down, down, diving for the water; will he make it? I hold my breath.

The delicate creature with a forceful roar pulls away from blissful annihilation just inches from the water (it seems to me) and swings a long arc back into the endless blue perspective. Again and again with variations to the extreme limits of physics and gravity. Breathless at the apex and breathless at the nadir, the pilot and spectator are both ecstatic with kinetic force driving the flow. I think of Antione de St. Exupery and his book about flying the mail route to Africa and flying during the First World War, *Wind, Sand, and Stars*. If you haven't read it, go immediately and find a copy.

## Intersections

You are on your way to somewhere from somewhere else. Completely unexpectedly, you meet someone you haven't seen in several years. This is someone from another era in your life. You and this other traveler—like "two ships passing in the night"—exchange a few pleasantries and off you go on your separate ways. This chance meeting is not simply an isolated incident. Imagine how this incident might be a confirmation of some dilemma in your life, or a resolution of a long-standing dilemma. Or that this sets off a series of consequences that have some significance in both lives.

## Parades, Festivals, and Fireworks

When we achieve "flow" of journeying (traveling, sojourneying) it seems to me we intersect with celebrations everywhere we go!

We took a long walk this morning from our apartment ("Didi's Apartment," Siemiradzkiego Str. North, of the old city center/Stare Miasto of Krakow, Poland) through the center and far southeast to the old Jewish city of Kazimierz. We wander, taking small streets and turning right or left based on what looks more interesting in that direction.

We came upon an old market square with a circular market building in the center. The building had window booths all round its perimeter. It seemed merchants were selling food and beverages from the windows. Vendor stalls sold fruit within the square, and local cafés lined the perimeter.

We walked toward a high garden or cemetery wall and then around to the left. It was more of a construction site in that direction so we followed the wall around another corner to the right this time and came upon the Jewish cemetery. Each of these small Jewish cities in Europe holds a tragic history of annihilation during the 1930's. (reread W.H. Auden's poem "September 1, 1939") The reality always comes home most vividly to me when I see photographs of the children who were murdered. We went to the museum in the Jewish neighborhood in Prague and read their writing and saw their photos. They were beautiful children, like my children, like my grandchildren, each and every one.

We continued to wander and came to a small cobblestone square that was more of a long triangle with a small park at the top (which was the base of the triangle). The open area was lined with small hotels, cafés and restaurants. This is much smaller than the main square of Krakow, but lovely, more intimate, on smaller scale.

Around another random corner or two we saw a sign for jazz and entered a café called Ptasiek on Dajwor Str. #3. Yes, music tonight, no cover charge, large club downstairs. We took a flyer thinking maybe to come back later.

We wandered toward the Vistula river which is not developed for tourism, but which attracted a small group of today's adolescent graduates, sitting and swinging their legs over the stone wall facing the water, laughing and contemplating the flow of their future along with the flow of the river.

Our next loose goal of wandering was to seek a café for a coffee, beer, mineral water, ice cream break. We wandered all the way back to the main square and out of the possibly 40 cafés lining this huge square, I randomly picked one for us to enter, and it was called Da Pietro! After our refreshing snack, we did errands—drug store for mouth wash, hotel for towels, bank to cash traveler's checks, delicatesy for sandwich fixings—and then back to our apartment for a nap!

Our general plan for dinner was to wander back to Kazimierz and find a place for a drink, dinner, and then possibly for music at Ptasiek (which we recalled as "Plastik"). On our way, we noticed preparations for some grand event. The main square (Rynek Glowny) was packed with people already drinking, and there were many soldiers around. There was a man making announcements from a stage in the center of three huge banks of bleacher seats. Possibly this is part of a big celebration of 750 years of Krakow? We couldn't understand this date as the university is much older than this we think. We thought the festival was already over, but something was going on for sure. As we walked away from the square towards Kazimierz, we noticed several locations where marching bands were gathering. The police seemed ready to block traffic on certain streets. We kept walking in the opposite direction of the crowds. Sometimes it's just as well to be away from the exact center of an approaching storm! We found the small intimate square again after passing through the market square where all local people seemed to be enjoying a beverage or meal at small cafés and stalls. We had dinner at Szera, a restaurant with pretensions and tablecloths on the long side of the triangle.

Walking back we encountered the full display of marching bands in uniforms leaving the square as well as a flow of the crowd away from the square. It looked like the navy, airforce, and army bands along with the boyscouts. I liked especially the gray uniforms with long capes and feathers in the caps.

## Magic

On a beautiful afternoon in Cologne, Germany, I walked through Hiroshima-Nagasaki Park and along the lake on my way to the University. A woman who had just been feeding the ducks and two snow-white swans was just leaving. I smiled at her, but I don't think she smiled back. I wondered, "Don't people smile at each other here?"

The ducks and swans accepted the exchange of women as I crossed paths with her and continued to walk along the lake. They kept their eyes on me. I took my time noticing the mallard pairs, males dramatic and females quiet brown; the amazing soft-looking, white feathers and graceful shapes of the swans, the smaller birds, light grey like floating pigeons, and one odd duck, larger than the mallards but with similar coloring. As I walked along the shore, ten birds followed alongside in the water. Oh, I felt like magic! The Pied Piper; Dr. Doolittle; Snow White! They glided alongside me for twenty or thirty yards until I realized that I must be honest with them and proclaim my lack of food.

Magic over. I turned away from the lake onto the path towards the street, and they dispersed to seek better options.

## Surprise

Upon entering our hotel in Cologne, Germany after lunch, we heard a deep bark as if from a very large dog. "Did you see the dog?" we later queried one another.

"No," I replied. "It might be an alarm that goes off when the door opens—an alarm that sounds like a big dog!"

"We should get one of those," said V. "It's very persuasive."

The next morning after breakfast, we stopped at the reception desk and heard the dog bark alarm again. This time we also heard the clerk say, "Hush!" I was thinking that this makes the alarm that much more persuasive because you picture a large dog actually behind the desk.

The dog I imagined was only half the size of the actual dog that emerged from behind that desk—larger even than the pony I saw saddled and ready for a child to ride on the pedestrian shopping street. This dog was more the size of the llama further down the street.

The only response that seemed possible to the dog's sudden presence, was to meet him (or her) eye to eye, to smile and offer a greeting.

"Hello, there!" I said, more startled than anything else.

The dog gave a menacing bark and a low growl to reinforce his (or her) reality as a dominant Irish Wolf Hound and dispel any further imaginings I might have about a warm and friendly nature.

CHAPTER EIGHTEEN

# Performance

*It may be that when we no longer know what to do, we have come to our real work, and that when we no longer know which way to go, we have begun our real journey. The mind that is not baffled is not employed. The impeded stream is the one that sings.*

—Wendell Berry

## Uncertainty and Certainty

Remounting our double-decker in Trafalgar Square, London, we traveled along the Strand and eventually crossed the Thames and were treated to the guide's enthusiasm for IMAX and wax museums as the most urgent destinations of every tourist. On our circle back around, we dismounted near the Duchess Theatre where *Copenhagen* was playing.

This dramatization of the mysterious meeting of Werner Heisenberg and his teacher Neils Bohr in 1941 is an exquisite meditation on the uncertainty principle, language, ethics, complementarity, and memory. Even after having read it months before, the masterful performance brought me to tears. Like particles in an acceleration chamber, the three actors traced emotional energy in complex patterns on the stage and in our minds. See it; read it; talk about it: it is then, but it is also now. Best performance of the trip!

Bohr: But, Heisenberg, Heisenberg! You also have been deflected! If people can see what's happened to you, to their piece of light, then they can work out what must have happened to me! The trouble is knowing what's happened to you! Because to understand how people see you we have to treat you not just as a particle, but as a wave. ..... ...

Heisenberg: And off he goes into orbit again. Incidentally exemplifying another application of complementarity. Exactly where you go as you ramble around is of course completely determined by your genes and the various physical forces acting on you. But it's also completely determined by your own inscrutable whims from one moment to the next. So we can't completely understand your behaviour without seeing it both ways at once, and that's impossible. Which means that your extraordinary peregrinations are not fully objective aspects of the universe. They exist only partially, through the efforts of me or Margrethe, as our minds shift endlessly back and forth between the two approaches. (69-70)

After this performance we turned a few corners and found a lovely restaurant called "Boulevard" on Wellington Street and made a snap decision to dine. Exquisite seafood risotto was my resulting good fortune. Even after a full day of touring, we decided to walk back to our hotel.

## Barefoot

A change of plans—we will not be going to the beach tonight. We will go tomorrow morning instead. We begin planning to get tickets for a concert by Maria Rita tonight at Citibank Hall in the faraway Moema district of Sao Paulo, Brazil.

Despite many efforts to get tickets without traveling there in person, we are forced to travel to Moema in the late afternoon and then spend five hours waiting for the concert to begin at 10 p.m.

After the taxi ride and purchasing our tickets, we duck into the first decent place to review our maps and books for ideas of what to do for five hours here. This place smells like kerosene so we don't linger for long! We begin to walk in one direction and then reverse to a more auspicious direction. We begin to encounter nice restaurants and bars. We stop for chopp and shrimp appetizers at Amazen Paulista where they sell scotch by the bottle and patrons seem to sit down for the whole day with a bottle of scotch, ice, and two glasses.

We continue further to come upon a wealth of four or five really nice places and it is hard to choose. We end up in Amalfi attracted by risotto. VC has seafood risotto with the most delectable shrimp I've ever tasted. I have a bountiful dish of sundried tomato and rucola risotto. We walk back and enter the theater (night club) at 8:30 pm when the doors open. We order Campari, take out our books and relax to read and watch the crowd slowly enter and take seats at tables around us.

The show begins at around 10:30 pm. Maria Rita is youthful, energetic, and an amazing singer with styles from blues to ballads and even a bit of rock and roll. She performs barefoot, and the crowd absolutely loves her! They know the words to every song and she gives them ample room to prove it. The heartfelt connection—almost a group ecstasy—of 1,000 plus people is very moving. She gives an encore of varied emotional tones in three songs and brings the entire room to closure.

## Small town Soccer

We went to a fútbol game (you know ... soccer) this afternoon in Cianciana, Sicily! Mostly there were men and boys there, but I asked everyone if it was ok for a woman to go. They laughed and said "Sure!" but there were hardly any women.

The players were vigorous. At the slightest bump, one of the players dives into the earth (not grass), grabs some part of his body (leg, head, chest), and rolls around. The first time I saw this, I thought there was a serious injury. But could everyone be injured so intensely and then, with 10 seconds of care from a teammate or coach, jump up and play soccer?? I soon realized it was all a masterful performance to gain time to breathe. One time the player who was supposed to be injured didn't notice until after the official blew the whistle on the offender. He immediately dropped down and clutched his leg until he was tended! Another time, no one noticed the performance and the game moved on. The "injured" player soon gave up and rejoined the game.

We won, 2-0, and went to the local bar –not at all like a U.S. sports bar – to have a drink of Averna, a Sicilian liquor, good for digestion.

A little later, we strolled along with nearly every other person in the town, up and down the main streets for passagiatta. Groups meet and recompose themselves. You meet someone who invites you to his home and you stroll there, others arrive, you all leave together and stroll to another bar with more relatives or friends to meet; half the group waits outside and new people join up. All strolling, arm in arm, conversing. No, wait, many men are sitting at tables on the sidewalk sipping or snacking or playing cards. Unbelievably, cars weave through the crowds on the street! This is just a normal Sunday evening! The stroll takes place every evening, but more on Sunday. I think this strolling is in my blood. And, by the way, Moonstruck was on TV tonight. It was so strange to hear it dubbed in Italian.

## Désiré by Breughel

I am looking at a Breughel, not a Rubens, from my window seat at Désiré de Lille Tea Room in Antwerp, Belgium. I would frame the artwork better by switching my own seat with the two ladies at a nearby table. Petite, well dressed, mature women. They both have silver hair, cut short and youthful. I think they are sisters catching up on family news, not just the what of it, but the why and the how, going deep inside the family stories to make meanings of new alliances and old fractures. They are wearing skirts and low heels. One wears glasses, one does not. The window begs to be bordered by their warm russet and brown brocades.

If they sit here in my place at the window table, the word Désiré will be just above their heads as read from the outside looking in. How would Breughel frame this? Will that word become the title of the entire piece? I like Breughel's busy composites of folk sayings or parables. Each tiny scene is an illustration of some human foible. What is going on in my Breughel?

A woman walks into a shop labeled with a blue fluorescent sign. It might be a jewelry store. I can't quite see from this angle. The name of the store is clear however. It is Choice. What is she going in there to choose?

Another woman, dressed in brown with short dark hair and glasses, walks out of a shop with a package under her arm. She is purposeful, stepping into the flow of pedestrian traffic to her right with eyes only for the next steps of the day. What is in her bag?

There is a large Buddha statue in the window of the shop she has just left. Buddha is holding a lit candle in his lotus-flower hands. The shop is called Rituals: Home and Body Cosmetics. Above and behind the Buddha is a board with writing on it. It begins ..."Onze filosofie ..."

Two women in slacks and short coats with their collars up walk a medium-sized black poodle. We see only their backs as they walk from the center of the canvas off to the right. The woman on the left is older, perhaps the mother to the daughter on the right, the one with longer hair and slighter build. They aren't touching, but their bodies proclaim intimacy

Two young men in shirt sleeves unload flats of water onto a hand cart just to the left of the center of the scene. Their bare hands grip the heavy trays.

A boy in a black coat is running, running through the scene. He is not alarmed, just late. Late to pick up a package from a shop closing soon? A package he has promised his mother he will bring home, but he was talking on his cellphone so long that he's late. The twilight is shading down on him and soon that sharp scimitar, Magritte's moon (in Breughel's painting!) will be hanging over his head.

Tequila tempts passersby two or three at a time. Tequila's final letter, the "A" is designed to look like the top of a minaret. The door of the minaret, as well as the spaces within the letter "e" and the letter "q" are filled with a deep pink, almost red color. What is Tequila offering besides a blush of intoxication? Costume jewelry, scarves, and bags are visible along with an elephant and a giraffe. Outside on a pole a deep pink package tied with matching ribbon beckons with an exchange of imagination for possession.

The clerk of Tequila keeps busy in the tiny, spot-lit shop: folding and unfolding scarves, organizing small leather wallets in a display box. A mother and daughter, arm in arm, pause, turn away, and then turn back and enter the minaret's door. They are darker than Northern Europeans. Are they from a minaret or from tequila? Drawn by the aura of the bustling shop, another woman enters.

A little family doing passagiata –two tiny girls, and Mom and Dad.

A shopgirl on her cellphone making plans for the evening.

Which of us is Icarus, falling from the sky with melting wings from the dizzy heights and fiery sol?

Behind the tingle of the minaret's door, is it the young woman in houndstooth trying on a scarf?

Or the young girl behind the Buddha who has just blown out the candle?

Or the young blond woman with a stiff-legged walk?

Or the woman with graceful packages pausing beside the "60% Off Sale" sign?

Or is it me?

The young man carrying two suitcases, one red, one grey, crosses from left to right and then from right to left ten minutes later. Where is the woman who belongs to the soft things in the red bag? Is she lost, or is he?

This tea room is really a series of rooms, each one lined in framed mirrors and deeper, deeper into the perspective of distance mirrored back smaller and smaller.

Tequila! Tequila! Number 11, the magic windows, the magic door. Did the woman whose face I never see put one irresistible gem among the fake chains and baubles?

The boy in the black coat runs across the scene again, in the opposite direction. On this little street, Schrijnwerkers Straat, are we at the fold of time? Every action will have its mirror, its reverse, sooner or later?

It's almost dark; our reflections go deeper within the lighted windows and enfold one another across the narrow street.

No one goes in or comes out of Hush Puppies despite the pastel-bright colors splashed across the windows. Perhaps Breughel's eyes cannot see into pastels. We'll ask Renoir for this perspective.

# CHAPTER NINETEEN

# Arriving

*All journeys have secret destinations of which the traveler is unaware.* —Martin Buber

## Island Hopping in Scotland

After breakfast, we drove 5 miles into Oban. We stopped and shopped a bit. Good prices! I finally got a kilt, N's shawl, and several inexpensive scarves for gifties. We found the ferry for the Isle of Mull, but it was confusing. We have to wait on line for at least an hour to maybe get on the ferry. We can't get back tonight. We have no petrol and no place to stay on Mull, and we must get back in time to shop and drive to Ayr on Thursday.

We did fit on the car ferry. Price was £ 17.00. Wow. We got expensive petrol and a room near the return ferry dock, and we booked a 9 am crossing for tomorrow. OK. We had lunch before heading across the island to catch another ferry to visit Iona. I ordered prawns, which seemed to be shrimp. Yuck! They had heads on, lots of eggs, and were tough to eat. Didn't really taste like shrimp either.

It was 2:30 before we headed out on 37 miles of one-track road to Fionnphort (spelling confirmed!) to catch the ferry for Iona. What an endless ride. It was very difficult driving because you have to be so alert to oncoming traffic. The island is really sparsely populated, and very beautiful with mountains and valleys and an indented coastline. Very green. Lots of sheep. We were both exhausted ninety minutes later when we arrived at the ferry terminal. I rushed down to buy tickets for 92 pence each for our round trip to Iona.

Iona is very pretty with small white sandy beaches and clear green water. We toured the Nunnery and Abbey and saw remains of St. Columba's mission (virtually nothing). Saw celtic crosses from about 800.

(After Castle Cawdor, we went to Clava Cairns near Culloden to see ancient burial mounds. They date from 1500 or 1800 B.C. Iron age? Bronze age?)

We listened to a tour guide for awhile. He was saying that no one really knows why the Celtic cross has the circle. Maybe just for structural stability. Perhaps to symbolize the sun or shape of the earth. Someone who had walked up in the middle of the talk offered another explanation. Then a woman interjected that the Celts didn't know that the earth was round. The fellow who had just joined the group—who must have been Irish—said, stingingly, "The Irish knew a lot of things before the rest of ye!" We all chuckled, but he was serious!

The Book of Kells was supposedly written here. There is also an old graveyard where Scottish kings are buried. Again, no evidence left.

They say many people here on the islands speak Gaelic still. I didn't hear any.

We walked back to the dock to catch the ferry. It was a long wait, about an hour, and the wind had picked up. We sat on the beach. I had my white sweater on. D was a bit chilly. He told me that I should give that sweater away when we get home. I agreed easily. I never liked it; it was merely convenient for the trip. (Why on earth did I bring something that wasn't attractive to wear on our trip???)

After awhile we went into the restaurant and had tea to warm up while waiting. We eagerly bought a wedge of "cheesecake" that was on the counter for our snack. What a shock to my tastebuds! It wasn't cheesecake, I discovered, with my mouth full. It was an onion and cheese lunch pie. D was brave to eat most of it. I marched back to the counter with clamoring tastebuds and found some tea biscuits for 14 p. to sweeten my mouth.

The ferry came at about 6:15 and we returned quickly to Mull. We were dreading that endless 37 miles to reach our room, a hot bath, and a glass of sherry. Despite this anxiety, we took the opportunity to have a hot meal in Fionnphort and we were pleasantly surprised. "A good meal always comes after something difficult," said D. In a tiny, family-run place with only eight tables, he had salmon; I had soup, salad, and gateau. The gateau was a bit heavy on the tummy, but my eyes insisted. I had coffee too, to keep wide awake on that drive back to our room at the other end of Mull.

We talked over our souvenir and gift buying strategies for much of the way back and there were many fewer oncoming cars for us to dodge. We made very good time.

I had a lovely hot bath and dropped off to sleep with a glass of sherry and my trusty book of poetry.

The next morning, we met the 9 am ferry back to Oban and arrived on the mainland at 10 am.

## Arrivals

We arrived late in Budapest. I chose a minivan taxi service rather than arranging our own private taxi because we have been cheated so many times recently. I also feel anxious when we are in a taxi alone without knowing the city or the language, particularly at night! It was almost 11 pm when we arrived at Hotel Anna, but we wandered out almost immediately. We had seen several cafes open on the main street two blocks away. We ordered drinks at a very nice restaurant just about to close. Feeling more relaxed after sitting there among local people for a half hour, we returned to Hotel Anna and were able to sleep despite the heat.

## Bogend Farm

Driving through Glasgow, Scotland was a nightmare. I was weary to death of roundabout signs and of reading maps. We finally pulled up in front of the Robert Burns cottage at 4:45 pm. Fifteen minutes before the time we expected it to close! Fortunately, it was open until 7 pm.

We toured the two room cottage attached to a two room byre. Unbelievable. Tiny, tiny. We saw the museum with manuscript copies of some poems. He wrote large. I saw a note he wrote in a Bible or volume of Shakespeare. It was funny. He had such a sense of humor. We saw Alloway Kirk, Brig' o Doon, and Monument.

We wanted a farm B&B so we went to the Information booth. The attendant called to make a reservation and gave us directions to Bogend Farm in Mossblown. What a name! We went to the Temple House for a pub meal. Then we took a walk on the farm. I wore one of my new sweaters because it was chilly and because the despised white sweater had disappeared! I really don't know what happened to it, but I'm glad it's gone.

I took a bath and went to bed with sherry and a book. It was windy and both the door and window rattled. I had a funny dream where N's hair was cut short.

## Boyana Church Day

We were put in a taxi by IV with clear directions for the driver to take the four of us to Tzarkvata Boyana where IM would meet us and guide us in visiting this UNESCO protected site. Our guide book begins to describe it thus: "At the foot of Mt. Vitosha, this settlement was a medieval fortress near the beginning of the 11th century. Today it is one of Sofia's wealthiest residential neighborhoods. In this area is one of Bulgaria's most precious monuments, the tiny, medieval Tzark-vata Boyana" (458)

I don't have the rest of the entry because I cut out the pages I thought we would need and left the "Side trips from Sofia" at home! This tiny church, or really, three joined chapels, was truly a moving site. The fresco paintings of warm rich colors were distinctive (according to our guide) for the personalized (rather than stylized) features of the many figures. It was easy to see why this is a treasured site; it was one of the most moving experiences ever at a religious site because the faces of the figures were so diverse and human.

Over a hundred years ago, someone brought giant sequoia trees from the US and planted three of them on the site. Even at a youthful 100 years of age, these trees are monumental.

I's wife, D, works at the Boyana church and she arranged a tour in English for us. Afterwards, we had a typical Bulgarian lunch at an outdoor café overlooking the city. The grilled trout that K and I's wife ordered was probably the best dish even though it attracted three cats to our table begging for the heads and other scraps.

We missed a downpour with hail by seconds after getting into a cab. I immediately fell into a two hour nap on returning to the hotel.

K picked us up at 7 pm to go to I and D's home for dinner. The building was a large apartment building with a locked entrance on the back side away from the street. How to describe the setting behind this building? Like a destroyed landscape, pockmarked, broken, abandoned space with a shed-like building deteriorating and piles of rocks and earth. As if it is orphaned land that no one belongs to.

Odd for us to find our colleagues living amidst this disorder. Inside, however, was very orderly and refined. It was a modest apartment with magnanimous hosts. Rooms at the front and back were filled with light and plants. From their small kitchen, they offered a buffet of appetizers that I thought was the dinner itself so varied and delicious were they.

I was looking forward to meeting the President of the University. He appears to be one of the efficient and humanistic people who inspire action. Clearly, he had a vision of a private university, flexible and modern; a new university for a new reality within a traditional culture recovering from an extreme condition. He created from nothing a university that within sixteen years developed the capacity to educate 12,000 students. New Bulgarian University is his brainchild.

In a leadership development program I am familiar with, participants in groups are given the challenge of creating a university. What is your mission? How will you organize the fields of inquiry? What will be the principles of leadership? How will you market this "product"? Professor B's achievement is the real experiment answering these questions, solving these challenges.

## Buda and Pest

Breakfast at Hotel Anna was very nice with fresh breads, smoked meats and ham, cheese, fruit, and granola.

After breakfast we walked to the train station—a gorgeous monumental structure—to purchase our tickets to Krakow for the 21st. After waiting on the wrong line (in-country travel) and the right line (international travel), we learned that our only option was a train once a day at 6:30 pm (18:30). We decided to leave one day earlier and spend the night of the 20th on the train rather than delay our arrival in Krakow, reasoning that with so much travel, the value of one place for longer exceeds having one more day in a short-visit city. With this train we arrive in Krakow at 5:30 a.m. We reserved a sleeper. Our total ticket was 175 Euro. After making these decisions and arrangements, we returned to Hotel Anna to change our reservation there so we wouldn't have to pay for the night of the 20th.

At around 11 am we set out again to stroll to the Széchenyi Iáchid bridge and the funicular up to the old city of Buda also called Castle Hill.

It was really hot! I had to plot our progress through the shade. We followed the main avenue near our hotel to the Danube River. We discovered a pedestrian street parallel to the river in just the direction we needed to get to the bridge.

I put my umbrella up to cross the hot bridge in the sun and we immediately bought round trip tickets for the funicular. A funicular usually feels very safe because it runs on a track with a huge chain pulling it up and guiding it down the steep hill. We recalled the tiny funicular in Salvador da Bahia last summer that ran down from a street level hotel to its water-level bar at the foot of a cliff. The little carriage held just ourselves ("and immortality" Emily Dickinson).

My first funicular was in Positano at the hotel Agave the year I organized a trip to Italy for my mother, sister, cousin, and children. Our room was so spectacular that I could not bring myself to sleep indoors. I dragged my mattress outside to the balcony and slept all night out there. Agave, like many hotels in Positano, is high up the cliffs where the road winds south from Sorrento to Amalfi. Each room or pair of rooms is down the steep hillside at a specific stop on the funicular. Like a personal, outdoor inclined railway! From the main hotel lobby balcony, we looked down on a tiny beach, the village of Positano, and the cruise ships and fishing boats below in the Mediterranean Sea. On the night of August 15th the fireworks shot upwards at us and burst below us, stunning us with great joy and excitement after our post-dinner Sambuca. I couldn't have been higher on any drug!

Back to Buda and a practical (not magical) funicular that lifted us as a machine task up to the top of Castle Hill. Our first priority was to find a café in the shade to have a beer and plan what to see. We sat down (in the shade) at a café on Tarnák utca to cool down and refresh. After a Fanta orange and a beer (and bathroom break) we continued along this street to Mátyás templom (under renovation) and Halász-bástya—a lovely castle-like fortification wall with picturesque arches, domes, towers, arcades, and views across the river to Pest. I think it is entirely a replica because it is so shiny and white looking so new. We wandered through a back garden of the lavish Hilton Hotel which resembled an antiquarian site blended with new elements—very Henry James—and very rich looking site for a wedding cocktail hour.

We wandered and peeked for another hour or so enjoying all the views, the breeze, the sky, the air, and the historic ambiance, all for free! We entered a labyrinth at least 2 stories below the street and looked around a bit, but decided not to take a tour since the wall paintings were not authentic. It was so cool down there that I wanted to stay!

# Wroclaw Day

J, A, and I boarded a train at 9:11 a.m. from Opole, Poland, to Wroclaw, Poland, about an hour away to the northwest. I became interested in this city because it is the home city of our friend JS, who lives just down the street from us at 440 East Irvin Avenue. So close to the conference, a nice daytrip away for three English-major wives of Peirce scholars: J from Anchorage, Alaska; A from Indianapolis, Indiana; and Jo from State College, Pennsylvania.

On the way out, J asked me about my work since we had last seen each other at a similar meeting in Alet les Bain in southern France possibly eight, or ten years ago.

When I came to talking about my current independent endeavor, they both gently asked me many questions and it felt like small warm hands gently massaging to loosen up muscles and mind. I didn't want this questioning to stop, yet it felt selfish to talk so much about myself and all the paths that led me to this moment and that nourished this dream. Articulated to these women, my dream sounded good to me; solid, full-bodied, and powerful. Unspoken it feels less so, more tentative sometimes, less certain of success. The hour ride went quickly as we again became familiar to one another and rediscovered our many common areas of interest.

After a few minutes of confusion seeking a map and an umbrella, we made do with exactly what we had with us and found the streets leading us to the market square, Rynek. It is magnificent with a highly detailed town hall, Ratusz, in the center and colorful buildings, some only two windows wide, surrounding the entire square. One building was covered with a huge cloth poster: "Wroclaw Expo 2012 Poland: The Culture of Leisure in World Economies."

We wandered through side streets, aiming towards the river and the many bridges we read about in our guide books, stopping frequently to window shop and browse in galleries. I bought a small gift for E and J from his hometown.

After reaching the river and walking on two bridges to islands, Mosty Uniwersyteckle and Most Macieja, we meandered back to the square to find a restaurant for lunch. We sat surrounded by flowers outdoors under an awning for a long, leisurely lunch of goulash, vegetable crepes, and Greek salad sharing many more compatibilities of our lives: religion, writing, reading, families, career paths, marriages, etc. We each had a first and second marriage to compare and early religious training to discuss. All three of us have had students moved by our teaching and we have all traveled to many different places with strange food, incomprehensible customs, and language challenges.

After lunch and rain showers we set a goal of going to the Wyspa Piasek (Sand Island) and Ostrów Tumski (Cathedral Island). There we wandered in and out of the many churches and along the winding streets, enjoying the sunshine in between showers and the sense of long ago lives lived in these spaces.

We retraced our steps as the rain increased in intensity. Our goal of reaching the train station for a 4:00p.m. train was delayed with a rain respite in a small shop where A bought a hat to cover her wet head and we just rested for a few minutes. We had almost reached the train station by 4 p.m., but decided to stop for a cup of tea and make the 5 p.m. train.

Refreshed, we located our platform and track along with hundreds of others, again glad we had purchased the more expensive first class tickets. Our hour-long ride back to Opole was congenial with quiet conversation in a cabin with two men and the three of us. We assumed they spoke no English and we talked almost as if we were alone. It was a picture perfect day, even with the rain! The sense of adventure was enhanced by sharing it with two women of similar sensibility, loving to see what is around the next corner, enjoying leisurely browsing, unforced conversation, and each other's company.

## Street Food, Istanbul

The four of us arrived at our hotel around 7:45 p.m. and met again at 9:30 p.m. to go out into the old city of Istanbul for strolling and dinner. We walked across several highway ramps near the hotel seeking a tram stop in front of a neighboring shopping center. As we puzzled next steps at a bus stop (not tram stop), a taxi-van stopped to offer us a ride for 3 Turkish Lira each. We took it. It was quite a long ride along the Sea of Marmara across a bridge and up a hill to Taksim square. We were coming to understand that Istanbul is a very geographically textured city. We began our stroll down Istiklal Caddesi, a long pedestrian street lit with tiaras across from side to side reminding me of the festival of San Gennaro in lower Manhattan. K says this warren of streets is busy every evening all year long.

On a side street we found a casual restaurant with food and beer available at tables outside. Three of us had grilled lamb parts sandwiches on exquisitely fresh bread. V had fried calamari. It was fun to sit and eat amidst the bustle of the busy street. Strollers were examining food and making decisions just as we had been minutes before. I watched a young couple eating musssels while standing at the large kettle filled with the dark shells: opening, squeezing lemons across their own fingers onto the warm flesh and then pouring/sucking the soft body onto the tongue for a quick bite or two and swallowing. A sensuous experience even for an observer!! Foreplay to analogous paddling in flesh.

Walking is wonderful! The scene gradually changed as we continued down the street; from the crowded multitudes and soccer fans thinning to a few couples walking home holding hands. Our way home included (again) crossing highway entry/exit ramps, walking across a long bridge, crossing 6 lanes of traffic, and negotiating for a fixed price with a cab driver with whom we shared no languages. The speed and maneuvering of the cab reminded me of a similarly terrifying ride in Rio de Janeiro.

CHAPTER TWENTY

# Live To Be Inspired

*It is my contention that favorite places have the capacity to heal.*
—Tim Cahill

DV

One day she woke up with the flu and a stiff neck.

Within days she was fighting for her life in a coma with meningitis—inflammation of the lining of the brain. At one point the doctors opened her skull in a dramatic attempt to save her life by bathing her brain in an antibiotic wash.

While she was in this coma, D could hear others talking about her and her condition. She recalls one physician saying, "If I were to slip and cut right here, she would be dead."

Today she is lively and articulate with a quick smile, rosy cheeks, and projects for the future. When she came out of the coma she couldn't speak. All that had to be learned again. Some colleagues and collaborators assumed she would die and wrote her out of joint projects that she had been an integral partner on.

She lived, she lives, she will live, and I am inspired!

# To Die or Not to Die

One of the ways I have made decisions about certain risks is by asking myself if I would be willing to die for the opportunity to have this experience. It separates the men from the boys (so to speak), the bliss from the bends. As I look back, three experiences come to mind and they all have to do with transcending the boundaries of earth's surface and the limitations of being a gravity-bound creature with feet. I fully recognize that my experiences are not earth shattering like those of explorers, warriors, astronauts, or survivors of cataclysmic events.

In my youth I had a recurrent dream of flying about a foot off the ground, posed in original superman fashion (BUT not hung from wires or lying on a transparent table as my siblings and I surmised). My three "worthy of death" experiences have to do with plunging head-first into a hole in the ground, sailing into a storm at sea with no previous sailing experience, and flying literally into the teeth of the wind. I wanted each of these badly enough to look death in the face and still say, "Yes, count me in!" This is not the same as asking myself who or what I would lay down my life for. I would certainly step in front of a bullet for my children or my beloved, and I'd think about the value of sacrificing myself for my principles or my country as so many others have done. Rather, this is facing a specific fear or risk that may or may not be life threatening at all, and deciding if the experience is worth the risk.

Spelunking is an old word for the habit of diving into caves and exploring. You might picture an opening about the size of your garage along a rocky trail or high up on a hillside. You might picture huge caverns with stalactites and stalagmites growing up or down drip by limestone drip. The cave that swallowed me was a mere dimple in a grassy field, an Alice-in-Wonderland rabbit hole that did not beckon enticingly nor appear inviting in any way. I was part of a group of about eight friends—not even my friends—who were led by two people who had previously survived this experience. Head first is somehow even more frightening than feet first! I don't know why, but it is. I was not the first to go down, nor the last. Somewhere in the middle or maybe towards the end, for my reluctance was a huge boulder blocking entry to the experience I craved. Head first, on the heels of the precious person in front of me, who would become my lifeline through this deep dark tunnel. We each had a flashlight, but there is nothing to see, only whispers and rough rocks and the feet of the person in front of you. Not even crawling on hands and knees, but slithering on forearms and shins, propelled by toes, prehistoric, pre-upright motion. Not an iota of sense about what is coming next or how to go forward or back; just this rock, this shadowy light, and these feet in front of your face. Occasionally, the tunnel led up and then we climbed awkwardly; or down, and then we dangled and handed one another through gaps that were longer than we were tall. There was only one cave-like space where we all fit at once and then turned off our lights. The dark seeped in through our pores and we were extinguished from the atomic core of our beings outwards through our eyes. Eyes that began to recede through negative evolution even as we counted ten seconds before illuminating the small space again with our meager bulbs. Annihilation more real than hell or death; imagination just barely diverted from flood, collapse, falls, seizures, stinging creatures, and so on. Despite the purple bruises that bloomed along my arms and legs a few hours after we regained the surface of the planet, the exhilarating rush of terror, deed, and bonding was worth the risk.

## Ring the Bell

At Jiming Temple in Nanjing, China, I held three smoldering incense sticks in the sticky humid air and bowed in four directions to the Buddha, beginning with the East. I inhaled smoke and then opened my hands and heart for a blessing. A few hours later, I paid 2 Yuan to sound the massive bell in an inner courtyard of the Confucius

Temple. A small log was wrapped in red cloth and suspended by two ropes. I pulled it back, posed for a photo and released it toward the bell and the boom reverberating through flesh and bone and air. I paid another 5 to hold mallets and play three rows of graduated bronze bells, a very big drum, and a long sound box with strings. My five minutes on that stage were not enough to perfect my style, but to confirm a hazy vision that this might have been my role in a past life at this temple.

On Monday, I climbed every available stair in the weaving workshop garden, the geometric and smooth ones as well as the water-shaped, rough and uneven ones, filling all of my frames with their textures. I looked and longed toward the roof garden that was inaccessible to my ascending desire.

I confess that I am the one who touches sculptures behind signs that say "Do not touch," and on Tuesday, I touched the lucky turtle along with the elephant and the camel, and also the lions. They were stone both before and after, but I was not.

At the gate of Linggu Temple on Purple Mountain, I ate slippery cold noodles of bean paste with shredded carrots and cucumber, sauced with sweet, pungent, and spicy. Though I held my sticks upside down, no one noticed my splashy style.

Today, I plan to touch silk and jade, perhaps to great excess. When the anti-phospholipid antibody syndrome rings the final bell in my head or heart, I will be ready.

CHAPTER TWENTY-ONE

# Travel Themes

*Give me a willow chair on a quiet deck, the world with its worries and noise and prejudices lost in distance, the glare of the sun, the cold light of the moon blotted out by the dense blackness of night. Let me rest rocked gently by the rolling sea, in a nest of velvety darkness, my only light the soft twinkling of the myriads of stars in the quiet sky above; my music, the sound of the kissing waters, cooling the brain and easing the pulse; my companionship, dreaming my own dreams. Give me that and I have happiness in its perfection.* —Nellie Bly

## Yellow Star

The transfer sticker from our airplane arriving in Shanghai to our flight to JFK is a center circle of yellow with a star over it. "Yellow Star" is the impression, shorthand for the Jews who were forced to identify themselves during holocaust. Certainly unintentional, but also poignant to attach this symbol to our clothes to make the transfer status obvious.

# Lanterns

We boarded the Thameslink train with London's morning commuters, and I was relaxed and ready for twelve to fourteen hours of reading and dozing in the airport and on the flight home. I had finished Marion Wright Edelman's *Lanterns* and was deep into the biography of Vita Sackville West. *Lanterns* is a book to take much from, but one of the most important messages I gained was a renewed sense of the importance we adults have in the lives of the children we are connected to regularly. Wright Edelman comments:

"Parents, teachers, leaders: pay attention. In an era in which mentoring has become increasingly professionalized or left to volunteers, these important supplemental programs and individual efforts are not substitutes for the daily adult examples in children's lives. The most important is not primarily about a few hours a week or month of volunteer time with a child. It is who we are and what we do and say every day in our homes, classrooms, work places, congregations, cultural, civic, and political lives that children absorb to develop their sense of worth." (45).

# Vulnerability and Survival

We stopped to ask for directions in Istanbul and both of our Bulgarian friends jumped out of the car to converse with a helpful pedestrian. As we waited in the back seat with the car running, my mind turned to "what if's"—"What if someone got into the driver's seat and tried to steal the car with us in it?"

I thought about what I have with me as possible weapon material: small black leather purse, pens, pencils, camera, books, straw hat, water bottle, straw bag, mints, gum ... no obvious defensive weapons, but I'd have to improvise. A sharp pen to the jugular or eye? Or could I strangle the thief with the leather strap of my purse like a garotte? Could I do it? Yes, I think so. Or should we jump out of the car?

My mind works like this and drives me crazy! Why does my mind go in this direction?? Is it human instinct to prepare for danger with a plan or am I infected with obsessive compulsive disorder of some sort? I have always done this, I realize. When I taught 7th grade, we read a wilderness survival story of a young boy who somehow is lost in the forest and has to figure out how to survive. I recognized then that I think this same way. If dropped into a situation, what are the skills and tools I have available? How do I/we drop back to a more primitive level of existence to survive? I think this is how I enjoyed my adolescent wanderings in the woods behind our house, imagining I was stranded and had to create a plan to survive. Even now, my bag always includes survival food and water. I think I could survive for a week on what is in my backpack when we travel. I sometimes think it is a remnant from being a mother with small children to be fed and watered frequently, but it persists even now when they are parents themselves, packing bags of snacks, water, and surprise toys (survival indeed) for their toddlers.

## Lost

We were lost so long this morning that local people are asking US for directions! After eight or ten times asking directions, two hours in traffic, and amazing patience of our driver, we recognize that we are back at our hotel where we started. Our driver says "Good, now we can do it right!" and he does, and it takes us less than 10 minutes to find the university. It is the wrong campus, but still, there is a shuttle van waiting outside the entrance and we decide to follow it to the main campus. Good thinking! The main campus is—as the crow flies—directly across several highways from the small campus we have found. BUT it takes us a good 10 minutes and complex circumlocutions of several counterintuitive ramps to get there, finally! We realize the problem wasn't really with the many languages we didn't speak in which we were receiving directions, but with the folded nature of the city, folded horizontally and vertically, and also it seems, in time. Italo Calvino must have visited Istanbul—Constantinople to the Greeks—before he wrote *Invisible Cities*. It certainly lends itself to Calvino's ethereal descriptions of the ineffable about a city. We learned that the word "sokak" which seems to be used in Istanbul to mean "very small street," means, in Bulgarian, "impossible to find." We laughed and kept searching.

We set out in the morning with high hopes that our directions would lead us through this multidimensional city to our goal. We asked directions at least ten times in two hours, found ourselves exactly back where we began and started over with (finally) more success.

At least two dozen Istanbul citizens were part of this journey offering their ideas of how to get somewhere—perhaps here, perhaps some other destination that sounds like what we might have said. The very city itself is a character in the search. Calvino's "Invisible Cities" are all alive and well here! The arteries clogged with molecules rushing off to purposes both infinitely diverse and yet coordinated by several general themes of economic advantage, stimulation of taste buds and satisfaction of desires, rushing together and rushing apart. In the capillaries the city shows how oxygen passes from cell to cell. One by one, packets of elements and positive or negative charges move through narrow lanes carrying information and nutrients, bumping against one another, exchanging zips and zaps of energy.

The hills and waterways might very well be shifting form moment to moment like sand castles transformed by each wave. Thus we are not chronologically lost between moments of foundness; here, in this shifting city, lostness is a perpetual condition of anyone who cannot become fluid like the terrain.

## Dancing Theme

Certain themes emerge from particular trips. One of the themes of this trip emerged during our first hour while we were still at the airport in State College, Pennsylvania. We encountered S, a former colleague of mine from ten years ago when we first arrived at Penn State. She was the Director of the Women's Studies Program and I was a new adjunct faculty member with an appointment in both Women's Studies and English. At my most memorable meeting with S, she told me that I would never advance by spending so much time with students when I should be focusing on scholarship. That semester I was meeting with each of my students in three classes several times to discuss their writing and projects. This was taking hours and hours of my time, but it was satisfying work because their writing was improving. S noticed and offered me this good advice, but, at the same time, I was devastated. I walked home that night without looking either way as I crossed streets, not really caring much if my life's energy was so worthless. In the years since then, we've both moved on to appointments where our energies are better aligned to rewards! S was at the airport on her way to Argentina to dance tango!! She told me that she had one pair of dancing shoes in her carry-on bag and two more pairs in her checked luggage. That's quite a commitment to tango!

The dance theme emerged again on the morning we left Sofia, Bulgaria to drive to Istanbul. KB, our colleague and host in Sofia introduced us to IA, a theater director and professional tango dancer and teacher who was also going to Istanbul. IA is a semiotics scholar, and he would present a paper at the conference on visual semiotics, but he was especially looking forward to dancing tango in Istanbul. Apparently, there are vigorous tango gatherings there. I was hoping to tag along to see this, having just glimpsed some amazing dancing on "Dancing with the Stars." We fell in love with Leila Ali, Mohammed Ali's daughter, who, though a tall and substantial woman, turned out to be a stunningly beautiful dancer. Grace, power, and precision are not owned by skinny women!! She and her partner came in at number two and we were very disappointed! Anyway, IA was frustrated one evening with the lack of partners at a tango gathering. His second attempt was more successful though complicated because a young female faculty member at the Istanbul Kulture University offered to guide him to tango. He danced with her, but then found other partners, until she reclaimed him for a taxi ride home without asking if he was ready to leave. Too much leading by this woman in a dance of another name!

Our travels continued, as did the dance theme, this time in Finland. We learned that tango has a Finnish version called, of course, Finnish Tango. Our conference organizers planned a tango evening for us late in the conference week.

Now we are in Opole, Poland for the final meeting of this European Tour. I am meeting and renewing acquaintance with many scholars. I know I've met KH before, but we didn't have an opportunity to speak and get to know each other until now. I remember her with brown hair, but now she has red hair. When I confirmed my recollection with V, he commented that, in addition to being a scholar and teacher, she is a professional dancer. I look forward to learning more about this, but with four instances of dance punctuating this trip, I can't help but notice the theme. I have a list called "On Return" to remind me of the ambitions I gather along the way as we travel. Some are very miniscule, like finding my ankle bracelet and wearing it for the rest of the summer. And some are learning goals, like making a commitment to finding an Italian class or teacher we can stick with and finally learn enough to communicate in another language. V has agreed that he will take dance lessons, with the condition that we learn with different partners. "Our relationship is complex" is the excellent reason behind this condition and I immediately understand. He laughs with good humor when I push him around on the dance floor, but it probably isn't the best way for either of us to actually learn skills!

## Local Knowledges

Travel day from Krakow to Opole: We bought our tickets days ago so the only puzzle this morning was getting a taxi from our

apartment to the train station. V went to the hotel where we regis-
tered to order a "Radio Taxi." Three of them showed up at the same
time! Someone on the street quickly jumped into one of them, and
we asked the second if he was called by Hotel Floryan. Of course, he
said "Yes." But number 3 may have been the actual summoned cab
because we saw him cruising the street looking for his fare. Anyway,
off we went with taxi number 2. He took a long route to bring us
to our actual track, not the train station, normal for this city I've
since learned. I asked specifically for the train station because we
had to change our second class tickets to first class at the advice of
friends who traveled the same route yesterday. From the drop off, we
asked directions several times, found an elevator, and worked (felt
like work!) our way to a waiting point for V while I walked "over,
under, around, and through" to wait on two lines, pay for first class
supplements, get water, breakfast, and a pretzel and return. V added
apple juice, a sandwich, grapefruit juice, and another pretzel to our
supplies for the three and a half hour ride.

We confirmed our track #4 and went to the elevator to go back
up to the platform level where we had been dropped off by the taxi.
Nothing happened when I pressed the up arrow button. After several moments of waiting, we turned to the long flight of stairs and
contemplated how we would get our suitcases up. At that moment,
as if synchronized with our thought processes, a woman selling pretzels at the foot of the stairs across from the elevator gestured to us to
push the buttons for the elevator more vigorously. Armed with this
assurance of results, I pushed the down arrow this time and lo and
behold the elevator door immediately opened and we rose effortlessly
to our track with luggage, saving our maximal effort for stepping onto
and off of the train itself, quite a dangerous feat requiring agility and
strength. The pretzel woman must have observed countless travelers
attempt and fail to access the convenience of the elevator. She gave her
local knowledge generously to us and certainly to others. With all of
our book knowledge and broad general knowledge, we were helpless

to manage the simple mechanical device without her help. She could easily have remained quiet and added our discomfort to some store in her experience of perhaps rude foreign people who deserve to suffer, but she extended herself to help us. As I turned to face the closing doors of the elevator, I waved to her and she waved back in acknowledgment of a shared instance of cooperation.

## Midnight Morning

We pretend to be asleep like babies in our car seats, heads lolling left, right, and that painful crook with the head hanging straight down. It's 8:00 p.m. We're not really sleeping; just pretending.

I am intimate with strangers coughing in my ear, leaning back onto my knees, smiling across our blue paper pillows, listening to each other's whispered conversations.

How different is this from the bunks in steerage we saw in that immigration movie. Well, clean for one thing! And shorter, by several weeks, for another! What's a sleepless, short, tight, seven-hour crossing compared to those weeks or months at sea?

After we pretend to sleep for a couple of hours, the attendants wheel carts up the aisle to alert us to the idea of "morning." Now, we pretend to wake up, even those of us who haven't slept at all. We stretch and blink our eyes against the cabin lights and raised window shades. We queue for the toilets. We eagerly receive the mysterious cellophane packets handed to us, and the soft simultaneous crackling all through the cabin makes me giggle. Hundreds of us, just finished pretending to sleep, now pretend to awaken with curiosity, if not appetite, for whatever is wrapped so smartly in cellophane: a small banana bread and strawberry yogurt. These breakfast treats come with a delightful surprise I haven't seen (or thought of) in years: a spork. I intend to keep mine as a souvenir, but get distracted organizing my stuff and forget all about the spork.

We had dinner at 7:30, tucked in at 8, and we're eagerly crinkling breakfast cellophane like starving toddlers at midnight-morning!

# La Chaloupe d'Or (The Golden Boot)

Not having slept at all, I was working at being bright and willing to stroll in Brussels, Belgium. Our hotel was kind enough to offer us breakfast when we arrived at 7:30 am local time, but resolute that we could not check in to our room until after 1:00 p.m. We relaxed in the lobby for a while and then set out to see something of the city with our sleepy eyes. We easily found our way to the streets leading to the Grand Place—the majestic old square surrounded with guildhalls. We took a detour along the Rue des Bouchers and watched as the restaurateurs prepared outdoor sculptures of fruits, vegetables and fish with artichoke, tomato, clams, mussels, shrimp, and other crustaceans and sea life.

The wind was cutting and cold, and we decided to retreat into a bar for a beverage by the fire. It was maybe 10 am local time on a Sunday morning. As we thawed by the gas fire in La Chaloupe d'Or, the place filled with Sunday morning folks having luscious café beverages or amber golden shades of beer, or bright wines.

We speculated on what the name of this café in the former tailor's guildhouse might mean. I thought it meant Golden Mermaid because of the statue near the door and a wooden coat of arms above the bar. Neither of us guessed Golden Boot.

A tour group of boy scouts in the square outside sent several "scouts" inside to steal (quite a few) or request (one) of the colorful beer coasters that were on all the tables. Is this a badge requirement or a prank? Are they flinging the coasters like Frisbees outside in the square? One of the elegant, dignified waiters locked the door against further pleas and incursions by scouts.

We sat over chamomile tea (me) and a glass of red wine (VC) for over an hour, hoping that we could rest long enough that the previous night's guest in our room would have left the hotel and that the room would soon be ready for our weary bones.

# Ultimatum

Lack of information makes traveling harder. We arrive in Antwerp, Belgium without much knowledge about our stay which is mostly arranged by university hosts.

I quickly decide to try to activate the Nokia cell phone that I've borrowed from our South African friend, G, who travels quite a lot. There is one convenience store in the Antwerp-Berchem station where we were directed to disembark. The proprietor speaks English and is very helpful. He recommends a particular SIM card for the phone at 10 Euro and offers to help me set it up. We would still be sitting in that station without his help!

The phone made it possible to call the office of the person who would pick us up. Well, no, three phone calls later we learn that he isn't picking us up. I phone the B&B directly and learn that we should just take a taxi.

There are hundreds of bicycles parked right outside the station exit, but not a taxi in sight. I walk into the Travel Center to ask about where we might find a taxi. The elderly couple at the only counter open is planning a complex trip and the line grows exponentially behind them. A long ten minutes later, I ask my quick question and we are directed to the opposite end of the station.

The B&B, Via Stefania, that has been booked for us is on a short, quiet street far from any of the places we need or want to go, but we have a whole, floor-through apartment that is spacious and very nice.

Was that a frustrating day? A thirty-eight minute train ride in the center of the day was the hub of a wheel that seemed to have us trapped in its spokes. Transfer days can be like that! Morning lost to being mindful of departure time; afternoon lost to the little broken expectations and arrangements of arrival.

Practice what you preach! Experience focused journeying, not destination-focused, not itinerary-focused, not tomorrow-focused: NOW focused!

We are in a bar/café called Ultimatum near the historic Grote Markt in Antwerp. I can see an incredible ferris wheel from here. Almost as big as the Millenium Wheel in London.

The beer is stronger here, and I've found my new favorite: Leffe Blonde Trappist. It is much stronger beer than I am used to and I feel it.

Serendipity, where are you? We need a rescue tonight!

There seems to be an outdoor movie playing on a screen in the small square outside these windows. Is this the gift that will lift us tonight?

No, we went even further into a "funk" as we walked away from all the bright lights of the main squares, Grote Markt and Groenplaats, towards our B&B. We were quickly on streets with no restaurants and we were getting hungry. Finally, on the other side of the street, we saw a lighted window with many guests at tables and one or two tables for new arrivals. We didn't notice that it was an Italian restaurant, which category we had been avoiding all evening! We chose the exact same meal from the menu and with a visit to the restroom and a glass of red wine each, we were back in our fortunate mood. We didn't expect to be so comforted by the Italian food, but we were. Sometimes, what you need is familiar comfort found in a far-away place to appreciate both more robustly.

CHAPTER TWENTY-TWO

# Invisibles

*It's not what you look at that matters, it's what you see.*
—Henry David Thoreau

## Invisibles

On a side street, I see three people negotiating a transaction ... are they delivering goods to a nearby business? One of them has a scarred face that is very red. I couldn't tell if this was a man or woman without turning to stare. Was this the same person I saw hours later smoking a cigarette and hovering over a trash can?

The beautifuls are on the front streets; the invisibles are on the side streets and back streets.

There was a stoic woman sitting in the center of a wide passageway under a busy street that separates the old city of Krakow, Poland from the train station and the shopping mall. She sits in the same spot each day with her full bags on one side of her and a box displaying her breads and pastries for sale on the other. Her face is blank. She does not meet your eye, nor solicit attention. The rolls are piled neatly like a pyramid of rounded bricks in the center and the small oval sweets are arranged at two ends of the pyramid. The arrangement looks exactly the same every day. Does anyone ever remove a piece in exchange for money? Are her baked goods as invisible as she is?

## Views From Trains and Bus

Graffiti and broken windows; platform at Trezbina, Poland; parking lot; bars on station windows; powerlines; chimney smoke; cargo cars parked on side rails.

Abandoned industrial facility with multiple buildings, chutes and ladders, broken windows, rusted towers.

Small villages; workers eating lunch; backyards, bird house, picnic tables, swimming pools, trees, cars, swing set.

Marshy lake with electric towers; small shacks with outhouses, summer shacks on shore, screened gazebo, boat-house, arbor, gas tank.

Industrial site, square stone house with square cupola.

Rusty farm equipment, treehouse or deer hunting stand, underbrush and trees, new field with brush piled up for burning.

Flowing streams, islands in river, junked cars in woods, fire clear-cut breaks up side of mountain.

## Training

From the train window on an
afternoon dark with night encroaching
from winter solstice,
in the dark distance,
small weebles in formation
under bright lights.
Somewhere beyond them
observers lining up with scarves and snacks.

Disembodied rooms lit by
soft lamps. Flowers on the tables
hung in chill air like baubles
on an invisible tree.
Like momentary bubbles on
a stream of time.
Is this what I'm meant to
learn today, then?
Sadly, you are a long ribbon
floating, trailing
in the beak of a soaring bird?
How will I return to you
if the eagle does not circle
back around and the train
does not reverse along this rail?
It is only a belief that
links us now. Still, I
hold a coherent universe
inside me with vigorous stretches of you,
though a screen flickers momentarily
in the air outside the fleeing train.

## Backstage to the Statue of Liberty

As long as I feel safe, I enjoy the somewhat grimy aspects of travel, especially train and bus travel. Air travel secludes the passenger from all of the "back of the house" activities, although if you are watching out the windows of the departure lounge or aircraft, you can observe some pretty gritty situations, i.e. luggage bouncing off carts and into puddles.

When my train from NY Penn Station arrives in Harrisburg, PA, I exit the train and take the padded elevator up several levels with two other women and their luggage. We cross over the tracks on open-air scaffolding and approach the station's waiting and ticketing areas. We are crossing a sooty, rusty, and littered backstage. I can see the brightly lit waiting room ahead like the moon viewed through a break in foggy twilight. I know this station from previous trips, and I am able to move quickly to the elevator taking me back down one level to the waiting room and ticket area for bus passengers. My first and only greeting is from a man leaning against the vending machines. "Sister, Sister," he begins, but I continue without diverting my path.

Every ticket purchase today seems to be complicated. The starkly groomed but efficient young woman behind the counter seems equipped to handle every inquiry and request, but still, each transaction takes a full five minutes with multiple exchanges of documents, pens, and plastic through the little round window usually reserved for talking. One woman, three or four ahead of me in the line, is purchasing a set of tickets to be mailed to someone else. A tall young man with long hair and a cap hiding most of his face leans sideways to talk right into the round opening inquiring for a ticket in his name that should have been wired and received by today. A second, older, ticket agent searches for it in several locations and then must disappoint him with bad news. He complains that this always happens. He will now have to get a transaction number so that another clerk on another day will be able to locate the record of the ticket lost somewhere in the ethernet. As he moves away, both windows become available. A woman and her young son move to the left and I move to the right. Producing a government issued ID and sixteen dollars in cash gives me a lovely three-part ticket home. One part becomes my luggage tag, the driver takes part two, and part three is my souvenir of this encounter.

Raise your hand if you've never ridden a bus. I'd like to see the data on this, and I'd like to make a bus ride across America mandatory before any high school graduate can enroll in college. I'm not sure of the hierarchy of transportation in this country, but the bus is one of the lowest on any scale. Students, grandmothers, and the poor of any age are the clientele. I sit first on the right side facing front to avoid direct sunlight, but then decide to switch to the left so that I can better view the river as we ride alongside for part of the way. But first, we have to pass by a huge junkyard where rusted metal of various origins is stacked in huge piles, maybe awaiting transport to China where, I read recently, much of American recycling goes to be fashioned into new consumables for us to buy back, most likely on credit. Soon, we are alongside the mighty Susquehanna, a very wide and shallow river. Today I think I could skip across on the rocks jutting up all the way across just where the small replica of the Statue of Liberty stands.

## With Edi

Edi arrives at the Tropical da Bahia hotel and we are on our way. Our orientation tour of Salvador da Bahia, Brazil is fabulous. We come to understand the blending of religion and culture and the pride people take in their Bahia. Surely, some of this is for commercial purposes—introducing us to stores and restaurants where he has connections, but still, it is authentic commercialism.

It wasn't the gold-leaf ornate churches that were the highlights of the tour. It wasn't the colorful Baianas laughing and coming close for our expensive photo with them. It was the glimpses into life that made the deepest, most lasting impressions. We saw the seams wide open in historic buildings under construction, a façade with a gaping hole behind. Still, if a hole can be punched through the façade, someone was living there. In the main historic center—Pelourinho—residents were moved out to the suburbs and all the renovated buildings were given to businesses; restaurants, art galleries, crafts, stores, bars, etc. We visited behind the scenes at a tee-shirt factory, literally behind the curtain and saw women sewing and then we went below this level to a workshop where two men were silk screening the images on fabric in layers of colors, one color at a time.

In the case of a percussion school we visited, going "behind the scene" meant going Upstairs rather than down to the instruction room where the booming, irresistible rhythm was coming from teacher Macambira and just one student with two or three drums each. That rhythmic fullness filled us up and stayed with us for the rest of the four day visit in Salvador.

At every step it seemed we were offered something to buy—clothing, jewelry, photos, food, and so on. I always see things I want, but hesitate to bargain and negotiate. Moreover, the deepest desire is to bring home the essence of the place and the way that I'm feeling in that place. The tee-shirts and baubles are sometimes not up to the task.

## Shades of Blue

Sitting at the "Shades of Blue" bar in terminal A at the Philadelphia International Airport, I watch fascinated as a neatly dressed "Philadelphia Marketplace" worker makes his trash rounds. In particular, I watch him use five trash bags to line a plastic bin. He uses the same efficient motion for each one—a touch of his fingers to the moist cloth on his cart handle and then he rubs the top of the thin plastic until he can grasp the opening edges to pull them apart and create the envelope. He shakes it open and catches the air to balloon it open. Then he shifts the shape to grasp the gathered bottom and create a stiffer shaft of the bag to push it into the bin. The shape of the thin plastic has already been transformed three times from a long sheet to a balloon, to a shaft! The heavier gathered bottom of the thin paper shaft leads the way into the bin. The worker opens the shaft of plastic again and folds the top of the bag over the edge of the bin, neatly and pulling it tight, knotting one corner to hold this layer tightly over the slightly wider top edge of the bin. Five times in quick succession.

In a red shirt and blue pants, the worker seems to take pride in his efficiency and forethought. The bartender at "Shades of Blue" signs his delivery sheet and points to the Corona box and other folded cardboard boxes for him to remove as he completes this stop on his schedule. He moves out of my line of sight to service other areas though his cart remains in front of this bar. He returns with a full bag of trash and places it on the cart and then pushes on to his next scheduled arrival. Did anyone else even see him? His quiet, calm rhythm and efficiency, his smooth dark confident face?

## Façade

Buildings, clothing, and businesses on the main streets in Nanjing, China are modern and bright. Immediately behind, a couple of centuries drop away into dust.

From our hotel room window on Zongshan Road I can see the blue corrugated metal awning that covers the bicycles and motor scooters parked by employees during their shifts at the hotel. These dozens of vehicles are behind a fence, but on every street there are multitudes of the same dusty, rusty, trusty wheels individually secured, or not.

This narrow street that I see behind the hotel.

Bright yellow and red signs.

Cooking instruments just inside doorway and seating further inside.

Simple, essentials-only restaurants, supplies for repairs piled up---still a culture where things are fixed rather than discarded or exchanged for new. Need all the parts and tools to keep repairing and patching? Here they are. They may even be used parts as there don't seem to be packages, just piles. They are not shiny, but they are ready. They have no instructions, no marketing, no wrapping or packaging.

Cracks in the façade: bicycles are old and rusty.

We rode the Yangtze River ferry with Temur and photographer friend. Just the wrong day to wear a loose fitting dress likely to billow up in the wind! This is not a tourist attraction, but a genuine experience. Muddy river, wide river, working river. Boats riding high (empty) and low (full). This is not an oil port. I see a crane moving piles of coal.

Other side of the river similar to behind the scenes. Still part of

Nanjing, but out of view. Small three-wheel boxes wait for passengers just outside the ferry station. They are all red. We are taking a little walking tour of this side of the river. It looks like a different city, like the scenes in Gatsby where they drive through coal territory between the bright mansions on Long Island and the glitter of Manhattan. We make a long loop through streets of partly destroyed buildings where you might see an elderly woman emptying a plastic pan of water out the doorway of a small habitable portion of a crumbling four or five story building. The photographer's eye draws ours to a small cat crossing a broken rooftop. Small restaurants and shops line the streets, but many are closed and look abandoned. At one corner a group of men stand loosely talking framed by the cranes and coal behind them. They become silent to observe the spectacle of four strangers walking down their street.

After re-crossing the river on the ferry, we cross again, this time in a car via the bridge built in the 1960's. The ferry crossing was much quicker and easier! In the car we talk about Ai Wei Wei and about the prejudices that make life uncomfortable for the minority Chinese groups who live and work among the Han Chinese (majority dominant). Temur is from Inner Mongolia and feels this bias from his students and from other faculty.

The driver brings us to a Muslim restaurant closer to downtown, our hotel, Gulou district. At dinner we see photographs taken by Temur's friend. Black and white photos of faces so crisp that you feel the complex emotions as if you are watching a film clip. Many of his photos cannot be published because they are politically sensitive photos of people and events that implicitly criticize. He will send us photos he took of us today. He teaches photography at a college here in Nanjing. He teaches students how to see the world. This is a very subversive education! His photographs are "invisible" behind the seen!

When we leave the restaurant there is a heavy mist falling and no taxi available on this street so we begin walking towards our hotel. We can see the Zifeng Tower (a landmark of the Gulou area) and Temur and his friend know the area well. We walk through narrow lanes similar to the one I see behind our hotel. I fall behind the others for the density of looking and seeing in this crooked aisle. A family sitting in the middle of a small open room that appears to be a used electronic parts shop, watching a small TV in bright colors towards the back of the dark room. Parted curtains framing women moving white tiles on small tables. I want to hear the tiles clicking. Tiny dark doorways. Small children and shrunken elderly. The vigorous and young must be working at a hotel or shopping center.

Temur says things have always been hard and they are getting harder. Inflation. More pay but also higher costs.

I feel that we don't understand China. What does this precipice into darkness behind the tall hotels and futuristic shopping centers mean in terms of globalization? We have access to endless new appliances heavy with metal, coal, and transportation while that woman empties a plastic basin in the dusty street. Has prosperity always been such a juxtaposition of hovels leaning against the castle walls?

## Las Vegas Report

People Watching: the customers/clients/tourists seem quite similar. They are typical American shopping mall patrons, many overweight and many senior citizens. There are few people-watching stations. Someone should do an analysis of the number of seats at gambling tables and slot machines, number of tables at restaurants, and the number of people watching. The workers are more interesting to watch than the patrons: more diverse, more energetic, purposeful, and talented.

Architecture: Façade is the only variety; interiors are all alike. Exaggerated exterior size and detail are intended to mask the lack of substance inside.

"Style": Style here is very stylized. Patrons are wearing aggressively casual clothing. All the service personnel wear standardized uniforms.

Women serving drinks on the casino floors seem to be uncomfortable in their uniforms.

Cleanliness: Yes

Overheard: "Assault to the senses!"

Depth: none

Geographic setting: Beautiful ring of mountains almost appear artificial in postcard coloring.

Bathrooms: Sumptuous! The reasoning must be that patrons who are comfortable will spend more time at slot machines and gambling tables.

Public Transportation: Designed to guide visitors to shops and casinos.

Thought-provokingness: Bring your own.

Shopping: All brand name products. Themed souvenirs. NO bookstores.

Wild Almond

# CHAPTER TWENTY-THREE

# Off Itinerary: Saying "Yes!"

*Destination no longer ruled. My only map was that of free association: I would follow each street only as long as it interested me and then, on a whim, choose a new direction.*

—Alice Steinbach

## Saying Yes To Off-Itinerary Experiences

I said "Yes" to an early morning walk around Xuanwu Lake Park in Nanjing, China with C and K. We met at 6 am and C asked me if I was hungry. What's the right answer to this? I sensed it was "Yes" and I was right. They wanted to take me for street food breakfast. We walked toward the university until we came upon a woman who was setting up her cart. She was pulling small snowball-sized lumps of dough off a large bucket full of dough in the lower part of her cart. She set out various containers of filings and checked the fire under her wide flat pan. We watched for a minute or two and then K spoke to her. Nodding seemed to indicate that she was ready to begin. She spread the dough over the pan and then cracked an egg over the dough. With a broad spatula she spread the egg over the dough. As these set and became a crepe of sorts, she spread the vegetables K had indicated over the egg. Finally, she folded this tortilla into a roll and placed it in a thin plastic bag for holding. By the time she had made one each for the three of us, a second and third cart had arrived on the scene and quickly set up for business. Each was a slightly different variety of the same thing. I could imagine that a worker or student might have a favorite cart for breakfast every day— one and only favorite out of these three and the dozens more we saw as we rode in a taxi to the lake. The top few bites were crepe only, but below that it was a crunchy, soft, wrap around oily veggies for a very satisfying, finger-licking good breakfast if you can let go of dry toast as a standard. 2 RMB each, about 30 cents.

The taxi dropped us off at one entrance gate to the lake park. A group of adults were doing tai chi with red flags just outside the arched opening in the old city wall. We entered and made a plan to walk the forest route and then the island route. There are broad wooden walkways through the forest and people are doing morning exercise routines alone and together. They move to the same principles, if not the same rhythm/drummer, in harmony and community even if each may be doing something individual. A man plays his trumpet to a tree. A woman stretches at a bench, couples walk briskly, small groups move through different forms of tai chi or chi gong. A man uses tree branches to do pull ups over a small water feature. It is 6:20 am. Someone plays a flute; someone else is doing primal screams, and a sole woman is singing opera to the lake. She has a beautiful voice, and I think the beauty of the lake owes something to the vibrations she infuses.

The care and artistry of setting is stunning here and almost everywhere else we went. There is not just simply a row of bushes along the highway—there is usually an array with depth and texture. Lower plantings in front, with medium thick hedges framing shaped trees or contrasting hedges of medium height and then one or two rows of trees standing taller behind. This would be along the highway. This level of quality in a park would be arrayed in groupings rather than along a road. The difference in the park is the inclusion of height and stone. Beautiful "scholar rocks" are cultivated near Xuanwu Lake by putting a "seed" stone in a crack and then the action of the water agitates and shapes openings in the rock.

## "Alabaster Feet"

Opole, Poland has not yet hit the tourism circuit. It is a small city of perhaps 100,000 citizens with a university of about 15,000 students. It takes almost four hours by train from Krakow, about an hour from Wroclaw. Most of the people we see on the street are Polish and local. The Mercure hotel across the street from the main train station or Glowny is very quiet aside from our group of only about twenty visitors. At breakfast, there are perhaps ten persons not related to our group. We saw a small group eating dinner when we had drinks at the bar, but in general, it is very quiet. I have not had to wait for one of the two computers in the business center. I haven't seen any other hotels at all.

There don't appear to be any American chains here yet, no McDonald's or Starbucks. There are no souvenir shops. We will search for a post card later today, perhaps at the train station? The restaurants do have menus in English, a sign that Opole is hopeful for tourists from the U.S. One waiter mistakenly handed us menus in German.

Our host tells us to stay away from the area on the other side of the train station because there is a lot of construction going on for the European soccer tournament scheduled to take place in Poland in 2012. It will have venues in several cities, including Opole. Perhaps this will put Opole "on the map" in terms of increasing tourism.

The last time I was here, three years ago, several of us wives (AH, GB, and I) took a train ride over to Wroclaw. It is the home of our friend and neighbor, JS. Wraclaw is a beautiful city of bridges, churches, public sculpture, and fountains. This time, with so many days "on the road," I was not eager to travel anywhere else, and fortunately, my friend E felt the same. We decided to stay here while our husbands are engaged with William James. We both have "work" to do in our rooms, and we both enjoy strolling to see THIS city and experience what it has to offer.

Our adventure on Thursday was to have a pedicure in a Polish salon. E made our appointments for 14:00 (2:00 p.m.) with someone who did not speak English after seeing a brochure that showed pedicure for 30 zl. This seems a genuine bargain at the exchange rate of 3 zl to $1. We listen to two academic discussions with our husbands and share their conference lunch of pancakes filled with mushrooms and then we walk to the salon. We experience some of the construction along the way.

As we enter, a petite woman dressed in black with short black spiked hair asks us to sit for a moment. She is a streak of energy and as she quickly moves around the shop, behind the curtain, through several doorways, she is talking to us. "Where are you from? I live San Diego two years. San Diego, Paris, London, eight years. My mother Russian; my father Polish." Already, this is more than a pedicure; this is an experience!

She asks for and remembers our names: "E, Josephine, come here. E first lady; Josephine number two lady. Sit here. Feet here. I love movies!" While Iola Maj, Dyplemenara Kosmetyezka, gives us hints of movie titles and actor, actress names, we happily play along and guess the English titles and names. "Tall, tall, handsome, not titanic, birds inside!" We keep up the game while she covers the couch with paper, settles E, arranges her feet under a magnifying light and peels the paper off a fresh razor. Iola has her back to me, but E and I are facing one another. My horror is clear ... don't let that thing near me! "Love Story, The Aviator, Al Pacino, Thelma and Louise, Susan Sarandon, Marilyn Monroe." We stir a rich goulash of names.

E is a good sport through all the shaving, buffing, clipping, and trimming with a variety of sharp, cheese-grater rough, and pincing instruments. Finally the hot wax comes out and Iola tells us this will produce "alabaster skin"! I tell E that I'd like to skip all the preparations and go right to the hot wax treatment and the wrapping in cellophane!

As the conversation shifts from film to transvestites shopping in Vancouver, Iola prepares a second couch for me. I devise a phrase that I hope will protect me from the blades! With E wrapped in cellophane, painted bright red, and resting inside a hot blower, Iola Maj turns her attention to "lady number two." I tell her, "I am a baby and my feet are baby feet! Please do not make my baby feet cry!" In other words, "No sharp implements for me, please!" Given that she has spent ninety minutes on E, I think she is pleased to hear that I want to skip a few steps. We go right to gentle buffing and sanding. I can't avoid the cuticle cutting, but I manage not to cry out at the little stabs of pain.

Iola Maj tells us that even when she was a little girl, her teachers told her she should be an actress. She was singing and performing early. As a younger woman she was cosmetologist for a TV program and had the opportunity to do make-up for many politicians who appeared on the show. We didn't have much success in understanding her Polish explanation of the election coming up in a few weeks other than realizing she has great disdain for someone in that race.

When we are released from cellophane and hot/cold blowers, and after we are touched up and cleaned, she asks us if we are happy. We both say, "Yes!" We take photos and then move to the other side of the curtain, back to daylight and closer to the street where construction has been going on for two and a half hours while we were being entertained. The brochure said 30 zl, but our bill was 95 zl each. We look at one another and pay in cash without a word. I leave a tip of 10 zl. Did we have a cultural misunderstanding or pay fairly for the "stage show with pedicure" we received? We chose not to ask. Whether Iola Maj gave us a tourist polishing in addition to a pedicure is not the point. We walked out happily on alabaster feet!

CHAPTER TWENTY-FOUR

# Meeting and Missing

*A small breeze of homesickness had been blowing over me for the last few days. I suspected, however, that I wasn't homesick for anything I would find at home when I returned. The long-ing was for what I wouldn't find*          —Alice Steinbach

## Homesick

We are in Oxford now doing a walking tour. I had to have this new pen. Lunch at Rosie Lee's. I was homesick last night. What is that? What does it feel like, sound like, taste like?

## B and J in Buckie

B and J were staying at the same B&B as we were. They live on the coast in Buckie, Scotland. It was fun talking with them. They are both retired. She was a music teacher. He works several days a week for a farmer—for fun. She loves Robert Burns and the Royal Family. They said we should visit. We might go there tomorrow.

B&B is a wonderful way to meet other travelers: Oxford and history of religion scholar; Australian family; Florida couple coming back from Scotland; and now, John and Betty .

She used some words not common to us, like "ken": "He didna ken his Mary." I knew what she meant from having studied old English in college. D did not. J was almost impossible to understand.

We drove back to Edinburgh to tour the castle. What a magnificent view from up there! Mary, Queen of Scots, had her baby James there. It is built right out of a rock. Extinct volcano?

We got in the car at 1 pm and headed north through Perth. Drove past Balmoral. Not open because the Queen is there right now.

Scenery is heather and mountains—barren, except for sheep. The road in some places is single track and a little tricky.

We drove until 6:30 or 7 pm looking for a B&B. Hard to find here. Found Mrs. McPherson in Abeldour for £ 5.50 each. We walked to the hotel for bar snacks. I am feeling so fat from eating snacks!

Tomorrow we(I) plan to enjoy a distillery tour in Dufftown, and then go to Buckie, and finally Cawdor. B promised to sing Robert Burns songs for me. Wasn't she telling me about "McPherson's Farewell" this morning? And here we are in Mrs. McPherson's house!

I'll have to be sure to tell B that they were right about Inverness. It is horrid—crowded, expensive, and with inferior, touristy goods.

We drove to Buckie, arriving at about 12:30 pm. I wasn't sure if they really meant it. When B opened the door, she seemed so genuinely happy to see us that I felt pretty sure they had meant it.

B sat us in the living room with some books and magazines while she went in to make some tea and snacks in the kitchen. She closed the door. People here always close the door between the living room and kitchen.

We originally intended to leave Buckie at 3:30 or 4 pm and go to Inverness by way of Castle Cawdor. After a few minutes of talking, B persuaded us to stay overnight

They were preparing for our visit even though they had only

arrived home the night before. B had a meat roll in the oven. They were overjoyed that we had kept our word to come and visit.

We had hit it off so well at the breakfast in Edinburgh. All four of us felt it. She and I are teachers and connect to the Royal Family and Robert Burns. (Her name is Elizabeth and I was born the same day as Charles). D and J are very much alike also. J was born on a farm, was a grocer/shopkeeper all his life and now is retired and works overly long hours on a farm to help his friend N.

After tea, D and I went for a walk through town and along the harbor. Buckie once had one of the largest fishing fleets in Europe. We saw boats being built in Thompson's boat yard, and also the Moray seafood company. Do Moray eels come from this Moray Firth?

We scavenged on the rocky beach for awhile also. It was very hot.

When we returned, D and J went to the garden, B cooked, and I took a bath and got dressed in my dress. I debated over the stockings, but she is such a lady I decided to put them on. She does make a big fuss over cleanliness. When they travel, they do not eat out; they always picnic. I'll really have a struggle if they come to visit us.

It was so comfortable to be with them. No effort to get along, only the slight tension of being "proper." After dinner, D and J went to visit N's farm. B let me dry while she washed the dishes in scalding water. Then we went upstairs to the piano room. She sang and played many of Robert Burns' songs for me, explaining the stories as we went along. I sang a few with her: Auld Lang Syne and another folk tune. We went down about 10 pm to wait for the 'boys.' B told me all about her family. She taught for twenty-four years before she married J. His first wife had died of cancer. She left teaching when she married seventeen years ago. (D and I have been married 15 years next Thursday).

In the afternoon before the men went to the garden, J noticed that his neighbors were moving a pile of cinder blocks from the street into their house which they are renovating. He rushed out to help them. He is a vigorous sixty-eight years old. He wears a three-piece suit to go to work on the farm or anywhere. He has to look decent because he peddles the produce of N's farm for him. When he goes into a grocery or butcher shop, he always buys something before he sells his goods. It is quite expected. N used to give him a good bit of trade when J had his own shop. B said she has to think of something she needs so he can buy it when he goes round to the shops. They don't speak too highly of farmers who try to wriggle out of this system by requesting some obscure grocery item, like rennet, says B, and then trying to sell you their goods.

D and J still weren't back by 10:30 so B put on some tea for us. When it was ready, we decided to have sherry instead. I went to bed. She walked me up the stairs and kissed me good night like a mother or a dear friend. D and J came in soon after. D had a splendid time. As soon as they reached the farm (20 mi), J set about trimming hedges. Luckily, D and N hit it off immediately and had a good tour of N's farm and another neighbor's farm of pigs. J worked all the while. I knew D would enjoy that. He said N has seven tractors! And also many of the same problems that we have with farming.

Next morning we were all up early. B wears pearls and looks like a lady even early in the morning. I don't think I do. We had breakfast about 7:30. J said good-bye, took our picture, and went off to work. Something about "Taties today."

I felt very dizzy, but we left at about 8:30. B gave me some address labels and napkins of her tartan plaid. Her maiden name was Mac-Beath, but they claim the MacBeth tartan. She seemed so sad to see us go. I know we will keep in touch. She is the type to write back. I'll start by thanking them, of course. I'd like to send a gift too. They were so generous with us.

## June the Third

It is our 12th anniversary today in Sofia, Bulgaria. The entire trip is a celebration of our life together! We spend the day with K, a PSU grad student, and his wife, P. They met while both were studying political philosophy at PSU. She is from a small town near Sofia, but went to Sewanee University for her undergraduate degree and PSU for master's. Finally, we have a walking day through the center of the city with excellent guides. It rains so we do spend a lot of time in a brasserie drinking and talking. When the rain tapers off to sprinkles, we go back out and manage to see and enter almost all the sites mentioned in the travel guide, in addition to wandering onto a movie set where shiny black cars converge for a dramatic scene and then speed off. Men with machine guns and masks also figure in the scene. The storms have interfered with the wireless connection at the hotel and we can't get on the internet in the evening. Am I getting "homesick" or just missing the weekly connection with my children and family?

## Young Wives Club

We've spent time with two young couples recently: M (Italian) and S (US Persian) who live in Turino, Italy and K (US) and P (Bulgarian) who live in Sofia, Bulgaria. Both young women are extremely personable, vibrant, and attractive. M and K are philosophers (or Ph.D. student on his way for K)) and their wives are educated but work outside the academy and they have varied ambitions and interests. S graduated from UC Berkeley with a degree in comparative literature. She is teaching English in Torino and working on a novel. P has a Master's degree in Political Science from PSU and she is working for a start-up Bulgarian web-development company as a project manager with clients in the U.S. I love them both!

Am I seeing my younger self in their bright, energetic goals and achievements? Am I like MS to them, i.e. the wife of an older distinguished professor with some interesting aspects of her own life? Who else might I be? SC's wife C; so lovely and engaged in her own career? JW? Do these young women see themselves years from now when they see me and V?

Another young woman who comes to mind is M in Sao Paulo,

the wife (a year ago) of VR who is a journalist and now a new Ph.D. with specialty in Peirce. We saw them several times last summer as couples, and with their two young children, C and P. M and I spent an afternoon together with the children while V and V talked philosophy and then we had dinner all together at least twice. Again, I think we bonded in a way. As wives of philosophers? As career women? As writers?

When I sense that young women are looking for a glimpse of themselves in their future I feel tremendous responsibility to project a positive image and also to invite their thoughts on being the partner of an academic. I haven't figured it all out yet myself, but I think I know a few things about letting go, about diverging and converging paths, about being the "spousal hire," and about respecting the achievements and goals along that other career path. In some ways, these young women and I are "ships passing in the night," but some of my most significant influences have been people I've met only a handful of times. MS was a dignified, intelligent and intellectual woman with achievements of her own and a very famous philosopher husband. She was always there, part of him in so many ways, but outstanding in her own right as well. I miss her.

CHAPTER TWENTY-FIVE

# Journey's End

*May your trails be crooked, winding, lonesome, dangerous,*
*leading to the most amazing view.* —Edward Abbey

## Leaving

We are staying in Imatra, Finland, one more day, leaving on the 11:09 am train back to Helsinki tomorrow, and then on to Budapest, Hungary in the evening. Already, many people have left for early trains today, and we've even noticed that several voices have been missing for a day or two now. It's good we had several conversations and one long evening at the Irish pub with PC because I discovered that he left shortly afterwards. We'll hope to see him again in London in September. Some of the "kids" left this morning: P, the lovely graduate student from Brazil, shared a cab with FA (not a kid!), and I think M and S also may have left this morning early. We are now in the final sessions of the week-long meeting (June 11 to June 17) and many people are leaving shortly after noon. A few are staying until tomorrow for the excursion to St. Petersburg. We tried to go, but couldn't get a visa in time. So, we are staying over until tomorrow because at the time I made our reservations, we thought we were going to St. Petersburg tomorrow. It will be fine though, as we'll have some time to relax and have dinner with Norwegian friends, D and her husband.

I'm ready to leave, although it takes a lot of energy to repack, and to do the taxi, train, luggage hauling, luggage storing, time in Helsinki, bus to airport, flight to Budapest, taxi negotiating, ride to Anna hotel, and orientation to Budapest. I think any leaving reluctance today is due more to the rigors of travel than to reluctance to leave this place. It has been a good place with lovely, interesting people to observe day after day: getting to know A and appreciate V's friendships with N, A, F, etc.; observing the trio of young academics of K, M, and N; experiencing the Imatra "surge"; seeing the light all night long; having some very inspirational learning sessions; but I am ready to leave the place itself, much more than I was ready to leave Helsinki. Helsinki is a place that would take many months to be ready to leave, especially with such a pleasant residence as our hotel and neighborhood.

Children often have such a difficult time with leaving themselves or experiencing others leaving. I noticed that D seems to bribe his daughter to behave during leaving with a promise of some reward if she can leave without resisting. She had a terrible time when V and I left after spending a weekend with them when their parents went away for two nights. She began to attack her sister and resist her mother's suggestions. She wouldn't hug or kiss us good-bye, but then she had made it crystal clear in advance that she didn't want us to leave. And, of course, we didn't act on her preference, but still took our leave, so no wonder her protest. It is gratifying to hear her say, "I want you to stay here!" But also painful, because of how genuine is her desire and how hard it is to leave when she wants us to stay.

What happens to this intensity of feeling as we grow older and conditioned to many leave takings? We suppress the anguish, I think. It isn't less; I sometimes feel a sense of panic as the moment of leaving approaches, and a visceral depressed spirit for some hours afterwards, but I feel myself pushing the panic behind or below the words and promises of adulthood: "we'll see you in six weeks," "I'll always have memories of this city and experience," "we'll write an email and stay in touch." None of this is ever enough for a four-year old, nor is it really for me, but convention dictates that we move on from place to place and person to person. The returns over time lay down continuity and build confidence that another return follows each leaving. Is that a true sentence?

## Last Night, Party Night

TAM flight 8080 from Sao Paulo to JFK is almost over. There was so much security at the airport! Each and every piece of checked luggage was opened and examined at the check-in desk, and every piece of hand luggage was searched. Still, all went smoothly and I had time for browsing, breakfast, money exchange, and to read today's International Herald Tribune before boarding.

I took several catnaps to make up for last night's very short sleep, but not enough to disrupt a good night's sleep later tonight! For our last evening, L organized a wonderful outing to hear Brazilian music at a small former machine shop called Ono Borogado (something like that) that means a "complete mess" I think. Music began after 11 pm.

I had one caiperinha to make up for the night before of two caiperinhas and a shared bottle of wine. The music was two guitars, a singer, and percussion. I am really inspired to take up classical guitar again. We sat and listened most of the night. C danced with several of the younger women in the group and then asked if I would like to try. Yes! I'm feeling very awkward, but I love moving to this music. He tries to explain the difference between samba beat and most US dance music. I hear it but I can't quite move to it. V gets up to go pay the bill and another man sees that I am released from C and begins to dance with me. I think he is intent to communicate the samba rhythm to this clumsy North American woman. It is a worthy try but I need some private time training my body to hear AND feel the beats. Dance lessons before returning to Brazil are a must!!

## Resolutions

We are in the air over the Atlantic right now, about half way home. I just put my headphones on to "I'm gonna live forever." It looks like we are at least going to make it home anyway. Before I leave on a trip, it doesn't seem like I'll get back.

I've been planning a regimen of exercise for myself. I don't have much wind. I have to tighten up this tummy. If I get up earlier, I can exercise either downstairs or in my room. I thought I would also jump rope. I'll start with one minute every day for a week and then work up from there. I will also do my aerobic set for stomach muscles. And my deep knee bends. I don't like anyone to see me while I'm doing this which presents a problem. I'll either have to get used to that, or find a private place and time.

This flight is a DC8. More cramped than our arrival plane. No lovers to watch. The air is very dry again. We will be a bit late getting into NY. I hope we get the 3 or 4 pm Airporter limousine with enough time for me to call home first. I am very anxious to hear that all is well!

Things to do when I get home:
+ Call NP about Weaving Course
+ Call CC
+ Write thank you note to B and J

## Towards Home

Today and two more days before our long journey home. We've been traveling for five weeks tomorrow and we are both ready to go home. (Is home a destination or an experience?) We've almost turned our heads, our eyes and noses toward the familiar beauties and away from days filled with new beauty. Toward knowing the menu at our familiar restaurants rather than meeting an adventure for every meal. Toward easy access to our children's voices and soon even to hugs and real, reachable sight of them, not photos on Snapfish.com! Toward our personal laundry—anytime of day or night. Toward the clothes we haven't worn steadily for 35 days. (All the bells are ringing at all the churches in Opole right now at noon as I sit in the square waiting for my Hungarian Goulash soup because I couldn't read anything else on the menu! Calling me into the present moment?) Toward a stretch of two weeks or more without negotiating train schedules, tickets, and hotels. Toward our own small town Arts Festival that we love. Maybe even towards a minor league baseball game. Towards work at our own desks with our books and wireless internet access. Towards beach week vacation with the kids. And also towards the next trips in Sept, October, November, and December. Towards next summer's events already being planned for Urbino and South Korea and Brazil. Toward my houseplants and plans for outdoor plants. Toward my blooming bee balm and my new rock garden with a red rock I named Balzac for its shape like Rodin's sculpture.

## After-Effects

Returned travelers speak about "jet lag" as if it is the only after-effect of travel. I've been having strange dreams. They all involve trains this week. I am running to catch a train. I am struggling with luggage to change trains. I am, of course, missing trains. I am in the train station confused (again). I am having to make a decision between my luggage on a train that is leaving and my purse which I've left on a bench on the platform. No wonder I'm waking up at 2 am ! It's not only 8 am for my body which seems to still think it's in Poland, but I'm suffering all night from train lag!

# To Do

I begin making a list for my return even before I leave town. The first things to go on the list are those on the "To Do" list from before the trip that didn't get done before I left! Next I begin to write names of people I want to see and get together with upon my return. This will be a gently growing list over the time of our travel, often with things I dream of doing to prolong the aura of the travel or of being in that wonderful frame of mind in between being here and being there ... open to new possibilities, full of old possibilities.

On this trip, V has been thinking that he would like for us to host several "cultural nights" at home for a congenial group of friends. We've begun to talk about who to invite and those "downer, high maintenance people" we won't invite.

# Flashes of Memory

Drawing upon the energy of our recent travels, we were reorganizing our books yesterday, making decisions to release many of them from our ownership to continue their life's journeys. As they passed through my hands, quite a few of these experiences (books are not objects, but experiences) opened to reveal travel stories!

*The Beans of Egypt, Maine* by Carolyn Chute handed me three small slips of paper: a receipt for "Ascension de la tour Eiffel" sponsored by "Société Nouvelle D'Exploitation de la Tour Eiffel," dated May 27, 1998. M was with us for this "ascension" and one of my favorite photos of her, the one I call the "Embrace Life" photo was taken there.

Another slip of yellow paper is Entrée No. 001178 to Abbaye d'Alet les Bains. After spending five or six days in Paris with M, V and I flew to Perpignan, rented a car and drove to Alet les Bain for a small philosophy meeting hosted by HP. This year we spent some time with H reminiscing about that region of France where he has a home and which is the region producing the wines for his new business as a wine merchant of philosophy wines, "Vinosophia." The meeting this year that brought us together was in Opole, Poland, and it was the occasion for me to reconnect with GB, the wife of another philosopher, JL, who was also at the 1998 meeting in Alet les Bains. G and I spent time together exploring the region and the four of us spent a lovely day in Carcassone.

The third slip of paper, a melon-colored "Billet à conserver en cas de contrôle" No. 00614, marked the day G and I spent "Sur les routes du Pays Cathare" visiting ruined castles. I see from the map on the back of the ticket, that we were offered the possibility of visiting Château, Abbaye, and Musée. Apparently, one of our selections was Le Château d'Arques and Le Muse du Catharisme et de ses Interpretations. I recall the country roads, the evocative piles of stones, some standing towers, and how lovely G was. Alet les Bains is a tiny town on a small swift river in the middle of a wine producing region. H arranged wine tasting for us and G and I also went to a winery to buy several bottles, none of which made it back to the U.S., some because we consumed them, and at least one bottle of champagne for exploding in G and J's room. *The Beans of Egypt, Maine* took a long trip that year and made it safely back home. More recently, we release our books along the way, imagining their new lives and travels as they are adopted by other travelers.

In my copy of Giuseppe Di Lampedusa's classic *The Leopard*, I discovered a yellowed page from The New York Review of Books, December 5, 1991. Under the title "The Melancholy Prince," it is a review of *The Last Leopard: A Life of Giuseppe di Lampedusa*. This book went to Sicily with me (and my cousin, Joseph D'Ambrosio) in October of 1991. I didn't get too far in reading it, but it has generously rewarded me with this review and with a greater treasure. Tucked inside the book is an air mail envelope with no stamps. It was sealed and opened with a slit across the top edge. Addressed to "Ms Jo Glorie, Italia" it was from "V, New York."

We had met in March of that year and by October we were deeply involved; much more than our original relationship of editor and author. My trip to Cianciana and all of Sicily was long planned, and though it was hard to be so far away from my new lover, it was good for us both to have this respite to reflect on and imagine a life together. In the letter, V described "The combination of deep (I almost want to say ancient) familiarity and utter newness is—again, for me— intoxicating." At another moment he promised me a perpetual honeymoon, and now, with sixteen years of experience, I often mention that promise, not to him because he lives it every day, but to others, just to describe the flavor of our relationship. He wrote this letter specifically for me to carry on my trip and to read somewhere in Sicily. While I was away, V stayed in my little studio apartment on 81st street in Manhattan and slept in my bed.

Occasionally we still slip a sealed letter into the other's suitcase. Most recently, I was gifted with a poem for Mother's Day, "to Jo on May 13, 2007." I am irresistibly drawn to a man who brings words upon words to enrich our lives every day: "children too are words, and stone, also tempo, thus poems, sculptures, rhythms, rimes, times, kept, lost, and every other possibility, especially in our dreams and delusions, our hopes and anxieties. Yet above all, They are Themselves. ... This you know, Above All." I will remove the letter and all associated memories from this book and keep these treasures close to me on my desk. The review will remain with the book.

In Carol Shields novel, *The Box Garden*, I find a bookmark from Livraria Cultura, our favorite bookstore in São Paulo, Brazil. It is located in a small shopping mall just a few streets away from the apartment hotel where we stayed last summer for over a month. We had been reading everything we could find by Carol Shields, including her children's books. What a treat to find this novel, in English, in our neighborhood book store in Brazil !

In a book of essays by Maria Laurino, *Were You Always an Italian: Ancestors and other Icons of Italian Americans*, I find a ticket from

February 15, 2002 for Castello Svevo on the "Circuito Castelli Della Puglia". That was the year I flew to Rome before V to visit with my student, AB. After my few days in Rome with A, V and I met in Bari for a semiotics conference.

## The Traveler's Stages of Regret

Inevitable, fleeting regrets (hardly worth mentioning)

I should have ordered the salmon; the lamb; the trout; the paella; the salade nicoise, the ice cream, etc. OR I should not have ordered the salmon, the lamb, the trout, the paella, the salade nicoise, the ice cream, etc.

Simple, situational regret:

Dining: We should not have been tempted by "our friend Ali" to eat in the restaurant along the bridge in Istanbul where all tourists inevitably stalk the perfect, "typical" dinner of succulent gigantic grilled shrimp and promises of free coffee and dessert.

Transportation: We should have paid only the pre-arranged taxi fare and not been intimidated by our lack of language skills and the front seat directive that the price is more now, meaning, now that we are separated from our fluent friends.

Health and medical care: I should have allowed the antibiotics my local physician gave me more time to work before spending over one hundred dollars to have a Brazilian doctor tell me that this was an "overkill" antibiotic that would cure me of anything, including the throat infection I acquired while visiting the authentic Feria de San Joaquin in Salvador da Bahia.

Transportation: We should have paid extra for first class tickets (reserved seating).

Hotel Accommodation: We should have asked for a repair to the shower drain immediately upon discovering that we couldn't leave the water on for more than 90 seconds without flooding the bathroom.

Excursions: We should have taken one more excursion in Iceland to ride the small horses.

Complex regrets:

Decision-making in groups: The two of us should have split off from our compatible group of five strollers that night in Istanbul when we came upon a serendipitous jazz club. Fear of offending the others with a sudden change meaning separate plans for the evening, fear of having to negotiate our own transportation home, slow signaling between the two of us?

Decision-making in groups: Eight people just arrived in a small town looking for a place to eat dinner equals a many-headed monster! We should have asked for a recommendation before walking from our hotel to downtown and back, entering several places en masse asking for accommodation and then leaving, choosing the fall-back option of eating in the hotel, and then hearing a recommendation for the one place downtown we hadn't discovered.

Communication: We should have learned to use Skype before leaving home.

Communication: We should have arranged a "contingency plan" with our friends who generously offered to pick us up at the airport and who, due to our delay (missed connecting flights, sudden change in itinerary, etc.), were waiting for hours, sometimes at the wrong airport.

Communication: We should have learned the correct phrases to request a visit to the family farm (which we desperately wanted to see) rather than use the same incorrect phrase and be taken to visit the marble factory several times, probably just as frustrating to our hosts as to us.

Destination Decisions: We should have gone to Buenos Aires for our Tenth Anniversary trip (instead of to Iceland)

# Desiderata For Travelers

*Why not turn this mishap into an adventure?*
—Alice Steinbach

## Desiderata for Travelers

I will allow myself to make more mistakes and when I do, I will enjoy them more fully.

I will pack lighter and lighter. Thoreau "Beware of any endeavor that requires new clothes and not rather a new wearer of the clothes."

I will wear comfortable walking shoes and walk comfortably in them as far and as deeply as my feet will take me.

I will seek out public transportation used by ordinary people of every country for my local travel and appreciate the joys of standing or sitting shoulder to shoulder with the essence and soul of the place.

I will eat ice cream (or gelato) at any time of day or night that I so desire and can find a street vendor with firm, cold flavor and fresh, crisp cones.

I will learn more words and phrases in more languages.

I will seek out and befriend international people in my home community.

I will stop judging customs and preferences of others and accept that fish, chocolate, and olives are excellent breakfast foods.

I will visit my own familiar places with a traveler's eyes.

I will approach the in-between and the meanwhile with as much eagerness as the destinations.

I will sample more food, listen to more music, drink more beer/ouzo/lassie/juice, wrap myself in more colors, and try on the shoes of more local people wherever I go.

## Recommended Reading

*I travel not to go anywhere, but to go. I travel for travel's sake. The great affair is to move.*   —Robert Louis Stevenson

- *Travels With Alice* by Calvin Trillin, Ticknor and Fields, New York, 1989
- *Writing Down the Bones* by Natalie Goldberg, Shambala, 1986, Boston & London
- *Without Reservations: The Travels of an Independent Woman* by Alice Steinbach, 2000, Random House, Inc.
- *Eat, Pray, Love: One Woman's Search for Everything Across Italy, India and Indonesia* by Elizabeth Gilbert, Penguin Books 2006
- *From Heaven Lake: Travels Through Sinkiang and Tibet* by Vikram Seth, Vintage, 1987.
- *In Xanadu: A Quest* by William Dalrymple, Harper Collins, 1989.
- *Jaguars Ripped My Flesh* by Tim Cahill, Bantam Books, 1987.
- *Around the World in Seventy-two Days* by Nellie Bly

# Travel Journal Writing Prompts

*Travel writing, I've come to think, is much more a matter of writing than of traveling—the hard part of the journey takes place at the desk ...As Thoreau puts it, ... 'It matters not where or how far you travel, the further commonly the worse, but how much alive you are.'*          —Pico Iyer

»   When does a trip actually begin? During planning? During packing? When departing home for the first stage of the actual journey?

»   What does it feel like to be ready for a trip, or for any experience?

»   Whom do you miss when you travel? What does missing feel like to you?

»   Reflect on encountering local belief systems.

»   Reflect on the power of our emotional states to affect events.

»   Set aside your mature self and regress to yourself at an age when you believed in old-fashioned pirates, Robin Hood, Peter Pan, Davey Crockett, Daniel Boone, dragons, and the knights of the Round Table. The stories that captured our imagination differed from generation to generation, family to family and from child to child. Who were you in your afternoon ramblings through the streets of your neighborhood on your bicycle? Who were you on the way through the woods to the ice-skating pond? Who were you on summer afternoons reading under the apple tree? If you are young enough to have an imagination supplemented by video games: what was your persona of choice in the depths of your favorite games?

» Take about 10 minutes to reconstruct your own "pirate persona," not necessarily a pirate, but possibly cut out of the same cloth as my Captain Blood: dramatic, larger than life, courageous and maybe a little wild, certainly not someone you introduced to your parents. What are the qualities of your "pirate persona" that you were once (and possibly still are) attracted to? Try to identify two or three core qualities of the persona that inspired (and perhaps inhabited) you as a youth. Write these in your notebook leaving six or seven lines blank in between each one. Now, think about what it would mean for you to transport that quality to your workplace or to your life in general. Once you get started, you can begin to think of small and large opportunities to seek out the experiences and develop the qualities you were once so very attracted to. Now, you try it.

» Do you try to replicate a remembered wonderful experience? If there is any occurrence of this during your trip, comment on whether it was successful or not.

» One of the pleasures or pains of travel is the shopping and purchasing of souvenirs or gifts. What is this like for you ... a pleasure or a burden? Describe one of your purchasing experiences that was especially gratifying or especially frustrating.

» Notice a difference in another culture and think about what this says about this culture's beliefs about people and their behavior? Are people basically good and law-abiding? Or are they basically transgressive, needing regulations and laws?

» Observe the work habits and practices around you. Can you notice cultural values inherent in the work practices you observe? For example, the closing of all businesses and stores in the middle of the day. What does this reveal about the culture and the people? What do you think about this practice?

» Recall a conversation among travel companions that seemed to be inspired by the momentum of travel itself.

» How likely are you to engage in conversation with strangers when you travel? Recall a memorable encounter with a stranger from one of your trips and describe it here along with your reflection about it.

» If you are traveling today, be attentive to those around you and allow a conversation to start.

» Write about your fear evoked by an experience during this day.

» Describe the value of being alone during travel.

» Write about transitions between experiences, cities, urban/rural environments, etc.

» The sounds of travel include far more than music! Focus on sounds for a morning and write about what you hear.

» Reflection: Instead of taking a photograph of an arresting scene, describe it in words.

» Something always goes wrong!! What is it; why did it happen to you ; what did you come to understand from this?

» What do you do when the plane trembles and shudders? Are these the same strategies you use for the dentist or any other unpleasant short experience? I remember using the entire poem of "The Raven" to get through a particularly difficult dentist visit. I experimented with the pain by filling my mind with the poem to crowd out the pain.

» Unpack the sensations of arriving at a particular destination.

» As you travel today, try to notice something that is going on "under the radar" of most others, invisible except to you.

» If possible, endeavor to pull aside curtains, or sink down another level behind/beneath the surface. What do you witness there? Especially when "touring" we see a staged surface level and can only imagine what is behind or below each level we can see.

# Acknowledgements

I appreciate everyone I have ever traveled with for their patience, persistence, suggestions, curiosity, and common sense! I am also grateful to so many friends and family members for the skills they encouraged that are part of a successful traveling toolkit. In particular, I am forever grateful to all of the following and many unnamed persons whose assistance turned me in the right direction.

My grandparents, Gabriel and Antonina Alessi and Andrea, Josephine, and Maria Carubia for enduring the rigors of migrations and wars and for the DNA that links me to all the Mediterranean cultures that swept our island home over millennia.

My parents for the choices that gave me both city roots and rural branches. My father, Joseph Carubia, for steadfastness and creativity, and the tools to sustain both. My mother, Anna Vincenza Alessi Carubia, for her spirit of adventure after many years of being virtually house-bound. When invited, she said "Yes!" eagerly and traveled good-naturedly.

To my cousin, Roz, a role model for negotiating life's twists and turns and making the best of every contingency.

To my cousins, Joseph D'Ambrosio and Ernest D'Ambrosio, along with Martha and Nicholas, who have invited me to share travel adventures abroad with them. We discovered deep compatibility along with fjords and a few trolls. To cousin, Andy D'Ambrosio, for persistence and a spirit of adventure, always, despite any and all obstacles.

To delightful young companions; Anna, Teah, Dakota, and Treyton; for trips both past and future. We discover ourselves along with new landscapes.

To friends, who first motivated extended travels and who generously made possible a wonderful trip by providing safe, secure childcare.

To Doug Sr., who safely drove through Europe on that first big international trip, and who customized a van so we could all enjoy our cross-country USA adventures, especially Las Vegas.

To my one and only, most favorite sister, Nina Snyder, for the spirit of always being open to experience and to art, both on the road and close to home. And for both past and future travels together. Let's go!

To my beloved adult children, Douglas James and Michele Joy, for all of our travel experiences, both past and future, and for so many moments of amazing comfort and adventure close to our homes and families.

To Teah Glorie, for the illustrations in this book and so many more.

And most deeply and dramatically, to Vincent M. Colapietro, my best friend, husband, and travel companion to cities and continents beyond my imagination, and who will give me a quotation or a poem for every experience along the way, now and forever!

# About the Author

Josephine (Jo) Carubia was born in a major metropolis on an island of Planet Earth. She learned to love city walking as a schoolgirl, imagining aerial views of her footprints. When her family moved to a small town upriver, she began to wander into woods, beyond fields, beside ponds, and across bridges. As an adult she crossed borders, learned to fly, and began a life-long career of exploring careers. She likes to say that she has been lost in cities on four continents. With limited experience of a fifth continent, she cannot yet claim this further distinction. Her DNA speaks of sea voyages, migrations, intersecting cultures, and persistence of survival. She currently lives beside the Atlantic Ocean where her ions resonate with aquatic frequencies and where horizons continue to beckon.

Josephine Carubia, Ph.D. is a writer, artist and educator. She earned the doctorate in literature from Fordham University with a dissertation on Virginia Woolf and feminist epistemology. In her career at The Pennsylvania State University, she taught courses in English and Women's Studies and directed co-curricular education for students of the Schreyer Honors College. She was awarded the year-long Penn State Administrative Fellowship, served as Chief Academic Liaison Officer for the medical campus, and was promoted to Associate Professor of Medical Humanities. She received an Achieving Woman Award from the Penn State Commission for Women, an NEH Summer Institute Grant, and the Rose Cologne Volunteer of the Year Award. Dr. Carubia is the author of articles on literature, semiotics, and organizational leadership and has edited and published several books, including *Complete Book of Waiting*.

Made in United States
North Haven, CT
14 February 2024

48710645R00163